17.11.04

Ethics and Action
A Series Edited by Tom Regan

Animal Sacrifices

Religious Perspectives
on the Use of Animals in Science

EDITED BY
Tom Regan

Temple University Press
PHILADELPHIA

Temple University Press, Philadelphia 19122
© 1986 by Temple University, except Ch. 4, which is © A. Linzey.
All rights reserved
Published 1986
Printed in the United States of America

Library of Congress Cataloging-in-Publication Data
Main entry under title:

Animal sacrifices.

(Ethics and action)
Contents: Religions and the rights of animals / John Bowker—
The use of animals in science / Sidney Gendin—Judaism and animal
experimentation / J. David Bleich—[etc.]
1. Animal experimentation—Religious aspects—Addresses, essays, lectures.   2. Animal experimentation—Moral and ethical aspects—Addresses, essays, lectures.   3. Animals—Religious
aspects—Addresses, essays, lectures.   I. Regan, Tom.
BL439.5.A55   1986   291.5′694   85-22093
ISBN 0-87722-411-0

All royalties from the sale of this book go to the
International Association Against Painful Experiments on Animals.

To Colin Smith,
for his vision and courage

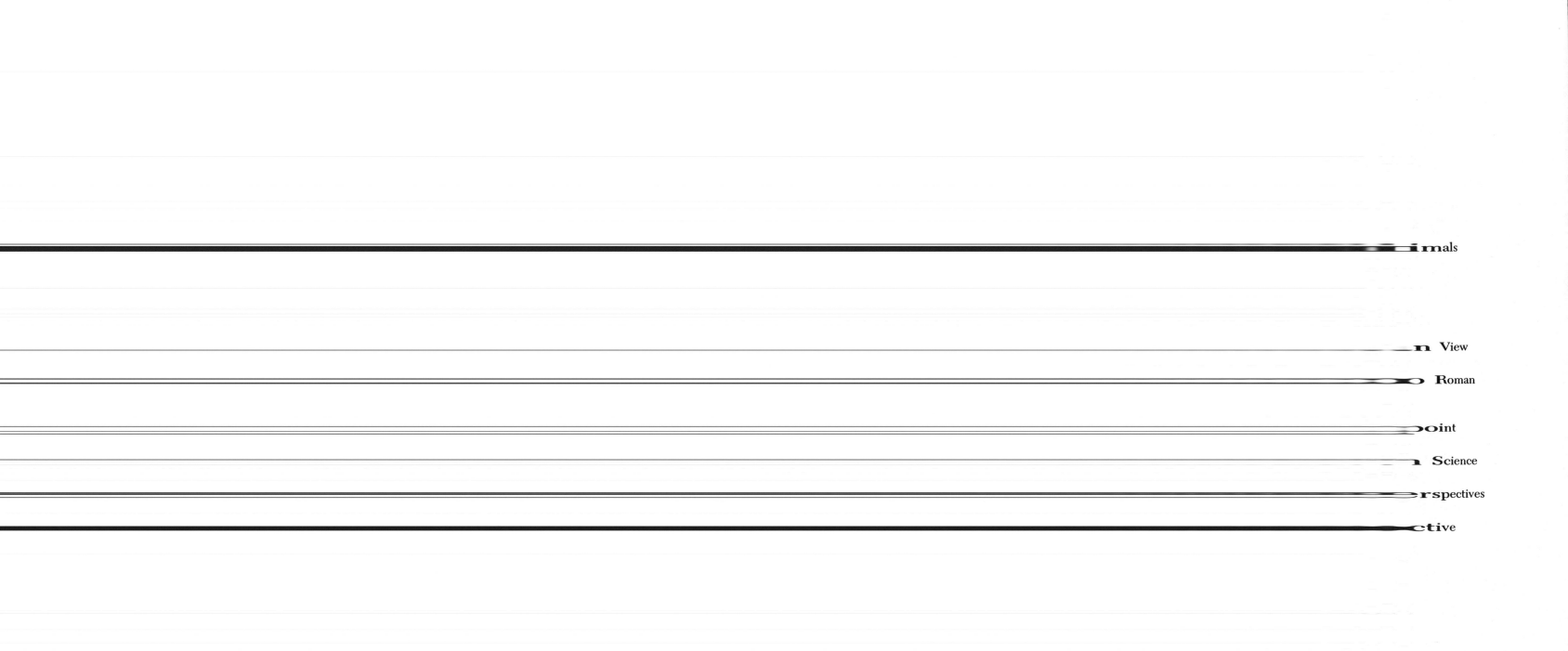

To Colin Smith,
for his vision and courage

Preface

Even as recently as a decade ago, not a single student in the thousands of philosophy courses offered annually in America's colleges and universities discussed the ethics of how humans treat animals. Today, each semester, many tens of thousands of students, perhaps as many as a hundred thousand a year, examine this topic. Usually part of a course on contemporary ethical issues that includes such issues as abortion, nuclear war, euthanasia, and world hunger, "ethics-and-animals" has become a staple in the diet of ideas in moral philosophy, at least in the English-speaking world.

The changes that have taken place in the classrooms of philosophy have occurred as a direct result of related changes in philosophy's scholarship. Previously relegated to occasional, brief mention in the footnotes of journal articles or to scattered, incidental passages in longer works, ethical questions about how humans ought to treat animals have come to be the principal subject not only of an increasing number of learned papers (indeed, several prestigious professional quarterlies in philosophy have devoted whole issues to essays on "ethics-and-animals") but also of a steadily growing number of books. Viewed historically, the increase in scholarly work carried out by moral philosophers in the last decade is nothing short of astonishing. And with this growth has come the burgeoning pedagogical interest in teaching "ethics-and-animals," with the result that today it is the exception, whereas only a decade ago it was the rule, to find a philosophy book or course on contemporary ethical issues that fails to include a significant sec-

tion devoted to moral questions about how humans do and
should treat animals.

To many, the curriculum in religious ethics at present is
the mirror image of the state of moral philosophy ten years
ago. Discussions of abortion, nuclear war, euthanasia, world
hunger, and other pressing issues in social and personal morality are common ingredients in courses in religion and ethics,
but not the ethics of our treatment of animals. As was true of
moral philosophers of earlier generations, the explanation of
this omission itself tells a tale. For it is not as if most religious
ethicists have asked searching questions about the many uses
humans make of animals and, after having given these questions a sustained, fair, and knowledgeable hearing, have de-
cided to exclude them because the questions lack ethical significance. Rather, the questions are absent largely because
they have not been asked.

This volume is intended to help foster growth in the area
of religious ethics and animals. With two exceptions, the papers collected here were presented at an International Conference organized around the theme of "Religious Perspectives on the Use of Animals in Science." Held in London,
England, on July 25–27, 1984, the Conference's sponsor, the
International Association Against Painful Experiments on Animals (IAAPEA), was, and is, hardly a morally neutral bystander
on the issue of animal experimentation. However, every effort
was made to ensure that compliance with IAAPEA's ethical
position on this issue was not in itself used as a criterion for
inclusion in the Conference program. A "Call for Papers," distributed more than a year before the Conference, was mailed
throughout the world to major Schools of Theology, Departments of Religion, Schools of Divinity, and Departments of
Religious Studies. The selection of speakers was based exclusively on the academic integrity of each respondent's record of
publication, the scholarly promise of the submitted abstract,
and the sponsor's interest in hosting a balanced conference, as
international in composition as resources permitted. IAAPEA
was, one might say, willing to risk truth's being on the program

Contents

rather than to try to program the truth. The quality of the papers chosen for presentation and reproduced here more than confirms the sponsor's elemental wisdom in this regard.

Although the stated theme of the Conference, adopted as the subtitle of this book, refers to the use of animals in science, it soon became evident to those involved in selecting Conference papers that the contributors inevitably touch upon the ethics of other uses we humans make of animals—as beasts of burden, for example, or as food. In their several ways, then, each paper serves as a general introduction to a wide range of ethical issues involving animals, as seen from the vantage point of one or another of the world's major religions. More than this, each provides a highly readable, informative introduction to the major ethical tenets of the religion under consideration, tenets whose scope reaches far beyond the ethics of the use of animals in science, and so provides an innovative, timely introduction to the ethical dimensions of one or another of humanity's enduring religions. Despite these many and possibly unexpected virtues, however, the ethical questions that serve most to unify the several essays, and the questions on which this volume, like the Conference before it, lays greatest stress, are those that concern the use of animals in science.

In preparing the conference presentations for publication, it became apparent that the papers assume a good deal of knowledge on the part of the reader concerning both the variety and extent of animal use in science. It thus seemed desirable to supply the necessary factual information about this use. This is provided in the second selection, "The Use of Animals in Science," which was not presented at the Conference. Another important addition is the synoptic overview of the essays provided by the Introduction.

My work as Chair of the Conference and as editor of the present volume was made easier and pleasanter because of the help of many people. Though space prevents me from listing them all, I must here acknowledge the special debts I owe to Colin Smith, Executive Director of IAAPEA; Ethel Thurston,

Director of the American Fund for Alternatives to Animal Research; Jane Cullen and Jennifer French of Temple University Press; and my wife, Nancy. Let us all hope that the "sleeping giant" will be roused!

Tom Regan
Department of Philosophy and Religion
North Carolina State University
Raleigh, North Carolina

Animal Sacrifices

1 Introduction: Religions and the Rights of Animals

John Bowker

Almost exactly a hundred years ago, in March 1885, John Ruskin wrote to the Vice Chancellor of Oxford University in order to resign from his position as Slade Professor of Fine Art. The immediate cause was the vote in the University on March 10 which, in Ruskin's phrase, "endowed vivisection."[1] In a speech the previous December, he had said:

> These scientific pursuits are now defiantly, provokingly, insultingly separated from the science of religion; they are all carried on in defiance of what has hitherto been held to be compassion and pity, and of the great link which binds together the whole creation from its Maker to the lowest creature.[2]

As he wrote to Joan Severn: "I cannot lecture in the next room to a shrieking cat, nor address myself to the men who have been—there's no word for it."[3]

In fact, Ruskin's resignation was not as simple as those two passages make it appear; but his abhorrence of vivisection was *one* of his two reasons, and there is, at least, no mistaking the passionate note in those words.

And now, a hundred years later, the same note of passion is unmistakable in the purpose and the preface of this book—"Let us all hope that the 'sleeping giant' will be roused!" Regan is right to regard religion as a giant, whether slumbering or not: it *is* the case that by far the majority of people alive today live religiously in some way and usually have some connection with religious systems and traditions that long precede them. The power of religion in human life can easily be seen in the many political disputes that seem particularly insoluble and intransigent, and in which the religious component is unmistakable. As I have said and written on many occasions,[4] virtually all the apparently intransigent and insoluble problems in the world have a deep religious root; not that religion alone is the cause of enduring hostilities or hatreds in Northern Ireland, the Middle East, South Africa, Cyprus, India and Pakistan, the Philippines, and so on, but it has its part to play.

There is, therefore, an urgent wisdom in Regan's recognition that the discussion of *any* global moral issue must take seriously the religious context in which so many people live, and from which they form, at least in part, their judgments. But what is obvious, and what is clearly illustrated in this book, is the fact that "the religious context" is not a single, undifferentiated whole. Exactly the opposite: there are many different religions, all of which are capable of holding sharply different (sometimes murderously different) views on almost all important issues. There is no way in which people speaking from different religions are going to come up with a single, unanimous opinion on animal rights and the uses of animals in scientific research.

But does that put the matter too strongly? There is one sense in which it does. It *is* possible to get religions to agree on certain major principles, goals, or ideals, or to find such agreement in their texts or traditions. Thus, to give an example, UNESCO celebrated the 20th anniversary of the Universal Declaration of Human Rights by "publishing a collection of quotations, drawn from a wide variety of traditions and periods, which, with their profound concordance enhanced by the very diversity of their origins, would illustrate how human beings everywhere, throughout the ages and all over the world, have asserted and claimed the birthright of man."[5]

But on a more detailed level, religions do not even agree on what constitutes human nature, and still less, therefore, on whether there are *rights* attached to or derived from the fact of being born. All religions would probably assent to a general proposal that we should love our neighbor and live at peace with him or her, "so far as in us lies." But when we ask what it means in practice and in detail to be loving toward our neighbor (what counts as loving behavior), the answers are very different indeed. And if we ask whether war is ever justified, all religions (including Buddhism) will say that sometimes it is; but the reasons they give and the circumstances they specify are extremely different.

So if religions have radically different anthropologies (accounts of what human nature is and what constitutes it), it is predictable that they will have different accounts of animal nature (what it is and what constitutes it). And from those differences, different estimates and evaluations of the status of animals, in themselves and in relation to human judgments and actions, will certainly emerge. That becomes very obvious in this book: you will not find a uniform statement to which all religions can subscribe. Or, to put it the other way around, religions do not provide different routes to the same goal where animal rights are concerned.

A particularly obvious example arises in the different anthropologies that occur in each religion. Three of the Eastern religions considered in this book—Hinduism, Jainism, and Buddhism—believe that either we (the living and continuing self) will be reborn or there will be a continuation in some future appearance even though there is no self being reborn, unless release from the whole process is won or attained. In all three religions it is possible to be reborn or reappear as an animal. Surely this must create a bond of caring and compassion for animals, since the animal on which you experiment today may be your future identity tomorrow.

Such beliefs both do and do not create such a bond, because despite the superficial similarity in the underlying anthropology of these religions, the applications are very different. In Buddhism, for example, in Chapter 8, the point is explicit that all living forms may have been any of the closest and dearest of your relatives, and may be so now, if the relative in question has died. Nor is that merely theoretical; it specifically generates the supreme Buddhist requirement in attitude and behavior, namely, compassion. In 1982 I interviewed[6] a Buddhist, a refugee from the Chinese invasion of Tibet who, as a young boy, had watched a Chinese soldier kill his father. Yet he said, "Of course, I don't think anything bad about the Chinese soldier or soldiers who were involved in killing my father."

Why not? Because for him the meaning of Buddhism is clear. As he put it, "Basically, I think, it is compassion, not limited to human kind, but extended to all the living creatures." How do you cultivate that kind of compassion? By remembering that it is possible for us, as happened for the Buddha, to be

> reborn almost innumerable times in various stages—
> maybe in terms of human beings, maybe in terms of
> birds, and fish, and all sorts of living creatures; and
> therefore each time he has taken birth, he has been a
> son, a member of a family or a tribe; so we believe that
> there isn't a single creature which has not been your
> mother at one time or another. And that is the basis
> on which one can build up some sort of compassion.[7]

Then surely Buddhists must oppose the use of animals in experiments? They may do so, but they do not *have* to do so, because the Buddhist understanding of no-self (of all appearance being fleeting stages in a process of impermanence and change) means that *within* the flow it is legitimate to work in such a way that the process is directed toward good ends. It is equally clear that the ultimate point of Buddhism is in any case extrinsic to such limited activities (since its purpose is to exhibit the way toward Enlightenment), and that consequently *some* use of animals might be legitimate, bearing in mind the way in which animals advance to a better reappearance (as do humans) by laying down their lives so that others may live.

However, the Buddha also contested the widespread rituals in which sacrifice was *imposed* on victims, because they cannot attain the goals for which they were intended, *i.e.*, they are ineffective. So the Buddhist point of view is not clear-cut.

Jains also strongly rejected the efficacy and practice of animal sacrifice, seeing, as Chapter 8 makes very clear, life and the living principle even in manifestations that others would regard as inanimate, "from a rock and a drop of water, up to men and women." Eckhart's remark, "Even stones have a love, a love that seeks the ground," could be understood in a Jain way, even though he meant something different by it. But Jains also accept the idea that within the long process of re-birth, there *are* appropriate actions for particular contexts, even though such contexts fall far short of true wisdom and release. An individual Jain might be sufficiently enlightened to refuse to participate in any use of animals involving their death, but he cannot, from the perspective of his own anthro-pology, prohibit others from so doing as they work their way toward a true perception.

Similarly, Hinduism believes that there are appropriate ways to proceed, according to the status and circumstance in which a living soul has been born. Indeed, there is a sense in which Hinduism can be described as the map of *dharma*—the guide to what is appropriate. This is particularly clear in the *Gita*, because the *Gita*, the Song of the Lord Krishna, is set in the context of Arjuna's sudden hesitation (on the threshold of a battle) about killing his relatives on the other side. Krishna en-courages him to fight, partly because it is his *dharma* to do so as a warrior and partly because, in the Hindu anthropology, it is impossible to kill anyone or to be killed oneself. It is pos-sible to bring the outer appearance to an end, but the essential inner self, *atman* (although projected into time and entangled in attachment to this world as *jiva*) *is* Brahman—is the un-changing reality, the unproduced Producer of all that is, which cannot be touched or affected, let alone killed.

> Know that that is indestructible,
> By which this all is pervaded;

Destruction of this imperishable one
  No one can cause.

These bodies come to an end,
  It is declared, of the eternal embodied [soul]
Which is indestructible and unfathomable.
  Therefore fight, son of Bharata!

Who believes him a slayer,
  And who thinks him slain,
Both these understand not:
  He slays not, is not slain.

He is not born, nor does he ever die;
  Nor, having come to be, will he ever more come not
    to be.
Unborn, eternal, everlasting, this ancient one
  Is not slain when the body is slain.[8]

Clearly, then, the sacrifice of an animal cannot kill what is essential in the reality of that animal, which is *not* its appearance but the underlying guarantor of *all* appearance, namely, Brahman. If you cannot kill your relatives, you cannot kill an animal, whether in sacrifice or in experiment, and you *may* indeed be helping it to fulfill its *dharma*; "for this thou wast created," as another religion puts it. Hinduism sees the whole process of creation, of the change and transformation of apparent forms, as a vast and necessary sacrifice. As Daniélou has summarized the point:

The universe appeared to the Vedic Aryan as a constant ritual of sacrifice. The strange destiny which compels every living thing to devour other things so as to exist, struck him with awe and wonder. The transformation of life into life seemed the very nature of the universe. . . . The principle from which the universe arises has a triple aspect, the devourer, the devoured, and their relationship, the devouring or sacrifice.[9]

It is in this context that we have to understand the remark in this book that "the sacrifice of an animal is *not really the*

killing of an animal." At first sight it must seem like special
pleading (especially when it is connected with the undiscussed
notion of "symbol"). After all, as Plutarch observed, "Boys
may kill frogs for fun, but the frogs die in earnest." But after a
closer look at the context of Hinduism's superficially similar
but in practice very different anthropology from the other religions discussed, a completely unique understanding emerges
of what is and is not appropriate in the interaction between
humans and animals.

This brief example of religious anthropology and its implications shows why it would be futile to expect a book of this
kind to come up with clear proposals to which all religions can
assent. Exactly the reverse is true: the stance that religions
take on particular issues has to be teased out by patient and
detailed argument, and very frequently it turns out that opposing attitudes can be maintained legitimately within the
same religion (legitimate, that is, in relation to what are agreed
to be the valid constraints and resources of that particular tradition). *A fortiori*, there are going to be differences *between*
the traditions, as this book well illustrates. (Consider, for example, in general the discussions of vegetarianism or in particular the different ways in which Judaism and Christianity
may interpret the same text in what they both regard as
Scripture.)

Nor is this difference confined to content alone. The religions argue in completely different styles, a fact that is very
obvious in this book. The style in which each of the chapters is
written is so different that you may well think, as you pass
from one author to another, that you are moving from one
world to another—and in a sense you are. Thus the chapter on
Judaism is a closely argued appeal to precedents, with every
step of the argument carefully referenced, because Judaism
rests on a belief that God has entrusted Torah, or guidance, to
His people in a way that includes specific laws and prohibitions. Similarly, Islam is a religion that rests on a revelation
bestowed on the world by God through His prophet, Muhammad, which (in contrast to other revelations) has not been cor-
rupted or contaminated by the recipients. As a result, the

chapter on Islam makes a comparable appeal to the revelation, Quran, and to its explication in Hadith—the narrations of how Muhammad and his companions first implemented Quran, as it was being revealed, in practice.

In contrast, Christianity, although believing itself to be a consequence of God's initiative in revelation, does not regard Scripture as establishing rules by way of constraint over all important aspects of life but rather as supplying the principles and offering the resources which, if adopted, will lead to the transformation of life into love. But the attempt to apply those principles and express the consequence of those resources leads to a wide range of conclusions, some more closely attentive to precedent and tradition than others—hence the inclusion of two chapters concerning the views of Christianity in this book. In contrast to the chapters on Judaism and Islam, the authors appeal more to working parties, reports, saints, and theologians than they do to Scripture.

Somewhat like Christianity, Confucianism has its equivalent to scripture in its revered books, but its major purpose is to apply Confucian principles to the formation of a well-ordered and harmonious life. Therefore in the conversation with a contemporary Confucian (see Chapter 9), neither Confucius nor the Confucian classics are quoted, but the Confucian ethic or teaching is brought to bear.

Equally remote from both the Jewish and Muslim styles of argument is the chapter on Jainism and Buddhism. Certainly, there are fundamental texts, but the point here is to gain insight as a prelude to enlightenment or release. For that purpose, stories, old and new, may be just as important as texts in opening the inner eye of perception. Halfway between the two is Hinduism, which is also a religion of revelation but in which the practice of the tradition is as sure a guide as the text. Hinduism comes down firmly on the side of precedent and tradition, but it also supports perception as the prelude to release; that combination is apparent in the style of that particular chapter.

Perhaps a more dutiful editor would have made a greater

effort to produce a more homogeneous style throughout the book. After all, the differences are *in part* a mere consequence of the origin of the papers in a conference, a notorious source of heterogeneous and uneven chapters when turned into a book. The editor can no doubt speak for himself, but in my view, it would have been a disaster to attempt any such thing. It is *essential* to recognize and grasp the fact that religions are deeply different, not just in *what* they say but in *how* they say it, and in what they regard as an appropriate argument. Religions are immensely influential in the forming of human judgments and that influence cannot be "locked onto" the huge problems or issues that confront us now (as inhabitants of a threatened planet) unless we recognize that the fundamental differences between religions lie not only in content but in method.

So at the conclusion of this book, is there nothing to be said but that religions cannot agree? Certainly not. There *are* important points on which they can and do agree—and the agreement is all the more impressive precisely because it comes from such different perspectives and routes of argument. Let me suggest some, arising from this book, by way of example. First, all religions agree that their traditions do not have a concept of animal *rights* but that animals do have valid claims upon us. Second, they agree that to ignore those claims, or to regard them as trivial in comparison with the pursuit of research, is to do long-term damage to the stature of being human—damage in which we will all be caught up, because the refusal, even by a single individual, of *moral* demand entails a chain of consequences, like the spread of a virulent disease. Even if the religious issue is not one of rights, it is most certainly one of human responsibility. Third, they agree that the validity of the claim of animals upon us is reinforced—perhaps even grounded—in the sense of the unity of life. This unity may be expressed in different ways (creation, Brahman, rebirth, sentience), but the claim is the same, that we belong to each other, not sentimentally (animals prey on each other) but, in the human case, with insight, responsibly: to touch the web in one place is to create a tremor in all its parts. Fourth, they agree that death is not the greatest evil one can imagine (which may create different priorities from those that obtain in the case of science and research) or conversely, that there are or may be more important things in life than living. Fifth, they agree that the various uses of animals must be differentiated: *some* uses *may* be justified, whereas others (for example, in relation to trivial ends, such as cosmetics or pleasure in hunting) cannot be. Therefore, sixth, they agree that the cultivation of pity, compassion, identification, and sympathy for animals is not, *ipso facto*, an expression of the pathetic fallacy but a necessary part of growing up. Perhaps indeed it is the quality of not losing the instinct of most children but of extending and applying it until the outrage is not simply endorsed (as, again, all these religions agree that it must be), but acted upon.

So this book is not the conclusion—it is the beginning of an argument and debate. It is a further point of agreement among these religions that in relation to circumstances that did not obtain in the earlier years of their histories (and that is certainly so in the case of the use of animals in scientific research), there can be movement and change. In some respects, what religions have had to say in the past is bad news for animals. The Japanese Confucian who holds a memorial service for the fish he has eaten is not, one would suppose, going to do much to protest against whaling fleets and their methods; and those who regard it as *normative* to make use of animals may moderate what happens but not ultimately whether it should happen, for example, in sacrifice. But this book makes it crystal clear that when religion is confronted by new and serious issues, there *is* a specifically religious sensitivity (the discussion of sacrifice in this book is an obvious instance). And certainly, the overriding impression from these religions is that one must (although for different reasons) take Boswell's side in his exchange with Dr. Johnson:

> *Johnson*:   There is much talk of the misery which we
> cause to the brute creation; but they are recompensed

by existence. If they were not useful to man, and therefore protected by him, they would not be nearly so numerous.

Boswell: But the question is, whether the animals who endured such sufferings of various kinds, for the service and entertainment of man would accept existence upon the terms on which they have it.

Religions insist that Boswell was right to raise the objection. What they then do is to ask whether those voiceless creatures (as the Christian tradition puts it) have rights or whether that long tradition of moral consideration (the rights of the voiceless), which is well rehearsed in human circumstances (*e.g.*, making decisions on behalf of those who are not competent, for whatever of many reasons) *is* applicable to the voiceless animals. That is a way of stating the issue that is hardly addressed in this book; indeed, at one point, it is implicitly denied as relevant. But I bring this up simply to reiterate that this is the *beginning* of a debate; that there are urgent issues here; and that religions are not unanimous in their preliminary judgments about them but in any case they cannot and should not ignore them. Let that sleeping giant indeed awake.

Notes

1. Pall Mall Gazette, *Library Edition of the Works of John Ruskin*, vol. XXXIII, p. lvi.

2. M. M. Johnson (ed.), *These Also*, p. 217.

3. Unpublished letter in D. Abse, *Passionate Moralist*, p. 311.

4. See, for example, "Only Connect . . . The Importance of Understanding Religions in Making Decisions Today," *Christian*, VII (1982).

5. J. Hersch (ed.), *Birthright of Man*, p. 7.

6. These interviews of how ordinary people understand and live their faith in today's world were originally broadcast in a series of BBC programs and are now contained in the book *Worlds of Faith* (BBC Publications, 1983). Hereafter referred to as *Worlds of Faith*.

7. *Worlds of Faith*, p. 87.

8. *Gita*, ii, 17–20.

9. A. Daniélou, *Hindu Polytheism*, pp. 63, 74f.

2 The Use of Animals in Science

Sidney Gendin

Although each year only about 5 percent of all animal deaths at the hands of human beings result from the use of animals in science, the number killed—in the neighborhood of 500 million—is not inconsiderable.[1] If we are to make an intelligent judgment about the ethics and scientific wisdom of permitting this many animals to be used in scientific settings, we must begin to inform ourselves at least about the broad contours of their use: for what purposes they are used, under what conditions, and with what legal protection, for example.

This chapter attempts to take us a modest way toward fulfilling this obligation. In Section 1, I offer brief descriptions of the major categories of animal use in science, adding, where appropriate, statistics concerning the numbers of animals used. A closer examination of some representative and, as it happens, controversial uses of animals is offered in Section 2. Virtually every critic of the use of animals in science believes that science can advance by relying on alternatives to using animals. I describe some of the major types of alternatives in Section 3 and canvass the opinions for and against their validity. Finally, in Section 4, I highlight existing and proposed legislation as it applies to the use of animals in science in the major English-speaking nations of the world. I restrict my attention to these nations not because the rest of the world is unworthy of our attention but only because of the limitations of space.

1. Categories and Numbers

Product Testing

Animals are routinely used to test the safety of consumer products. Acute and chronic toxicity tests are carried out on animals to establish toxic effects of low or high doses of such items as insecticides, pesticides, antifreeze, brake fluids, bleaches, Christmas tree sprays, silver and brass polish, oven cleaners, deodorants, skin fresheners, bubble baths, freckle creams, eye makeup, crayons, inks, suntan lotions, nail polish, zipper lubricants, paints, food dyes, chemical solvents, and floor cleaners. The test animals may be force-fed these products or have them rubbed or injected into their skin or dropped into their eyes. The Draize test, an eye irritancy test, is one such test, and will be described in more detail in Section 2. Not all product tests on animals are tests for toxicity. For example, animals are used in crash tests to analyze the adequacy of seat belts, helmets, and shoulder harnesses.

Behavioral Research

Behavioral research using animals may or may not involve pain. In many cases the experiments are the classic learning experiments in which mice or rats are required to run through mazes, move levers, or perform some comparable task. These may involve reward and punishment for success and failure. If the animal does not move the proper lever or does not move it quickly enough, it may not be fed or it may receive a small shock. Other psychological experiments typically performed on larger animals (usually primates) differ. For example, chimpanzees may be taken from their mothers, and a soft chimplike toy may serve as a surrogate mother. The baby chimps may experience different discomforts, while the scientist observes their degree of reliance on the mother-substitute. Details of one such experiment will be given in Section 2.

Instructional Purposes

Animals are used for study in the classroom. High school students learning some elementary anatomy frequently dissect frogs. The frogs are often dead, but sometimes the students themselves must first deliver the *coup de grâce*. High school students, and particularly college students, are not limited to frogs. Mice, rats, hamsters, guinea pigs, and cats are used to teach students, the majority of whom have no plans to become biologists, the elementary facts of anatomy by way of "hands-on" learning. No reliable tabulations are kept concerning how many animals are used for these teaching purposes, but the lowest sensible estimate would be two to three million per year in the United States. Over one million such animals are used annually in the International Science and Engineering Fair alone.[2]

In Vivo Tests

Animals are used whole and alive in so-called *in vivo* tests in the pharmaceutical industry. New drugs and vaccines are routinely tested on animals for their efficacy and safety before they are made available to humans.

Emergency Medicine

Animals are used in emergency medical situations. For example, primates have been killed and their organs have been immediately transplanted into humans to serve as very short-term support until satisfactory donors arrive. However, such cases are rare. Indeed, late in 1984 there was much publicity concerning an infant, "Baby Fae," who received a transplant of a baboon's heart. ("Baby Fae" was a pseudonym given to the child in order to preserve the privacy of the family.)

Long-Term Medical Research

Animals are used in long term medical research, including research on cancer, AIDS, and herpes.

Biological Research

Animals are used in "pure" biological research. Frequently investigators have no particular medical aims in mind but, rather, are trying to advance scientific knowledge. It is a commonplace in science that some of the most important medical advances have come about serendipitously in the course of pure research.

A statistical tabulation of the number of animals used for scientific purposes in any country can at best be only a good estimate. Despite claims to the contrary, nobody is keeping very close count. What is counted, in the United Kingdom for example, are the number of animals used in experiments that are funded by government agencies and, to a lesser extent, the number of animals used by pharmaceutical companies. In the United States, the convention is to estimate the number of animals used for such purposes at about 70 to 90 million per year. Some estimates, however, are as low as 15 million per year. Yet there are a few persons who claim that the best estimate is 120 million per year.[3] The difficulty lies in trying to extrapolate figures based on research reported to grant-funding agencies. Research that is not funded need not be reported. Moreover, rats and mice, the most commonly used laboratory animals, are currently exempted from the reports required by the Animal Welfare Act of 1966. Hence statistics concerning them are incomplete.

The Office of Technology Assessment (OTA) released some figures on November 18, 1983, breaking down percentages of use of laboratory animals as follows: 40 percent for biomedical research; 25 percent for commercial drug testing; 20 percent for toxicity testing; 10 percent for teaching; and 5 percent in a catch-all category called "other." But these percentages may not be accurate. To begin with, they are based on an estimate of 70 million animals used annually for science. This is the lower end of the conventional estimate. Second, the OTA's breakdown of each of these categories lacks precision. What counts as biomedical research is problematical. In fact, any research done by a biologist, any biological research done by an experimental psychologist, and anything done by a physician is automatically classified as "biomedical research," a classification that seems loose in many cases. In a not untypical case, researchers at Yale University devised an experiment in which cats were given ample opportunities to attack rats. The investigators claimed that the experiment "may help man to master his own violent instincts."[4] The Museum of Natural History in New York City did sexual experiments on cats after having first blinded them, and the director of the experiments claimed it would be a major contribution to learning how to control hypersexuality in humans.[5] The OTA routinely places such research in the category of "biomedical research."

Whatever the numbers or classifications, only in a minority of experiments are the animals given anesthesia, as illustrated by the following figures for the United Kingdom, released by the Home Office's Statistics of Experiments on Living Animals.[6] These concern experiments by licensed experimenters only. Generally these experimenters are persons using government monies for their operations. The statistics are for 1982 (see Table 2-1).

As one can see, in only about 4 percent of these experiments are the animals fully anesthetized, in another 15 percent the animals are partially anesthetized, and in 81 percent no anesthetic is given.

According to Richard Ryder, author of the widely read and respected *Victims of Science*, about 540,000 experiments on animals go entirely untabulated in official figures. These include tests for riot control devices and weapon ballistics, tests in which anesthetics presumably are not administered. Ryder also claims that 32.8 percent of experiments in the United Kingdom now serve a clearly identifiable medical purpose

Table 2-1.

Species of Animal	No Anesthesia	Anesthesia for Part of Experiment	Anesthesia for All of Experiment	Total
Mouse	2,131,358	296,105	15,239	2,442,702
Rat	554,630	273,701	104,004	932,335
Guinea pig	119,674	10,676	24,390	154,740
Rabbit	150,685	8,295	6,013	164,993
Other rodents	23,543	10,870	2,372	36,785
Primate	3,740	1,421	493	5,654
Cat	1,170	817	5,354	7,341
Dog	7,774	1,387	3,985	13,146
Other carnivore	561	523	792	1,876
Horse, donkey	356	106	13	475
Other ungulate	26,138	6,606	830	33,574
Other mammal	1,735	552	420	2,707
Bird	244,061	6,728	1,029	251,818
Reptile/amphibian	1,316	5,382	1,124	7,822
Fish	131,004	33,849	980	165,833
TOTAL	3,397,745	657,018	167,038	4,221,801

compared with 62.02 percent for such purposes in 1920.[7]

When the United Kingdom passed The Cruelty to Animals Act of 1876, it made provision for government inspections of laboratories. In that year there were about 300 experiments performed and about 15 government inspectors. By 1964 there were over 500 registered laboratories with over 8,000 licensed experimenters. The number of inspectors remained the same—15—now handling a combined caseload of several million experiments. The situation appears to be better in the United States. For example, statistics released by the United States Animal and Plant Health Inspection Service (APHIS) seem to show that the use of anesthesia is more common there (see Table 2-2).[8]

However, this covers only a listing of research facilities registered with APHIS and includes only about 1,660,000 animals. If we assume that figures for hamsters, wild animals, and

Table 2-2.

Animals	Dogs	Cats	Primates
Total no. in experiments	188,783	68,482	56,024
Experiencing pain— no anesthetic	2,684	6,531	942
Experiencing pain despite anesthetic	129,014	39,227	21,610

so-called "others" are proportional to the above, then the use of anesthesia may not be as prevalent as APHIS suggests.

Statistics for other nations are not as neatly broken down, but gross totals exist. In Denmark, for the year 1971, the Danish Ministry of Justice reported 1,400,000 as the approximate number of live animals used in experiments. For that same year, Australia reported 850,000 animals, India 870,000, Israel 323,000, Canada 2,768,000, and Japan 19,000,000. Sweden used approximately 1,000,000 animals in 1974, and finally Switzerland used about 3,000,000 animals.[9]

2. Behind the Statistics

Besides statistics, the details of some uses of animals need our attention. The Draize test, an eye irritancy test, will concern us first. Then, in turn, we will examine some specific uses of animals—and the controversies they have inspired— in behavioral research, drug testing, and cancer research. Our aim is not to resolve but to better understand the ethical and scientific divisions these uses engender.

The Draize Test [10]

In the cosmetics industry, one of the more commonly used methods to screen products for their safety is the Draize test, named after its inventor, John Draize, who developed the method in 1944. The test consists of placing rabbits in stocks that immobilize their heads and then dropping the substance to be tested into one eye, using the other eye as a control. The testing takes place over several days and may lead to opacity of the cornea, hemorrhage, ulceration, blindness, and nearly always to considerable irritation and pain. Indeed, the pain is sometimes so great that rabbits have been known to break their backs in efforts to free themselves from the stocks.[11] Rabbits are particularly well suited for this experiment because their tear ducts are too inefficient to wipe away or dilute the product being tested.

In the United States, retail cosmetics sales amount to about $10 billion per year and there are approximately 24,000 different cosmetics containing about 8,000 ingredients. Revlon Incorporated annually uses about 2,000 guinea pigs and 2,000 rabbits in acute oral toxicity tests, subacute dermal toxicity tests, immersion studies, and the Draize eye test. Revlon says in its annual reports that "No anesthesia is administered in any of the above procedures. This is due to the nature of the studies involved."[12] Avon, Gillette, and Elizabeth Arden use about the same number and types of animals. They, too, concede they use no anesthetics or analgesics. There is no effort by the Food and Drug Administration (FDA) to monitor the tests, and the FDA, as will be seen further on, does not contest the cosmetics industry's claim that analgesics cannot be administered "due to the nature of the studies involved."

A cosmetic is defined by the Food, Drug, and Cosmetic Act as an item that may be "rubbed, sprinkled, or sprayed on . . . or otherwise applied to the human body for cleaning, beautifying, promoting attractiveness . . . without affecting the body's structure or functions." Although cosmetics have been in the jurisdiction of the FDA since 1938, that agency has no power to require any testing whatsoever much less any specific test such as the Draize. What the Food and Drug Act, section 740.10, does require is a warning on any product that has not had adequate substantiation of safety. The law, then, does not require that tests of cosmetics be done on animals.

Indeed, there are hundreds of small firms, such as the by-now well known Beauty Without Cruelty, that produce lines of cosmetics, toiletries, and clothing that are neither tested on animals nor made from animal parts. Such companies appear to be flourishing and none has been implicated in lawsuits for harm done to consumers. Finally, the FDA lacks even the authority to compel cosmetics manufacturers to submit ingredient lists or any test data. In 1978, testifying before the House Subcommittee on Oversight and Investigations, Dr. Donald Kennedy, Commissioner of the FDA, stated: "In the absence of a specific statutory mandate to require test data and plant and product registration, and to do inspections, one relies, out of necessity, on programs that are essentially voluntary."[13]

Behavioral Research

There is a considerable disparity of opinion among psychologists concerning the nature and extent of behavioral research on animals. In a frequently cited article, it was maintained that a review of 608 animal experiments appearing in journals published by the American Psychological Association proved that none exceeded the bounds of humane treatment. Only 10 percent involved the use of electric shock and, of these, only a small fraction used shock above a moderate level. Only four animals were deprived of food, and none for longer than 24 hours.[14]

Nevertheless, there is conflicting evidence. In part, there is a problem determining what "extensive use" and "moderate level" mean. It is probably best to give a sampling of some of the more apparently extreme experiments so that readers may determine for themselves whether or not any of them exceeds the bounds of humane treatment. Although behavioral research is not the exclusive domain of psychologists, and although psychologists sometimes report their findings in nonpsychological journals, we shall limit the survey to what appears in psychology journals because that is the area in dispute.[15]

In a 1975 paper in the *Journal of Abnormal Psychology*,[16]

researchers reported investigations of the facial expressions
and social responsiveness of blind monkeys. First, the eyes of
five macaque monkeys were removed prior to the 19th day
of life. The young monkeys were then separated from their
mothers, who were placed in separate cages. Upon the mothers' uttering calls of alarm, the time required for the monkeys
to contact their mothers' cages was measured. These interactions were compared with those of young monkeys who were
not blinded. The researchers concluded that all the usual
facial expressions of sighted monkeys are also observed in
blinded ones.

Cats are often used in brain lesion experiments. Several
such experiments are reported in the *Journal of Comparative
and Physiological Psychology* in 1977. A team of researchers
from the Department of Psychology at the University of Iowa
offered this report:

> Because an abnormal grooming behavior that is medi-
> ated by the superior colliculi is elicited from cats with
> pontile lesions, an ablation study of the structures was
> conducted to specify quantitatively the changes in
> grooming behavior. Cats that underwent the surgical
> procedure except for the lesion and cats with lesions of
> the auditory and visual cortices served as control
> groups. [17]

The researchers found that "grooming behavior in cats
with pontile or tectal lesions [was] deficient in removing tapes
stuck on their fur."

Experimenters at Harvard University utilized squirrel
monkeys trained to press a lever under fixed-interval schedules of food or electric shock presentation. The purpose was to
compare hose biting induced by these two methods of sched-
uling. The monkeys were strapped in restraining chairs and a
bite hose was mounted in front of them. Shocks were administered to the monkeys' tails and the frequency, duration, and
pressure of biting were measured. The responses were compared with those induced by food presentations in various so-

phisticated ways. The animals were also studied under a range of doses of amphetamines. Various findings were duly reported in the *Journal of Experimental Analysis of Behavior*, vol. 27, 1977.[18]

At the Veteran's Administration Hospital, Perry Point, Maryland, dogs were placed in an experimental chamber and restrained on a table. They had to press a response panel to escape electric shock. Later their bladders were removed and ureters were externalized so that urine samples could be taken without storage in the now missing bladders. After surgery, the "animals were subjected to lengthy experience with various aversive schedules." In fact, they were subjected to 140 sessions of unavoidable shock with an intensity of 8.0 mA. The sessions lasted five hours per day, five days per week. Tranquilizers were administered, and the researchers concluded that "chlorpromazine consistently reduced avoidance response rates in dogs, producing consequent increases in shock rate." They also discovered that heart rate and urinary volume "showed no consistent pattern of results in response to drug administration."[19]

Drs. Steven Maier and Martin Seligman did "learned helplessness" studies on 150 dogs over a four-year period in which inescapable shock was studied. These responses were compared with responses in cats, rats, primates, and other species. It was noted that when response is totally debilitated and nothing can be done to escape pain, then "the learned helplessness effect seems rather general among species that learn."[20] Elsewhere it is argued that learned helplessness serves as a laboratory model of depression in humans. The effects of uncontrollable events influence a person's self-concept, assertiveness, aggressiveness, and even spatial localization. It is argued that to the extent that a person's depression makes him deficient in these various traits "the learned helplessness model is confirmed or disconfirmed."[21]

Behavioral research on animals remains one of the most controversial areas even within the psychology community itself. Several researchers, most notably Donald Barnes and

Roger Ulrich, who did years of animal research, are now staunch critics of it, insisting that none of it is worthwhile. Dr. Alice Heim, the former President of the Psychology Section of the British Association for the Advancement of Science and a person with 40 years of experience in experimental psychology, agrees.[22]

Heim discusses an experiment by Harry Harlow on maternal deprivation in which Harlow separated newborn rhesus monkeys from their mothers and gave them two "substitute mothers." One was a plain wire-framed object crudely modeled after a monkey; the other was also wire-framed but covered with soft terry toweling. Harlow reported that the infants preferred the model with the soft terry toweling. The monkeys were followed up in adult life, and it was noted that their responsiveness to the other sex had been seriously interfered with. It was the final conclusion of the project that "Thus the normal pattern of mating is a result of the interaction of the hereditary make-up of the animal and its own individual life history."[23] Heim expresses her amazement that one should have to conduct an experiment to discover this. She seems to regard this as a fairly typical experiment, and she holds that most animal experiments rest on a conceptual error. Her argument is that experimenters do experiments on animals that would be unthinkable to perform on humans and justify them on the grounds that animals are utterly different from us. On the other hand, they believe that the results gained from these experiments may be extrapolated to form conclusions about people. Heim believes that this is inconsistent.

Dallas Pratt, in his *Painful Experiments on Animals*, takes the position that the standard laboratory method of studying animal behavior, paradoxically, does not really study animal behavior. What is studied is only the pathology of behavior, the fragments that remain after mutilations of the functioning organism. The investigators are more interested in the reflex jerks that are "teased out by any of the myriad of prods, punishments, or pleasures which the ingenuity of a researcher can devise."[24]

On the other hand, many psychologists argue that very few behavioral animal experiments involve invasive techniques or high levels of stress. In a recent speech before the American Psychological Association, Perrie Adams argued that while *in vitro* nonanimal alternatives may prove very valuable for medical research, they must forever be inappropriate to the needs of psychologists because an isolated system "cannot replace the functioning intact animal to study its behavior."[25] Moreover, many psychologists argue that most of our knowledge concerning mother-infant bonding, compulsive eating, aggression, and depression originates in animal studies.[26] Indeed, Adams goes so far as to maintain that "virtually every medical advance" originates in experiments on animals.[27]

Despite Adams' confidence in the value of behavioral research and Coile and Miller's assurances (note 14) that the ethical treatment of animals in psychological studies may be taken for granted, American academic psychologists are clearly polarized as to the worth of behavioral studies and the manner in which animals are treated. Critics of existing practices recently organized a society called PsyEta (Psychologists for the Ethical Treatment of Animals). It is much too early to say what influence PsyEta will exert in the psychology community.

Drug Testing

Drug testing is a central part of medical research, and the former use of the drug thalidomide highlights most dramatically the grave problems encountered in this area. Thalidomide was introduced to treat morning sickness in pregnant women and tested on a wide range of animal species before being made available to humans. Its use by pregnant women caused severe abnormalities in newborn babies.

Why did it happen? Well, for one thing, the early tests on thalidomide were for its lethal effects only. No matter how much of the drug animals were given, it did not kill them. Also, prior to 1961 it was an entirely new concept that a drug not toxic to the individual taking it could produce severe congenital anomalies in their unborn fetuses.[28] In the case of thalidomide, specific deformities occurred in very few species of animals. In fact, teratogenic susceptibility to thalidomide is not universal in every species. There are only a few strains of rabbits, mice, and rats in which any abnormalities occurred as a consequence of the administration of thalidomide. Animals that might be expected to suffer the same problems as humans proved unaffected by the drug. Attempts to reproduce the teratogenic effects in monkeys have still not been successful. It is now known that tests on cultured human embryonic tissue clearly indicate the danger of the drug.[29] Had these tests been done when the drug was developed, tragic results might have been avoided.

As the thalidomide tragedy illustrates, there is an inherent difficulty in trying to predict adverse reactions to humans from studies in experimental animals. One simply cannot automatically extrapolate information from animal studies that yields either necessary or sufficient conditions concerning their safety for humans. In other words, drugs that are highly dangerous for species of test animals other than humans often prove valuable to us, whereas drugs that are harmless or positively beneficial to other species of animals sometimes prove highly dangerous to us. Penicillin is an interesting example of a drug that is fatal to guinea pigs even in very low doses. Other drugs useful to humans that are deadly to many animals include epinephrine, salicylates, insulin, cortisone, and meclizine. Drugs are not only dose-specific but species-specific. Species specificity is a function of differences in absorption, metabolism, excretion, gestation periods, and a host of other common biological functions.

A second problem inherent in toxicity testing of drugs on animals is that the animals cannot describe their experiences, including the aches and pains that are sometimes the side-effects of drugs. For example, they cannot inform us of headache, giddiness, and feelings of nausea. Finally, animal tests are nearly all short term, and some chemicals may take the length of a human life time to produce their delayed effects.

In the final analysis, then, no matter how many preliminary screenings are done upon animals, further preliminary screenings have to be done on humans. Should we therefore conclude that the preliminary screenings on animals count for nothing? This is a difficult question, but it is relevant to point out that in several suits the courts have ruled that it has not been substantially proved that the results of Draize testing on rabbits and thalidomide testing on mice can be applied to humans.[30] And many pharmacologists agree. Dr. Louis Lasagna of the Department of Pharmacology and Toxicology, The University of Rochester, maintains that it has long been known that toxic effects of many drugs are species-specific. Lasagna does not deny that some drugs are mainly dose-specific, but the failure to bear in mind this fundamental dichotomy of drugs gives rise to what he calls the "pathetic illusion" that "simply doing enough animal testing will predict all human toxicity."[31]

Lasagna is not alone. Many toxicologists and pharmacologists are convinced that routine drug testing on animals is neither valid nor reliable. They see a more reasonable alternative, namely, more extensive clinical trials coupled with postmarketing surveillance. Some point out that such drugs as penicillin, digitalis, quinine, and aspirin would not be on the market today if they had been subjected to the rules of current animal testing. Yet no drugs of more recent vintage have matched them in value.[32]

On the other hand, it should be borne in mind that ever since the thalidomide disaster of 1962, drug manufacturers have been held to more rigorous standards of safety. The Kefauver Committee, formed in 1959 to investigate drug advertising, prices, and the monopolistic nature of the drug industry, was inspired by the thalidomide cases to recommend more formidable regulation of the manufacture of drugs. The recommendation led to the Kefauver-Harris amendments to the 1938 Food, Drug, and Cosmetic Act. It is now generally conceded, even by such severe critics as Lasagna, that although considerable problems remain with respect to teratogenic, carcinogenic, and mutagenic assessments of drugs, routine animal toxicology tests "are more or less" satisfactory predictors of effects upon humans.[33]

Cancer Research

The most feared of all diseases is cancer, and for that reason I shall focus the medical discussion exclusively on animal cancer research, but to a great extent the following remarks are generalizable throughout the entire area of medicine.

The infectious and nutritive-based diseases that ravaged the people of previous centuries are now in decline. It is generally conceded that progress made against infectious diseases owes most to personal hygiene and community-wide sanitation, the concern for these factors having been inspired by the discovery of germs. The foundation of nutritional science was the discovery of vitamins, and their role in health owes almost nothing to animal experimentation.[34] In any case, the decrease of these diseases has meant the rise of deaths attributable to other causes. Today, about one in three deaths in middle age is due to cancer. There are of course many kinds of cancers and these tend to affect specific parts of the body: the breast, lung, lymph glands, pancreas, esophagus, rectum, and stomach are the principal areas. Over the last 30 years or so, the incidence of cancer of the rectum and stomach has declined but most of the other cancers have increased. The greatest increase is in lung cancer. In England there was a 136 percent increase from 1951 to 1975. Yet even as far back as 1914 epidemiology successfully identified the causes of a variety of cancers. About 85 percent of them are environmentally induced: excessive exposure to sunlight (skin cancers), smoking cigarettes (lung cancer), smoking pipes (lip and tongue cancers), industrial pollution (a range of blood, lung and other cancers), and carcinogenic food additives (a similar wide range). Smoking accounts for 40 percent of cancers in men. Meat consumption has been found to be associated with cancer of the colon, and breast cancers are related to dietary fats. Asbestos, vinyl chloride, and benzene are examples of industrial carcinogens. X-rays used to counter cancer (radiation therapy) and anticancer drugs are ironically also implicated in the production of cancers.

How was all this discovered? Not by animal experimentation but mainly by studies in epidemiology. Accordingly, many see a bitter irony in the experimental production of cancers in animals. In the vast majority of cases, they claim, the tested substances are *already known* to be carcinogenic to humans.

Treatment of cancer is terribly important. Given the fact, however, that 85 percent of cancers are environmentally produced in known ways, critics frequently argue that prevention deserves primary attention. We have the means right now, they say, without one further bit of research, whether on animals or not, to make a dramatic reduction in cancer. To be sure, these things cannot be done without considerable cost, not only in terms of the economic costs to the tobacco industry, for example, but also in terms of the psychological hardships that we are certain to experience if we make drastic changes in our lifestyles. Moreover, critics allege that animal-based research, despite public relations to the contrary, tends to be unproductive. The favorite cancer research animal is the mouse. Since 1955 the National Cancer Institute (NCI) has screened about half a million chemicals on mice in its search for a useful drug against cancer. NCI does not just test chemicals on mice to see if they are effective; it also uses these chemicals to induce cancers in the animals. But most mouse cancers are sarcomas (cancers arising in the bone, connective tissue or muscle), while most human cancers are carcinomas (cancers arising in membranes). Thus, although the screening has had some good results, critics claim that none of the drugs discovered as a result of it are as effective nor useful as the ten major anticancer drugs discovered before the screening began.[35] Of course, one wonders what role animal research played in the discovery of the ten anticancer drugs. According to the biostatistician, Irwin Bross, the incentive for testing those drugs came only *after* clinical observations on humans. Animal studies data were ambivalent, but because of the observations already made on people, the decision to try the drugs on humans had already been made.[36]

Despite this cynicism, some authorities, particularly those associated with NCI, believe there has been great progress in "the war against cancer," and this claim is backed by The American Cancer Society. Dr. Vincent DeVita, the Director of the NCI, claims thousands of lives are being saved today that weren't saved 20 years ago.[37] The yardstick the NCI uses is the five-year survival rate. In the 1950's only 33 percent of cancer victims survived another five years. Today 50 percent survive five years after diagnosis. Defenders of cancer research on animals claim that a good part of this improvement is due to animal studies.

Some authorities think otherwise. Dr. Richard Peto, an epidemiologist who is the author of a major study on cancer mortality for the Congressional Office of Technology Assessment, has said: "There has been little progress in curative treatment since the middle of this century . . . and there is no reason to expect substantial progress for the rest of the century."[38] Dr. John Cairns, of the Harvard School of Public Health, has publicly stated that the statistical advances are inflated and meaningless.[39] Cairns says it is not the integrity of the NCI that is in doubt but its methods of statistical analysis. The same point is made by Dr. John Bailar, eminent biostatistician at Harvard, who is the statistical consultant for *The New England Journal of Medicine*.[40] And finally, Dr. Haydn Bush, the Director of the London, Ontario Cancer Center, also maintains that cancer cures have not increased during the last 25 years.[41]

The reason there appears to be an improvement in the five-year survival rate, these scientists believe, is that diagnostic techniques now allow physicians to find disease that pathologists classify as cancer but which, in the normal course of events, would not kill anyone in five years. But these tumors would not have been detected 20 years ago. Bailar says that this is unquestionably true in the case of prostate cancer and to a lesser extent in breast cancer. It may also be true in other sites as well, and he specifically mentions the thyroid, the ovary, and the lung. Lesions that look bad microscopically may not manifest the biological behavior we associate with cancer. Moreover, some genuine cancers are now discovered much earlier than they used to be—most typically, cancer of the breast—and the result is that even if the patients received no treatment at all, they would survive longer than five years if the cancer took its natural course. This, too, starts the survival clock ticking a little too early when compared with previous periods. Finally, while the accuracy of recording cancer deaths is the same now as it was 30 years ago, there has been improvement in the registering of nonfatal cancer cases in recent years. This inadvertently makes it seem as if a higher proportion of cancer victims are surviving today. In short, according to the critics, the "war" against cancer is not being won, although billions of dollars are being spent on it, and the "true soldiers" in this war, the animals, are dying in vain.

Why, then, these critics ask, do we continue to fund such research? Lung cancers can be reduced by 80 percent without medical interventions of any sort. Heart disease can be reduced almost as dramatically by simple programs: improved diets, reduced smoking, moderate exercise, reduced stress, and even owning a pet (although perhaps the last factor is not an independent variable, as its undisputed value may be related to such things as reducing stress and even the fact that walking the dog is a form of moderate, regular exercise).

In 1972, a typical year, The University of Rochester's School of Medicine used 66,000 mice, 31,000 rats, 2,900 hamsters, 900 dogs, and some thousands of other animals in radiation experiments alone.[42] Given that the production of these radiation-induced cancers correlates poorly with cancers in humans and so is not likely to reduce human disease substantially, many persons allege that what we have are losses piled on losses. According to the critics, it is therefore not a matter of comparing what we stand to gain with what animals stand to lose; rather, it is a matter of comparing what we now lose in human life and animal life with what we might gain by adopting alternative methods of approaching the causes and treatment of human diseases.

3. Alternatives

Those critical of the use of animals in science do not argue that we ought to forgo science. Rather, they insist that we must explore alternatives. What are these alternatives and what are their possibilities? Here, briefly, is a list of the major ones:

(i) Mathematical and computer modeling of anatomy-physiology relationships.

(ii) The use of lower organisms, such as bacteria and fungi, for tests of mutagenicity.

(iii) The development of more sophisticated *in vitro* techniques, including the use of subcellular fractions, short-term cellular systems (cell suspensions, tissue biopsies, whole organ perfusion), and tissue cultures (the maintenance of living cells in a nutritive medium for 24 hours or longer).

(iv) More reliance on human studies, including epidemiology, postmarketing surveillance, and the carefully regulated use of human volunteers.

I shall discuss only the first three of these because it is in these areas that scientists who use animals in medical research have been the most skeptical.

Models

The development and use of models lies at the very heart of science. The classic picture of an atom as a tiny solar system is an instance of a model for the fundamental nature of matter. In the advanced portions of the pure sciences, models are not just heuristic devices to aid the imagination but are intrinsic to theory itself.[43] In the applied sciences, too, models are essential. New cars and airplanes are designed by testing their aerodynamic qualities on models. Architects build scale models not merely to illustrate what the finished projects will look like but also to test them in order to anticipate possible problems in exactly the way aeronautical engineers do. Indeed, when animal experimenters use animals, they do so because the animals are regarded as models for humans.

Computer simulations are often mentioned as a better model for scientific purposes than any animal. Although this claim may be a bit of hyperbole, the fact is that for many purposes they are as good, and future dependency on them can only result in their becoming much better. In particular, where physiological systems are well understood and definable in mathematical terms, good programs are already available. (In the ensuing discussion, a number of examples will be offered.) Some complex systems are poorly understood and therefore programs don't exist in these areas. Of course, in such cases, critics claim that relying on animals as models cannot be much better. But unlike the programs, the animals are already available.

It is important to understand that when mathematicians speak of computer models, they do not mean tiny replicas of large things. Mathematicians construct systems that they hope will mirror biological systems. Although the mathematical details are intricate, we can at least say this: These systems consist of equations into which biological data are input and analyses of data are output. Perhaps an example will elucidate. It is from a report by Dr. Alan Brady of the Bowman Gray School of Medicine, Winston-Salem.[44]

According to Brady, the glucose tolerance test is an example of something that may be simulated by a computer in a way that actually facilitates research. The computer model offers researchers the opportunity to explore situations that are not practical or ethical with animal experiments. Computer simulation also organizes material more systematically than animal experiments do and thus is better suited for teaching physiology students. A computer user first enters starting and stopping times for glucose infusion, the rate of glucose utilization, and the initial insulin concentration, then data on blood pressure and certain rate constants. The programmed algorithms manipulate the figures to generate the simulated results. Plainly, glucose tolerance can be calculated more quickly, for a vaster array of "animals," and over a range of values far more inclusive than would occur in real life. As an added benefit, Brady points out that computer simulations in physiology are much cheaper than animal experiments because costs are pretty much limited to initial outlay for program development.

Brady's example is not an isolated one. Ryder, in *Victims of Science*,[45] mentions computer techniques taught to medical students at the University of Pittsburgh that simulate the absorption and metabolism of drugs. Ryder also mentions computer simulations of cardiovascular defects constructed in 1970.

In general, a computer model is a program consisting of a series of equations known to express certain physiological systems. They may, for example, be related to cardiovascular dynamics. To this core program are added equations important to the regulation of blood acidity, heat movement, respiratory function, and blood pressure. Just such a program is used at the University of Texas Medical School.[46] It has been well received by students there for many reasons. Students may examine "patients" at their convenience, even stopping in the middle of an "examination" to attend classes. If serious errors occur, an experiment may be repeated. This is not usually possible with animal subjects. Simulations may be made to happen more slowly or faster than "real time." An electrical discharge takes a small fraction of a second, but the computer simulation may be slowed down so that the student observes changes as they develop.

The University of Texas is also experimenting with a program for teaching students the physiology of the digestive system. Since digestion is mainly a chemical process rather than a mechanical one, there is not much to see by peering into the gastrointestinal tract in operation. Thus, Texas scientists take data from hundreds of experiments in which the acidity and quantities of enzymes have been recorded and incorporate them into a computer program. Students then select appropriate data to study in accordance with the "experiment" they are currently performing.

Are there drawbacks to computer programming? Certainly. Even the University of Texas scientists willingly list them. For example, only by examining living tissue can one learn its normal and abnormal appearance, and medical students must learn by touch the proper amount of force to be applied to parts of the body. And if students do not observe the beating heart, the contracting muscles, and so forth, then they can never be completely sure what their computer models represent.

In 1974, the Director of Computer Research at the National Institutes of Health, Dr. A. W. Pratt, said that computer research is not designed to reduce experiments on animals but is done for its own intrinsic interest and worth. He claimed that computers must validate their predictions on live systems. Nevertheless, he conceded that technological systems are less expensive than animal models and that at some time in the future their validations might be carried out on human models.[47]

Opponents of animal experiments who cry out for greater reliance upon computer simulations frequently exaggerate what is currently available, but those who are content simply to insist upon the current limitations perhaps reveal their own biases as well as a failure of the imagination. Without a doubt there was a time when people insisted that the only way to learn to fly was to get into an airplane and fly. Anything less was inconceivable as a way of learning. Today, modern simulators are so realistic that an experienced pilot taken in his sleep and put inside a simulator, awakened, and told he had been put aboard an airplane and was now at the controls, would have a very hard time deciding whether he was being told the truth. Not only the controls but also the visual expanse as he peers through the window are all but indistinguishable from the real thing. Pilots today can become fully licensed without ever having flown a plane. Of course, the development of such simulators takes years, at a cost of hundreds of millions of dollars. Presumably, it is worth it.

Some anatomy departments have begun interesting experiments in simulation. They have found that they can teach dissection and a host of other important surgical techniques to medical students using pseudo-animals. These can bleed, blink, cough, vomit, simulate gas exchange, and even "die" when necessary. Recently, Dr. Charles Short, Chief of Anesthesiology at Cornell Veterinary College, developed a dog mannequin called Resusci-Dog. It responds to a broad range of techniques necessary for practicing and refining "hands-on" cardiopulmonary skills. For example, if a student applies excessive pressure while doing cardiac massage, a certain signal bleeps; if pressure is misplaced, there is a different bleep; and a white light indicates proper massage. Typically, veterinary students induce heart attacks in real dogs and only then begin to practice their resuscitation skills. Death may show they have done the massage poorly. Resusci-Dog has a femoral pulse, and it can also be used for practice in certain syringe injections.[48] The American Fund for Alternatives to Animal Research (AFAAR) has purchased one and intends to loan it free of charge to all veterinary schools willing to try it. It is engineered in modular fashion, and more sophisticated accessories can eventually be added on. AFAAR estimates that 25 Resusci-Dogs would fill the needs of all the veterinary schools in the United States.

The Use of Lower Organisms

We may now turn, although more briefly, to some recent and interesting research involving either the use of lower organisms or portions of organisms in novel ways. Consider the latter first. Dr. Joseph Leighton, with funding provided by AFAAR, the Lord Dowding Fund (of England), and the American Anti-Vivisection Society, has been at work developing a substitute for the Draize eye irritancy test. Since the Draize test is intended to stimulate inflammatory responses, it seems to require intact animals whose responses involve an ensemble of changes in blood vessels, connective tissues, and white blood cells. This suggests that isolated cell systems and tissue cultures are not suitable substitutes. Leighton overcomes the problem by using the chorioallantoic membrane of a live chicken embryo. This membrane has no nerve fibers for transmitting pain and is therefore especially suitable for the ends promoted by those funding agencies. The chorioallantoic membrane is a large, temporary structure lying just beneath the shell. Thus it is very accessible. It serves as a substitute lung during the chick's development. It has blood vessels that react to injuries in the normal ways. After about 20 days of incubation, it normally dries up. Chemicals that are usually tested in a rabbit's eye are injected into the membrane, and it has been found that the same gross changes that occur in the rabbit's eye are observable in the membrane. Moreover, the changes are proportional; when severe irritations are produced in the rabbit, they are also produced in the membrane; mild irritations in one also produce mild irritations in the other.[49]

The best known of all tests on lower organisms as a replacement for animal tests is the Ames test, developed by Dr. Bruce Ames at the University of California at Berkeley. Although the Ames test actually discovers mutation-causing substances (mutagenicity), Ames believes it also screens for cancer-causing substances (carcinogenicity). This idea is based on the view that most carcinogenic substances are also mutagenic. Ames takes the suspected cancer-producing substance and puts it into a nutrient medium in which a strain of *Salmonella* bacteria is growing. If the tested substance really is mutagenic, then the *Salmonella* will develop the indicated mutations. About 80 percent of the carcinogens tested this way have resulted in mutation. When substances known not to be carcinogens are tested this way, only about 10 percent of them result in mutations. This corroborates the very close association of carcinogenicity and mutagenicity and makes the Ames test an excellent way of screening presumptive cancer-producing agents.[50] The Ames test, however, is not quite what some critics of animal-based tests claim it is. The medium in which the *Salmonella* grow is actually treated with a rat liver preparation first. Some liver preparation or other is needed at this point in the development of the test, but it need not be rat liver. In fact, Ames has used human liver obtained from autopsies, and his preference for rat liver is dictated by convenience. Nevertheless, the humane killing of a rat to induce mutagenic changes in *Salmonella* is much preferred by many opponents of animal tests to inducing cancers in rats themselves. The test is now fairly standard in about 3,000 laboratories.

Another interesting use for bacteria is in tests of water pollution. The standard procedure is to immerse fish in different concentrations of the effluent to be tested and observe what concentration kills 50 percent—one more variation of the LD-50 test. But Beckman Instruments company uses a strain of luminescent bacteria as the bioassay organism. The light-producing metabolism of the bacteria is six times more sensitive to toxicants than are fish, and the test takes half an hour in contrast to the 96-hour test used for fish.[51]

Finally, work has begun in utilizing plants both for synthesis of useful drugs and as the subjects of *in vivo* research. Indeed, recent progress has been so significant that it has been argued that "there are sufficient numbers of bioassay techniques described in the current literature so that almost any biological activity of interest can be studied without utilizing intact animals."[52] The National Cancer Institute has now screened over 40,000 species of plants for *in vivo* antitumor activity and has identified many that are highly active antitumor agents. Of course, their safety is first screened on animals before they are allowed to be included in clinical trials on humans. But Dr. Robert Sharpe has argued that plants themselves can have cancer induced into them. In particular, he claims, there is research supporting the replácement of mice by potatoes in traditional tests of leukemia.[53] Although NCI has been doing plant tumor research for 25 years, it remains a fairly exotic frontier.

Tissue Cultures

Tissue culture research requires keeping cells alive outside a total organism. Animal cells have been cultured in laboratories since the 1920's. In the early days, the possibility of bacterial contamination imposed immense limitations on the use of tissue cultures. Today, antibiotics have removed those restrictions and tissue culture is available in nearly all research institutes in the world.

A tissue cell is typically cultivated in a medium such as a salt solution supplemented by various plasmas and serums to make the environment as natural as possible. The establishment of cell lines out of tissue cultures is essential for modern virology. Most viruses grow nicely in these media, enabling biochemists to observe all their changes. This, of course, is exactly what is needed for clinical diagnosis of viral disease. The best-known commercial application of virology is the production of vaccines for the polio virus, originally grown in kidney cells of monkeys but now normally grown in human cells. Rabies vaccines also are now grown in human diploid-cell cultures rather than in live animals.

Cell cultures are important in cancer research. For example, we can study the effect of certain hormones on tumor cells in cultures that have been obtained by the surgical removal of a cancerous breast. If the hormone inhibits the growth of the cells, this would be a promising sign for therapy. Another promising piece of research involves putting known cancer cells into a fertilized hen's egg. This causes the embryo to put outgrowths of cells toward the cancer cells, and the extent of the growth is related to the malignancy of the tumor. Some researchers maintain that the standard practice of introducing cancer cells into live animals to observe the development of the malignancy is not as sensible, since tumor development in animals is far slower than in fertilized eggs.[54]

Dr. John Petricciani and his colleagues believe they have an even better *in vitro* system than the chicken embryo organ culture system can provide. The problem with the chicken embryo system is that it does not mimic the immunological rejection potentials found *in vivo*. Petricciani has discovered that human muscle used as an organ culture system overcomes that problem. It is easily accessible (his own tissue samples were obtained from the Pathology Laboratory at NIH) and can be kept intact and usable even after a month of storage. It is true that muscle tissue is an infrequent site for tumors under natural conditions, but the researchers discovered that "the use of human muscle under the *in vitro* conditions described here did allow human tumor cells to express their proliferation and invasive potentials in the same way that they do under experimental conditions *in vivo* after IM inoculations."[55] This method offers a possibility not only for studying the biology of cancer cell growth but also for testing a variety of potentially important antitumor drugs such as interferon.

There is a thorough review by Dallas Pratt in *Painful Experiments on Animals* of the many medical diseases in which significantly greater progress, in his view, might be made by more reliance on *in vitro* experiments than on *in vivo* ones. Two illustrations must suffice. Tuberculosis has long been diagnosed by injecting material suspected of being infected into guinea pigs. The problem with this is that the organs of the guinea pig may not show a positive reaction to the tubercle bacillus for many months. Human cell cultures will be flooded with the bacillus only five days after infection. Consequently, one experiment showed that in 41 out of 2,000 tests the cell cultures were positive for tuberculosis when it seemed none of the guinea pigs had contracted the disease.

Second, Pratt mentions a cancer research experiment in which 86 beagles were forced to inhale smoke from 415,000 cigarettes over two and one-half years. The same results could have been obtained, according to Pratt, by exposing human lung cultures to tobacco smoke in an *in vitro* experiment perfected by C. Leuchtenberger.[56]

It is often necessary to determine whether the body's immune defenses to toxins are produced by humoral or cellular factors, i.e., whether they are due to antibodies circulating in the blood or to certain groups of white cells, the lymphocytes. Traditionally, drug tests are performed on live animals because there are well-known general limitations to the use of tissue cultures, at least so far as extending their use in the development of drugs is concerned. These are:

(i)   A drug has to be metabolized in order to express its toxic effect.

(ii) Tissues in the body are composed of many cell types, and these cells are integrated in a functional way. Cells in a monolayer culture seem unable to serve as a model for a nervous system.

In other words, if one raises questions about the transportation of a toxin through the body and not merely how it acts on a cell, or if one raises questions about the interactions of one part of a body with another part, then it seems that tissue cultures are of no use.

Nevertheless, advances are being made. For example, the liver is the main site of drug metabolism, and it is possible to incubate a drug with a liver preparation before putting it into a tissue culture. Some recent work has been successful in testing for a drug's carcinogenic activity. Hence the reliance on living creatures with livers may be overcome. In fact, it is the opinion of Dr. Philip Hanawalt, biology professor at Stanford University, that that day has already arrived. Hanawalt maintains that studies utilizing only cultured cells can elucidate the differences in how mouse cancers and human cancers originate. "New experimental techniques such as the analysis of cloned DNA from one cell to another, and the use of hybrid cells are particularly powerful and now render obsolete many approaches that have utilized animals to study mechanisms of carcinogenesis."[57]

It is of the very nature of scientific revolutions that major advances are unpredictable from the perspective of the old paradigms. This is why the claim of some animal-based researchers that such and such is quite impossible (for example, that one cannot screen a pain-killing drug by *in vitro* methods) may only point to their failure of imagination and has little bearing on what is or is not physically possible. Thus the claim of many animal-based researchers that they will be happy to use alternatives when they become available strikes so many advocates of alternatives as empty. Alternatives strain the imagination, and they simply will not appear unless they, themselves, are the objects of intensive investigation.

Other Alternatives

Shocking as it may now sound, human subjects can now be experimented upon in a variety of ways without running any risks. As Dallas Pratt puts it, "The increasing refinement and sensitivity of testing techniques, with the use of methods such as gas and thin layer chromatography, mass spectrometry and immunoassay make it possible to test in humans the metabolism of potentially toxic substances administered in doses minute enough to be harmless. Analytical polarography, for example, operates in the parts per billion range for many substances."[58] Actually, since the publication of Pratt's book, the range has been changed to parts per trillion by some of the newer developments in gas chromatography.

Chromatography and spectrometry eliminate risks to humans in the following way. Chromatography is the means by which substances are broken down into these trillionths of a part; spectrometry is the means by which these minute particles can be traced in their journeys. A portion of an otherwise toxic drug can be administered to a person and its path traced in his or her body. Much can be learned from watching this journey, and it is obviously superior to extrapolating results from crude, massive infusions of a chemical into an animal in doses no person would ever be subjected to. For example, the so-called LD-50 test requires giving animals chemicals in doses high enough to ensure that 50 percent of the sample dies, no matter how low the toxicity. Chromatography and spectrometry offer the promise of a much more efficient way to learn about the actions of toxins.

Finally, there is the matter of cost effectiveness. Mirkovic of the Salem Research Institute in Munich has made a detailed study of the comparative costs involved in fitting out a medium-sized animal experimentation laboratory and a tissue-culture laboratory.[59] She has calculated that the cost of installing a tissue culture laboratory is 11,390 English pounds sterling and its monthly upkeep is 1,680 pounds. The cost of installing an animal experiment laboratory is 82,689 pounds, and its monthly upkeep is 4,507 pounds.

These figures were calculated for West Germany for the year 1976. Obviously some of these values are too low and others too high when appropriate adjustments are made for different nations. But the deficiencies in one direction are cancelled by excesses in the other and, on the whole, these tremendous differences between costs of animal-based and *in vitro* laboratories are valid. Thus, healthy business instincts, even if unaccompanied by ethical considerations, should make pharmaceutical and cosmetic houses reconsider their standard way of doing business.

Although the availability of alternatives is now plentiful and scientists claim they prefer nonanimal alternatives to animal studies "wherever feasible," critics are skeptical. They point to the fact that 34 percent of American physiology departments have now found alternatives to the use of animals for teaching purposes.[60] They regard this as evidence that the remaining 66 percent are not utilizing feasible alternatives (presumably on the ground that physiology departments have similar needs). These critics of animal-based research point to such findings to support their point that it is not just a matter of a lack of funds to support a systematic search for alternatives that is retarding their use. Something much more fundamental is at stake, they claim—a plain resistance to take animals seriously.

4. Legislation

It is interesting to compare the legislation concerning use of animals for research in different nations. Such a review reveals something about different attitudes toward the treatment of animals and about what is known concerning the need for reliance on animal studies. Because of space considerations, I will limit my survey to existing and proposed legislation in the larger English-speaking nations.

Australia

Nearly all animal research is conducted by the federal government, some goes on at the state level, and surprisingly little is done by private industry. However, all this must only be a guess, because the government does not collect any statistics. There is something produced by the National Health and Medical Research Council called the Code of Practice for the Care and Use of Animals in Research in Australia, but it applies only to federally supported university-based research. Overseeing compliance with the code is the responsibility of "ethics committees," but the code is a guide with no enforcement provisions. Only two Australian states have licensing or inspection requirements. Australia is not an area of major activity in animal experiments, so inspection is not a large issue there. Less than 1,000,000 experiments per year involving animals is the most recent estimate. Thus, for example, although Australia was once a major importer of macaque monkeys when they were being used to make polio vaccine, there is very little trade in these animals now (14,000 macaques were imported in 1957 but only 155 were imported in 1982). Critics of the use of animals regard this as an encouraging trend, but other animal rights and animal welfare spokes-persons point out that Australia counterbalances this trend with their export of threatened kangaroos. The Australian government has recently requested that the United States remove kangaroos from its list of threatened species so that it can again become an export marketplace for Australia.

Canada

There are no federal laws at all governing the use of animals in science, the annual number of which approximates 3,000,000. Although the government does not supervise animal experiments, there is a Canadian Council on Animal Care (CCAC), an autonomous and supervisory body operating under the aegis of the Association of Universities and Colleges of Canada and supported by the Medical Research Council that proposes guidelines on animal care. These cover such things as how laboratory facilities should be constructed and maintained, environmental control, feeding of animals, waste control, transportation, preoperative preparation and postoperative recovery, and dozens of other things. There is not a word on what sorts of experiments are worth conducting. The manual of the CCAC says "The fundamental concept on which animal care in Canada is based is that of control from within the institution exercised by the scientists themselves." Nevertheless, CCAC publishes a regular newsletter, *Resource*, which from time to time carries articles that are critical of some scientific studies on moral grounds. Although CCAC endorses the reduction and replacement of animals in scientific experiments, it advocates a gradual, moderate approach. In 1981, the Convention on International Trade in Endangered Species (CITES) proposed new guidelines for the more careful transportation of animals. CCAC's Executive Director, H. C. Rowsell, successfully fought for the exclusion of mice, rats, and any animals specifically bred for laboratory use from the CITES guidelines on the grounds that they were not members of endangered species.[61]

United Kingdom

The Cruelty to Animals Act of 1876 amended the then existing law relating to cruelty by extending it to animals that while alive are subjected to experiments calculated to inflict pain for scientific purposes. It lays down the conditions under which experiments may be done with and without anesthesia. It requires that all experiments be performed by persons holding licenses granted by Her Majesty's Principal Secretaries of State. There is a provision that anesthesia must not frustrate the purpose of the experiment. Presumably, the use of anesthesia typically does frustrate these purposes for, as the statistics presented in Section I make clear, the administration of anesthesia is the exception, not the rule. Provision also exists for an inspector to demand that an animal be destroyed if it appears to him that the animal is suffering considerable pain. Since there are only a handful of inspectors who make infrequent inspections, it is not clear that there has ever been a case in which this provision was put into effect. Moreover, inspectors do not normally witness experiments; rather, they review the conditions of laboratories. The Act makes the usual exemption for invertebrate animals found in the laws of most nations regulating the use of animals.

English law regulating the use of animals in science has been virtually unmodified since 1876 despite persistent lobbying by various animal welfare societies. At this particular time the British government is not sympathetic to drastic reforms in this area. It has, for example, reaffirmed its commitment to the use of the LD-50 toxicity test,[62] and it has repeatedly said that the high moral character of scientific practitioners ensures that laboratory animals receive the most humane care possible. The Home Office Chief Inspector said that although "suffering considerable pain" is hard to define, its interpretation may be left to the discretion of scientists. "Were the licensee not a responsible enough person to be considered capable of defining these terms conscientiously, he would not be granted a license."[63]

Members of Parliament frequently put questions to the administration during parliamentary sessions, and these are often about animal matters. In the course of one recent session, MP Thomas Cox asked the Secretary of State for the Home Department whether he would seek to ban the use of animals in smoking experiments. The reply given by Mr. Raison was that "it would not be right to deprive the public of the safeguards that research into the risks to health involving smoking are designed to afford."[64]

In early September, 1982, Mr. Raison responded to a member of Parliament's inquiry as to the government's official position on animal research in these words: "The Government intends to improve and modernize the Cruelty to Animals Act 1876 when parliamentary time permits."[65]

In the light of Mr. Raison's representation of the government position, it will be most interesting to observe what its response will be to the rather remarkable recommendation by the parliamentary-appointed Committee of Enquiry into Human Fertilization and Embryology. This Committee recommended by a vote of 11 to 5 that on a small scale, and "under very particular circumstances," human embryos be used to test new products for toxicity and teratogenicity.[66]

United States

Because of the limitations on federal power laid down in the Constitution, the U.S. government can only make laws concerning animals provided they involve interstate shipments and foreign commerce. It is up to the individual states to impose cruelty laws or laws regulating what scientists may or may not do. Given the powerful traditional claims of scientists to be free to pursue what they judge to be in the best interests of science, no state in the Union has challenged the scientists' right to say what the limits of research are. Cruelty laws are all aimed at the occasional abuser—scientist, farmer, pet owner, or whatever. There are an incredible number of federal laws dealing with animals, but because of constitutional restrictions they come into play only in a roundabout fashion. There is no one federal agency that handles all animal-related matters. There are agencies to supervise marine mammal matters, endangered species, food processing, slaughter of farm animals, wildlife preserves, free-roaming horses, migratory birds, and animal experimentation.

Public Law 91-579, the Laboratory Animal Welfare Act of 1970, is enforced by the Department of Agriculture (USDA) and the several agencies under its dominion. Initially, the statute was concerned primarily with regulating the buying and selling of animals for research. Amendments to the Act during the 1970's widened its scope to include the exhibition of animals and strengthened conditions concerning their care and handling. The Act's definition of animals is such that only warm-blooded ones fall under its purview. Thus neither reptiles nor invertebrates are covered by it. As for warm-blooded animals, it is up to the Secretary of Agriculture to designate which ones are to be given the protections falling under the Act. Among rodents, hamsters and guinea pigs are covered but mice and rats are not. These exemptions are important, because mice and rats are the most commonly used laboratory animals. The Secretary has also not accorded birds the protections provided by the Act. Further, nothing in the Act addresses the question of what kinds of experiments may be done. What is regulated is the manner in which animals are handled, transported, and given pre- and postoperative care. In this regard, the United States is precisely like every other nation. Investigators conducting research sponsored by a grant from any federal agency are required to comply with policies set forth by the sponsoring agency and by policies set forth in the Public Health Service (PHS) Manual chapter entitled "Responsibility for Care and Use of Animals." The PHS has recently proposed some significant additions in its guidelines, including the following:

(i) Research should be such as to yield fruitful results for the good of society and not be random or unnecessary in nature.

(ii) Statistical analysis, mathematical models, or *in vitro* biological systems should be used when appropriate to complement animal experiments and to reduce the number of animals used.

(iii) The scientist in charge of the experiment must be prepared to terminate it whenever he or she believes that its continuation may result in unnecessary injury or suffering to the animals.

The proposed new guidelines continue to exempt scientists from using anesthesia, even in very painful experiments, "in those cases where the anesthetization would defeat the purpose of the experiment and data cannot be obtained by any other humane procedure."[67] However, such determinations are not unilaterally made by the investigator. His or her home institution must appoint an Animal Research Committee (ARC) to oversee the program. At least one member of the Committee must be unaffiliated with the institution and unrelated to anyone who is affiliated. This ARC is empowered by the institution to terminate research that it determines cannot be brought into compliance with PHS policy.

This is the fifth revision of the PHS guidelines since 1962. These guidelines actually precede the Animal Welfare Act. The current guide is used by the American Association for the Accreditation of Laboratory Animal Care (AAALAC) as the basis for its accreditation of institutions. Exactly what the force of accreditation is remains unclear, since of 123 medical schools only 59 were AAALAC-accredited as of the end of 1983.[68] Of course, if scientists breed their own animals they are free from rules concerning interstate shipment and foreign commerce. Moreover, if they seek no funds to help them engage in research, they are free from any regulations at all, including PHS guidelines. No one can say with authority how many scientists are doing such research since they are not required to report their activities.

Approximately 80 bills concerning animals were introduced in state legislatures during the 1984–85 session. The majority of these called for repeal of state laws permitting the release of animals from pounds to be used in research. The U.S. Congress is also busy considering bills related to animal research. As of September 1, 1985, the three most significant pending bills were:

(i) H.R. 2653 is the Improved Standards for Laboratory Animals Act, introduced by Representative George E. Brown, Jr. (D-Cal). This bill, as its name implies, does not address the issue of abolition of any kinds of experiments. Its reforms are, in the opinion of some animal advocates, very modest and put no serious restrictions upon scientists. Some of its provisions are somewhat like those proposed by the PHS. It goes beyond the PHS guidelines, however, in calling for the establishment of a data base center to provide information on improved methods for minimizing pain and maximizing the use of alternatives to animal experiments. At 1984 hearings of an identical bill (H.R. 5725, also introduced by Brown), several people testified that agencies like NIH place too much emphasis on voluntary compliance with federal guidelines.[69] Indeed, the Director of NIH, Dr. James Wyngaarden, admitted as much, although he denied that there is sufficient widespread abuse of animals to justify legislation.[70] A very contrary view was expressed by Dr. John McArdle, who testified that he had had ten years of experience doing surgery and "was told by my superiors not to worry about postoperative pain because animals don't feel pain."[71]

Dr. G. L. Van Hoosier testified that the bill rested on a fundamental error. Alternatives do not come about, he said, by research on research, and this is what the bill tries to encourage. Rather, alternatives come about incidentally, as it were, in the course of basic medical research. He urged an 18-month study before legislating. The final witness was Christine Stevens of the Society for Animal Protection Legislation. She had collected data under the Freedom of Information Act that showed that major and frequent deficiencies or violations of the minimum standards of the Animal Welfare Act existed in 23.7 percent of a sample of 186 institutions doing animal research that had filed annual reports. Another 22 percent had less frequent major deficiencies, and 28.5 percent had minor ones. An increase in NIH funds was given to 77.3 percent of the institutions with severely deficient standards during the second year of their grants.

The essential difference, then, between the Brown and PHS proposals is that Brown puts the onus on the federal agencies to monitor the requirements it calls for.

(ii) S. 1223, introduced by Senator Robert Dole (R-Kansas), is much like H.R. 2653. Although there are differences between the two, the pros and cons of the Dole and Brown bills are about the same. Accordingly, a detailed presentation of the Dole bill is unnecessary.

(iii) H.R. 5098 is a bill introduced by Representative Robert Torricelli to establish a center for scientific literature whose resources would have to be searched by any investigator seeking government grants. The bill is designed to eliminate unnecessary duplication of research. In a speech in which Torricelli introduced his bill, he explicitly said its purpose was in no way to deter or reduce "legitimate" research. The bill is somewhat controversial even within the animal rights and animal welfare movement; some of the spokespersons of the movement regard the plan to give scientists wider access to animal research as self-defeating.

What is the future of animal research? There are those in the animal rights and animal welfare movement who are overly sanguine about achieving their goals. They believe it is only a matter of time before the laws they wish to see passed are passed. They believe it is inevitable that scientific progress will make animal research obsolescent and that the public will be educated to rally behind their cause. They believe that this is only part of a greater movement—that factory farming will cease, hunting and trapping will end, and nearly all people will become vegetarians because they will realize that it is morally imperative, ecologically wise, and nutritionally sound. In all these expectations they are unquestionably mistaken. With the one exception of slavery, history reveals no profoundly divisive moral question that has ever been completely resolved.

One need only look at the abortion and capital punishment issues to see that there is an ebb and flow of opinion that is inherent in any complex moral matter. Moreover, the "other side" is forever working to maintain and advance its views with the wavering middle. For example, for every lobbyist against hunting and trapping there are about two lobbying for its continuance. The disinterested public is not likely to come down firmly on one side or the other in the foreseeable future. A recent survey shows that the public's feelings about animal-based research are mixed.[72]

It appears, then, that such values are in strong conflict in different segments of the population. The resolution for value conflict lies not with science but with ethical theorists. In the last decade, secular philosophers have begun to pay much attention to the question of whether the advancement of science or even human welfare may be purchased at any cost to animals.[73] It remains now to see what enduring contributions can be made by ethical theorists working within the traditions of the world's major religions.[74]

Notes

1. This is an estimate of the number of animals killed for scientific purposes throughout the world. No figures are released by either the U.S.S.R. or China. Estimates for the United States range as low as 15 million to as high as 200 million. Conventional estimates are approximately 70 to 120 million. Among nations releasing data, Japan ranks second, with 19 million. My own estimate assumes that figures for the U.S.S.R. and China are comparable to those for the United States.

2. The International Science and Engineering Fair (ISEF) is administered by Science Service in Washington, D.C. In 1980, the National Association of Biology Teachers and the National Science Teachers Association both developed new guidelines to discourage students from conducting painful experiments on vertebrates. ISEF immediately announced its opposition to these guidelines. See *Scientists Center for Animal Welfare* (SCAW) *Newsletter* (June, 1981), pp. 8–9 (hereafter cited as *SCAW*).

3. For a "traditional" estimate of 70 million, see *SCAW* (June and October, 1984), p. 2. For 100 million, see B. E. Rollin, *Animal Rights and Human Morality* (Buffalo: Prometheus Books, 1981), p. 91 (hereafter referred to as Rollin, *Animal Rights*). For 200 million, see R. Ryder, *Victims of Science* (London: National Anti-Vivisection Society, 1983), p. 24 (hereafter referred to as Ryder, *Victims*). Ryder only reports this estimate, he does not endorse it. He suggests 120 million. For the low estimate of 15 million, see Perrie Adams, "The Need to Conduct Scientific Investigations," address to the American Psychological Association, 1984 (hereafter referred to as Adams, "Need").

4. Quoted in Dallas Pratt, *Alternatives to Pain in Experiments on Animals* (New York: Argus Archives, 1980), p. 9 (hereafter cited as Pratt, *Alternatives*).

5. Pratt, *Alternatives*, p. 8.

6. Colin Smith, editor, *Animals' Defender* (September–October, 1983).

7. Ryder, *Victims*, p. 16.

8. *SCAW* (September, 1981), p. 4.

9. Ryder, *Victims*, p. 26.

10. The Draize test is one of the two major commercial tests that have aroused the ire of animal welfare and animal rights groups. The other is the LD-50 test. LD stands for lethal dose. In this test, animals are force-fed a dose of a substance that is being screened for toxicity. The amount of the dose is gradually increased to the point at which 50 percent of the test animals succumb. Further details may be gleaned from the aforementioned books by Pratt, Rollin, and Ryder.

11. T. Ward and L. Hunt, "Animal Rights in the Classroom," *National Anti-Vivisection Bulletin* (Fall–Winter, 1983), p. 19.

12. Pratt, *Alternatives*, p. 229.

13. Testimony before the House of Representatives Subcommittee on Oversight and Investigations, February 2, 1978.

14. D. C. Coile and N. E. Miller, "How Radical Animal Activists Try to Mislead Humane People," *American Psychologist* (June, 1984), pp. 700–701. In contrast to the Coile and Miller study, the

Department of Agriculture stated that in fiscal year 1983, 139,411 animals were subjected to serious pain or distress without the benefit of pain-relieving drugs. See *Animal Welfare Enforcement FY 1983*, U.S.D.A., APHIS, Table 3, p. 11. For this information I am indebted to Dr. Michael Giannelli, who showed me his forthcoming "Pro-People, Pro-Science, Anti-Vivisection" article to appear in *Cogitations* (hereafter referred to as Giannelli, "Pro-People").

15. More details of all five cases reported under Behavioral Research, including author citations, can be found in Jeff Diner, *Physical and Mental Suffering of Experimental Animals* (Washington, D.C.: Animal Welfare Institute, 1979), (hereafter referred to as Diner, *Suffering*). Diner's survey of over 200 experiments covers just the years 1973–1978.

16. Diner, *Suffering*, p. 6.

17. Diner, *Suffering*, pp. 59–60.

18. Diner, *Suffering*, p. 81.

19. Diner, *Suffering*, pp. 105–107.

20. Diner, *Suffering*, pp. 111–117.

21. Diner, *Suffering*, p. 116.

22. Biographies of the professional careers of Barnes and Ulrich have appeared in dozens of animal rights and animal welfare magazines. See, for example, the accounts in Pratt, *Alternatives*, pp. 42–45. Alice Heim's discussion of Harlow is found in "Experimental Psychology and the Use of Animals," Speech to the National Anti-Vivisection Society (U.K.), May, 1980 (hereafter referred to as Heim, "Experimental Psychology").

23. Heim, "Experimental Psychology."

24. Pratt, *Alternatives*, p. 31.

25. Adams, "Need," p. 7.

26. F. A. King, "Animal Research: The Case for Experimentation," *Psychology Today* (September, 1984), pp. 56–58.

27. Adams, "Need," p. 1. Adams' claim may be conceptually incoherent. As Michael Giannelli puts it, "The attainment of scientific knowledge is not analogous to collecting driftwood at the seashore." What percentage of the development of advances in open heart sur-

gery is due to animal experimentation? Obviously, as Giannelli points out, the development would have been impossible without previous advances in the fields of mathematics, physics, plastics, and so forth. And, in turn, one cannot begin to meaningfully say what percentage of advancement in these fields is due to animal experimentation. See Giannelli, "Pro-People."

28. William McBride, M.D., F.R.C.P.G., in a letter to the Sydney *Daily Telegraph*, reproduced in Ryder, *Victims*, pp. 174–175. McBride was among the first physicians to discover the dangers of thalidomide.

29. J. Lash and L. Saxen, "Effects of Thalidomide on Human Embryonic Tissue," *Nature* (no. 232, 1971), p. 634.

30. Pratt, *Alternatives*, p. 219.

31. Louis Lasagna, "Toxicological Barriers to Providing Better Drugs," *Archives of Toxicology* (vol. 43, Oct., 1979), pp. 27–33.

32. Brandon Reines, "Cancer Research with Animals," *NAVS Bulletin* (Summer, 1984), (hereafter referred to as Reines, "Cancer Research").

33. W. Wardell and L. Lasagna, *Regulation and Drug Development* (Washington, D.C.: American Enterprise Institute for Public Policy Research, 1975).

34. Among dozens of skeptics and their publications concerning medicine's role in reducing infectious diseases are Rick Carlson, *The End of Medicine* (New York: Wiley, 1975), James Giles, *Medical Ethics* (Cambridge: Schenkman, 1983), and Victor Fuchs, *Who Shall Live?* (New York: Basic Books, 1975).

35. Reines, "Cancer Research," p. 5.

36. Ibid.

37. Associated Press dispatch to *Ann Arbor News*, October 22, 1984.

38. *Ann Arbor News*, October 22, 1984.

39. Ibid.

40. Ibid.

41. Ibid.

42. Pratt, *Alternatives*, p. 64.

43. Norman R. Campbell's *What Is Science?* (New York: Dover, 1921) remains the classic exposition of the role of models in science.

44. Alan Brady, *SCAW* (September, 1983), p. 8.

45. Ryder, *Victims*, p. 115.

46. Bernard Conyers, "Progress in Texas," *Lord Dowding Fund Bulletin* (no. 20, Autumn, 1983), pp. 6–9.

47. A. W. Pratt's view is mentioned in Dallas Pratt (no relation), *Painful Experiments on Animals* (New York: Argus Archives, 1976), p. 162 (hereafter referred to as Pratt, *Painful Experiments*).

48. American Fund for Alternatives to Animal Research, *News Abstract* (Winter, 1984–85 and several earlier issues).

49. Joseph Leighton, "Development of a Procedure Using the Chick Egg As an Alternative to the Draize Rabbit Test," in *Alternative Methods in Toxicology*, vol. 1, *Product Safety Evaluation* (New York: Mary Ann Liebert, 1983), pp. 163–177. Also, "The Chick Embryo in Toxicology," publication forthcoming. I am indebted to Dr. Leighton for showing me this and other of his publications.

50. Bruce Ames is the author of over 140 articles on the subject of mutagenicity. I am indebted to him for having sent me a considerable number of these. Among the more recent are "A New Salmonella Tester Strain, TA97, for the Detection of Frameshift Mutagens: A Run of Cytosines as a Mutational Hot-Spot," *Mutation Research* (no. 94, 1982), pp. 315–330; "Revised Methods for the Salmonella Mutagenicity Test," *Mutation Research* (no. 113, 1983), pp. 173–215; and "A New Salmonella Tester Strain (TA 102) with A:T Base Pairs at the Site of Mutation Detects Oxidative Mutagens," *Proceedings of the National Academy of Science, USA* (no. 79, 1982), pp. 7445–7449.

51. Pratt, *Alternatives*, p. 214.

52. N. R. Fransworth and J. M. Pezzuto, "Practical Pharmacological Evaluation of Plants," *Lord Dowding Fund Bulletin* (no. 21, Spring, 1984), pp. 26–34.

53. Robert Sharpe, "Science Now," *Lord Dowding Fund Bulletin* (no. 20, Autumn 1983), pp. 40–44.

54. The claim these researchers are making is not necessarily true of brain cancer but it is true of the far more common cancers of the breast and the lung.

55. J. C. Petricciani, I. Levenbook, and R. Locke, "Human Muscle: A Model for the Study of Human Neoplasia," *Investigational New Drugs* (vol. 1, 1983), pp. 297–302. My thanks again to Dr. Petricciani for supplying me with his research papers.

56. Pratt, *Alternatives*, p. 107.

57. Quoted by Dr. Robert Sharpe in "Cancer Research: Moves Away from Laboratory Animals," *Animals' Defender* (July–August, 1982), p. 62.

58. Pratt, *Alternatives*, p. 168.

59. O. Mirkovic, "The Economic Aspects of Tissue Culture Research," in *The Moral, Scientific, and Economic Aspects of Research Techniques Not Involving the Use of Living Animals: Speeches Given at the Brighton Conference*, March, 1976 (London: National Anti-Vivisection Society, 1976), pp. 27–30.

60. Report of the American Physiological Society Before the House Agricultural Committee, September 19, 1984.

61. CCAC, "Lab Animals Not Endangered Species," *Resource* (Spring, 1981), p. 3.

62. See *supra*, note 10, for more about LD-50.

63. Dr. J. D. Rankin, in reply to an inquiry at the British Association for the Advancement of Science, in Alternatives to Laboratory Animals, *ATLA* (June, 1982).

64. Hansard's *Parliamentary Debates*, July 5, 1982.

65. Hansard's *Parliamentary Debates*, September 11, 1982.

66. CCAC, *Resource* (Fall–Winter, 1984), p. 1.

67. "Public Health Service Policy on Humane Care and Use of Animals by Awardee Institutions," 1984 draft of revised proposals. My thanks to Dr. Alan R. Price, Associate Vice President for Research, University of Michigan, for showing the draft to me.

68. J. Zola, J. Sechzer, J. Sieber, and A. Griffin, "Animal Experimentation Issues for the 1980s," *Science, Technology, and Human Values* (Spring, 1984), pp. 49–50 (hereafter referred to as Zola *et al.*, "Animal Experimentation").

69. Hearings on H.R. 5725, September 19, 1984, before the House Agriculture Committee. Reported in *Animal Welfare Institute*

Quarterly (Summer, 1984), pp. 1, 4–5, 8. (Not the result of clair-voyance, the issue was delayed until after the hearings; hereafter re-ferred to as Hearings on H.R. 5725, September 19, 1984.)

70. Hearings on H.R. 5725, September 19, 1984.

71. Ibid.

72. Zola *et al.*, "Animal Experimentation," p. 45.

73. Any list of the more important recent works would surely include the following: Tom Regan, *The Case for Animal Rights* (Berke-ley: University of California, 1983); Peter Singer, *Animal Liberation* (New York: New York Review, 1975); Mary Midgley, *Animals and Why They Matter* (Athens: University of Georgia, 1983); and Bernard Rollin, *Animal Rights and Human Morality* (Buffalo: Prometheus Books, 1981).

74. Special thanks are due to several persons for their assistance in preparing this paper: Dr. Robert Sharpe, Science Advisor for the National Anti-Vivisection Society (U.K.), and Mrs. Christine Stevens, President of the Animal Welfare Institute, both of whom discovered and pointed out to me several important errors in an earlier draft; Dr. Ethel Thurston, Director of the American Fund for Alternatives to Animal Research, who proved to be a valuable resource person; and Professor Tom Regan of North Carolina State University for his all-around valuable assistance, too extensive to try to document.

3 Judaism and Animal Experimentation

Rabbi Dr. J. David Bleich

While our teacher Moses was tending the sheep of
Jethro in the wilderness a kid ran away from him. He
ran after it until it reached Hasuah. Upon reaching
Hasuah it came upon a pool of water [whereupon] the
kid stopped to drink. When Moses reached it he said,
"I did not know that you were running because [you
were] thirsty. You must be tired." He placed it on his
shoulder and began to walk. The Holy One, blessed be
He, said, "You are compassionate in leading flocks belonging to mortals; I swear you will similarly shepherd
my flock, Israel."

Midrash Rabbah, Shemot 2:2

1. Concern for the Welfare of Animals

In a provocative comment, the German philosopher
Arthur Schopenhauer remarked that the denial of rights to
animals is a doctrine peculiar to Western civilization and reflects a barbarianism that has its roots in Judaism: "*Die ver-
meintliche Rechtlosigkeit der Tiere ist geradezu eine em-
pörende Rohheit und Barberei des Okzidents, deren Quelle im
Judentum liegt.*" [1]

Whether denial of rights to animals is or is not barbaric is
a value judgment regarding which reasonable men may differ.
Whether or not Judaism actually denies such rights to animals
is a factual matter that is readily discernible. The Bible abounds
in passages that reflect concern for animal welfare. Concern

for the welfare of animals is clearly regarded as the trait of
a righteous person: "A righteous man regardeth the life of
his beast; but the tender mercies of the wicked are cruel"
(Proverbs 12:10). Divine concern for the welfare of animals is
reflected in numerous passages: "And His tender mercies are
over all His works" (Psalms 145:9); "The eyes of all wait for
Thee, and Thou givest them their food in due season. Thou
openest Thy hand and satisfiest every living thing with favor"
(Psalms 145:15–16); "He giveth to the beast his food, and to
the young ravens which cry" (Psalms 147:9); "Who provided
for the raven his prey, when his young ones cry unto God and
wander for lack of food" (Job 38:41); ". . . and should not I
have pity on Nineveh, that great city, wherein are more than
six score thousand persons . . . and also much cattle?" (Jonah
4:11); and "Man and beast thou preservest, O Lord" (Psalms
36:7). *De minimus*, these verses serve to establish the theological proposition that divine mercy extends not only to humans but also to members of the animal kingdom.

It further follows that, as a religion in which *imitatio Dei*
serves as a governing moral principle,[2] Judaism must perforce
view compassion toward animals as a moral imperative. It is
told variously of one or another of the leading exponents of the
Mussar movement that he kept a cat as a pet and insisted upon
feeding the cat personally. That individual is reported to have
remarked to his disciples that his motivation was simply to
emulate divine conduct. Since God extends "His tender mercies . . . over all His works" (Psalms 145:9), man should ea-
gerly seek opportunities to do likewise. The story is perhaps
apocryphal in nature but remarkable nonetheless because of
its wide currency in rabbinic circles.[3]

These sources, however, serve only to demonstrate that
animal-directed conduct that is compassionate in nature constitutes a "good deed"; they do not serve to establish a system
of normative duties or responsibilities. Particularly in light of
the strong nomistic element present in Judaism, the absence
of normative regulations might well be regarded as indicative
of the absence of serious ethical concern for the welfare of

members of the animal kingdom. But this is demonstrably not the case, for, in Jewish teaching, there is no dearth of *nomoi* designed to protect and promote animal welfare. The most obvious example of a regulation having such an effect and one that is clearly biblical in origin is contained in the verse, "If thou see the ass of him that hateth thee lying under its burden, thou shalt forebear to pass by him; thou shalt surely release it with him" (Exodus 23:5). The same concern is manifest in the prohibition against muzzling an ox while it is threshing so that the animal can remain free to eat the produce while working (Deuteronomy 25:4). Similarly, Scripture provides that both domestic animals and wild beasts must be permitted to share in produce of the land, which grows without cultivation during the sabbatical year.[4] Although the literal meaning of the biblical text may be somewhat obscure, talmudic exegesis understands Genesis 9:4 and Deuteronomy 12:23 as forbidding eating a limb that has been severed from a living animal. Jewish law teaches that this prohibition, unlike most other commandments, is universally binding upon all peoples as one of the Seven Commandments of the Sons of Noah. Sabbath laws contained in both formulations of the Decalogue reflect a concern that goes beyond the mere elimination of pain and discomfort and serve to promote the welfare of animals in a positive manner by providing for their rest on the Sabbath day: "But the seventh day is a Sabbath unto the Lord thy God, in it thou shalt not do any manner of work . . . nor thine ox, nor thine ass, nor any of thy cattle" (Deuteronomy 5:14). Even more explicit in expressing concern for the welfare of animals is the verse "but on the seventh day thou shalt rest; that thine ox and thine ass may have rest" (Exodus 23:12).[5]

Judaism posits still another regulation regarding the welfare of animals that is regarded as biblical in nature, even though the law is not reflected in a literal reading of Scripture. The biblical statement "I will give grass in thy fields for thy cattle, and thou shall eat and be satisfied" (Deuteronomy 11:15) is understood in rabbinic exegesis as forbidding a person to partake of any food unless he has first fed his animals.[6]

This regulation is derived from the order in which the two clauses constituting the verse are recorded. The passage speaks first of providing for animals and only subsequently of satisfying human needs.[7] Amplifying this rule, the Palestinian Talmud, *Yevamot* 15:3 and *Ketubot* 4:8, declares that a person is forbidden to purchase an animal unless he can assure an adequate supply of food on its behalf.

Nevertheless, it does not necessarily follow that a general obligation to be kind to animals, or minimally, a duty to refrain from cruelty to animals, can be inferred from any of these biblical regulations or even from all of them collectively. These regulations have been understood by some Sages of the *Talmud* as establishing particular duties, not as expressions of a more general duty. Nor is it demonstrably certain that even these limited and particular duties are designed primarily for the purpose of promoting the welfare of animals. Even with regard to the particular duty concerning removing the burden borne by a beast, the commandment does not necessarily reflect concern for the welfare of the animal. The obligation to release the ass from its burden (Exodus 23:5), that is, to assist the owner in unloading merchandise or materials carried by a beast of burden, and the similar obligation to come to the assistance of a fallen animal (Deuteronomy 22:4) are understood by many classical commentators as duties rooted in a concern for the financial loss that would be suffered by the animal's master if the animal were to collapse under the weight of the burden. Thus, in formulating the rationale underlying this commandment, R. Aaron ha-Levi of Barcelona, *Sefer ha-Hinnukh*, no. 80, declares:

> The root purpose of the precept is to educate our spirit in the trait of compassion, which is laudable. It is unnecessary to state that a duty lies on us to take pity on a person suffering physical pain;[8] however, it is incumbent upon us to pity and rescue even a person who is in distress because of the loss of his money.

Yet, Judaism most certainly *does* posit an unequivocal prohibition against causing cruelty to animals. The *Gemara*,

Baba Metzi'a 32b, carefully defines the limits of the obligation to assist in "unloading" the burden carried by an animal but hastens to add that assistance not encompassed within the ambit of the commandment concerning "unloading" (*perikah*) is required by virtue of a general biblical principle prohibiting cruelty to animals and requiring that measures be taken to alleviate "*tza'ar ba'alei hayyim*—the pain of living creatures." Thus, for example, the commandment concerning "unloading" imposes no obligation in a situation in which an inordinate burden has been placed upon the animal. This exclusion may readily be understood in light of the earlier-cited analysis of *Sefer ha-Hinnukh*. Since the master has brought the impending loss upon himself by reason of his own imprudence, there is no obligation to come to his aid. However, assistance is nevertheless required by virtue of the obligation owed to the animal. The *Gemara* proceeds to indicate that proper categorization of the nature of the obligation is not of mere theoretical interest but yields a practical distinction. No fee may be demanded for assisting in unloading an animal when such assistance is required by the commandment concerning "unloading," that is, when the concern is conservation of property; however, compensation may be required if the sole concern is for the welfare of the animal.[9]

The source of the obligation concerning *tza'ar ba'alei hayyim* that imposes a general concern for the welfare of animals is far from clear. Indeed, the *Gemara, Baba Metzi'a* 32b, cites a dispute with regard to whether the obligation with regard to *tza'ar ba'alei hayyim* is biblical or rabbinic in nature.[10] As has been indicated, if it is biblical in nature,[11] according to most authorities this duty is not directly derived from the obligation of "unloading." One notable exception is Rashi, *Shabbat* 128b. Rashi states that according to those sages of the *Talmud* who maintain that binding regulations may be inferred from the rationale underlying precepts, obligations concerning *tza'ar ba'alei hayyim* are directly derived from the verse "thou shalt surely release it with him" (Exodus 23:5).[12] Maimonides, *Guide of the Perplexed*, Book III, chapter 17, and R. Judah ha-Hasid, *Sefer Hasidim* (ed. Reuben Margulies), no. 666, regard the biblical narrative concerning Balaam and his ass as the source of the biblical prohibition against cruelty toward animals. These authorities indicate that the verse "And the angel of the Lord said unto him: 'Wherefore hast thou smitten thine ass these three times?'" (Numbers 22:32) serves to establish a prohibition against conduct of that nature.[13] Me'iri, *Baba Metzi'a* 32b, is of the opinion that obligations concerning *tza'ar ba'alei hayyim* are derived from the prohibition against muzzling an ox while it is engaged in threshing (Deuteronomy 25:4). *Shitah Mekubetzet, Baba Metzi'a* 32b, suggests that these obligations may be derived from the prohibition against muzzling an ox engaged in threshing or, alternatively, *tza'ar ba'alei hayyim* may simply be the subject of *halakhah le-Mosheh me-Sinai*, i.e., an oral teaching transmitted to Moses at Mount Sinai with no accompanying written record in the Pentateuch.[14]

Other scholars advance less obvious sources as constituting the scriptural basis for obligations concerning *tza'ar ba'alei hayyim*. R. Moses ibn Habib, *Yom Teru'ah, Rosh ha-Shanah* 27a, finds a source for such obligations in the verse "'and thou shalt bring forth to them water out of the rock; so thou shalt give the congregation and their cattle drink'" (Numbers 20:8). Water was miraculously produced from the rock for the benefit of animals as well as humans. Water was provided for the animals, states R. Moses ibn Habib, in order to obviate *tza'ar ba'alei hayyim*. In the opinion of this authority, Scripture specifically records that the miracle was performed on behalf of animals as an admonition to man directing him likewise to alleviate the suffering of brute creatures. R. Moses Sofer, *Hagahot Hatam Sofer, Baba Metzi'a* 32b, similarly regards obligations with regard to animal welfare as predicated upon emulation of divine conduct. Thus *Hatam Sofer* cites the verse "And His tender mercies are over all His works" (Psalms 145:9) as imposing an obligation upon man to exercise compassion toward animals. Earlier, *Sefer Haredim*, Chapter 4, expressed the opinion that compassion toward animals is mandated by the commandment "and you shalt walk in His ways"

(Deuteronomy 28:9). Maimonides, *Hilkhat, gi'ot* 1:6, apparently basing himself upon *Sifre*, Deuteronomy 11:22, renders the verse as meaning, "first as He is merciful so also shalt you be merciful."

It is nevertheless probably incorrect to conclude that concern for *tza'ar ba'alei hayyim* is predicated upon a legal or moral concept of animal "rights." Certainly, in Jewish law no less than in other systems of law, neither the animal nor its guardian is granted *persona standi in judicio*, that is, the animal lacks capacity to institute judicial proceedings to prevent others from engaging in acts of cruelty of which it may be the victim. This is so despite the unique provision in Jewish law that an animal that has committed an act of manslaughter is subject to criminal penalty but is entitled to due process of law, including a right analogous to the Sixth Amendment right of confrontation, *viz.*, that the proceedings take place only in the presence of the accused animal.

In all likelihood, the rationale governing strictures against *tza'ar ba'alei hayyim* is concern for the moral welfare of the human agent rather than concern for the physical welfare of the animals, i.e., the underlying concern is the need to purge inclinations of cruelty and to develop compassion in human beings.[15] This is certainly the position taken by many early authorities in their discussion of the rationale underlying specific commandments dealing with comportment *vis-à-vis* animals. Thus, in discussing the prohibition against muzzling an animal while it is engaged in threshing, *Sefer ha-Hinnukh*, no. 596, states:

> The root purpose of the precept is to teach ourselves that our souls be beautiful, choosing fairness and cleaving to it, and that [our soul] pursue lovingkindness and mercy. In habituating [our soul] to this even with regard to animals, which were not created other than to serve us, to be kindful of them in granting them a portion of the travail of their flesh, the soul acquires a propensity for this habit to do good to human beings and to watch

over them lest he cross the boundary with regard to anything which is proper with regard to them and to com-
pensate them for any good they perform and to satiate
them with whatever they travail. This is the path which
is proper for the holy, chosen people.

In a similar vein, Maimonides, *Guide of the Perplexed*,
Book III, chapter 48, declares, "The reason for the prohibition
against eating a limb [cut off] a living animal is because this
would make one acquire the habit of cruelty." Maimonides,
Guide, Book III, chapter 17, makes the same observation concerning the general obligation with regard to *tza'ar ba'alei
hayyim* in stating that that duty "is set down with a view
to perfecting us that we should not acquire moral habits of
cruelty and should not inflict pain gratuitously, but that we
should intend to be kind and merciful even with a chance animal individual except in case of need."[16]

The concern expressed in these sources is that cruelty to
animals consequentially engenders an indiscriminately cruel
disposition. Acts of cruelty mold character in a manner that
leads to spontaneously cruel behavior. *Tza'ar ba'alei hayyim* is
forbidden because cruelty is a character trait to be eschewed.
Practicing kindness *vis-à-vis* animals has the opposite effect
and serves to instill character traits of kindness and compassion. Development of such traits results in spontaneous acts of
kindness, compassion, and mercy.

2. Slaughter of Animals

Since the concern is for the moral and spiritual health
of the human agent rather than for the protection of brute
creatures, it is not at all surprising that concern for *tza'ar
ba'alei hayyim* is less than absolute.

The most obvious exception is the slaughtering of animals
for meat, which is specifically permitted by Scripture to Noah
and his progeny: "Every moving thing that liveth shall be food
for you" (Genesis 9:3). Maimonides, followed by *Sefer ha-
Hinnukh*, regards this exception as circumscribed by the pro-

visions surrounding the requirement for ritual slaughter in order to eliminate pain.[17] According to Maimonides, those provisions are designed to limit pain insofar as possible. Thus in the *Guide*, Book III, chapter 26, Maimonides states: "As necessity occasions the eating of animals, the commandment was intended to bring about the easiest death in an easy manner. . . . In order that death should come about more easily, the condition was imposed that the knife should be sharp." The same concept is reiterated by Maimonides with even greater clarity in Book III, chapter 48 of the *Guide*:

> For the natural food of man consists only of the plants deriving from the seeds growing in the earth and of the flesh of animals. . . . Now since the necessity to have good food requires that animals be killed, the aim was to kill them in the easiest manner, and it was forbidden to torment them through killing them in a reprehensible manner by piercing the lower part of their throat or by cutting off one of their members, just as we have explained.

Sefer ha-Hinnukh, no. 451, similarly states:

> It has also been said with regard to the reason for slaughter at the throat with an examined knife that it is in order that we not cause pain to animals more than is necessary, for the Torah has permitted them to man by virtue of his stature to sustain himself and for all his needs, but not to inflict pain upon them purposelessly.

Maimonides, *Guide*, Book III, chapter 26, makes it clear that the concern evidenced in the prescription of the mode of slaughter is identical to the consideration underlying the admonition concerning *tza'ar ba'alei hayyim*. Both the prescriptions concerning ritual slaughter and the prohibition against *tza'ar ba'alei hayyim* are regarded by Rambam as having been imposed "with a view to purifying the people," in order to prevent internalization of cruelty as a character trait and to promote the development of compassion.[18]

Although Jewish law permits consumption of meat only if

the animal has been slaughtered in the prescribed manner, there is no explicit statement in the various codes or in the writings of early authorities prohibiting other forms of slaughter in situations in which the animal is killed for other purposes. If, as Rambam explicitly states, ritual slaughter is ordained to obviate *tza'ar ba'alei hayyim*, it might well be presumed that other forms of slaughter are entirely excluded. Yet, as is well known, the ramifications and applications of Jewish law in fulfilling any specific commandment frequently are not coextensive with the rationale underlying the precept.[19] Thus it cannot be assumed that other modes of killing animals are proscribed by Jewish law, particularly if the method utilized is painless.[20]

In point of fact, there is some controversy among latter-day rabbinical decisors with regard to the permissibility of putting animals to death other than by means of ritual slaughter. Some authorities maintain that the very act of killing an animal constitutes *tza'ar ba'alei hayyim*; others maintain that considerations of *tza'ar ba'alei hayyim* pertain only to the treatment of animals while they are alive but do not preclude killing them by any available method. Stated somewhat differently, the second group of authorities maintains that the act of putting an animal to death is excluded from the prohibition against *tza'ar ba'alei hayyim*. The authorities who forbid putting an animal to death (other than for the satisfaction of a legitimate human need, as will be shown later) apparently forbid even "painless" methods, since the act of killing the animal *ipso facto* constitutes *tza'ar ba'alei hayyim*. Thus, according to those authorities, the destruction of an unwanted pet, for example, would be forbidden.

The most prominent latter-day authority to address this question directly is the pre-eminent 18th-century rabbinic decisor, R. Ezekiel Landau, *Teshuvot Noda bi-Yehudah, Mahadura Kamma, Yoreh De'ah*, no. 83. *Noda bi-Yehudah* declares emphatically that the mere killing of an animal does not involve transgression of the prohibition against *tza'ar ba'alei hayyim*, a prohibition that he regards as applicable "only if he

causes [the animal] pain while alive."[21] In support of this ruling, *Noda bi-Yehudah* cites a narrative reported in the
Gemara, Hullin 7b. The narrative, in part, illustrates the
Gemara's assumption that a wound inflicted by a certain type
of mule may be particularly dangerous in nature. It is reported
that R. Judah the Prince invited R. Phinehas to dine with him.
The *Gemara* relates:

> When R. Phinehas ben Yair arrived at the home of R. Ju-
> dah he happened to enter by a gate near which were
> some mules. He [R. Phinehas] exclaimed, "The angel of
> death is in this house! Shall I dine with him?" Rabbi
> [Judah] heard and went out to meet him. He said to him
> [R. Phinehas], "I will sell them." He [R. Phinehas] said
> to him [R. Judah], "Thou shalt not put a stumbling block
> before the blind" (Leviticus 19:14). "I shall abandon
> them." "You would be spreading danger." "I shall ham-
> string them." "That would cause suffering to animals."
> "I shall kill them." "There is a prohibition against wan-
> ton destruction" (Deuteronomy 20:19).

Since R. Judah suggested killing the animals after having been
apprised that mutilating them is forbidden, argues *Noda bi-
Yehudah*, it may be deduced that killing animals does not constitute a proscribed form of *tza'ar ba'alei hayyim*. Moreover,
R. Phinehas objected to this proposal only because it would involve "wanton destruction" but not on the basis of considerations of *tza'ar ba'alei hayyim*. An argument based upon the
narrative recorded in *Hullin* 7b identical to that of *Noda
bi-Yehudah* was advanced earlier by R. Gershon Ashkenazi,
Teshuvot Avodat ha-Gershuni, no. 13.[22]

It is nevertheless clear from the discussion of *Noda bi-
Yehudah* that it is forbidden to put an animal to death in a
manner that involves pain. For that reason, *Noda bi-Yehudah*
refuses to sanction withholding of food and water from an animal in order to cause its death. The method employed must be
relatively swift in order to avoid pain.

The argument advanced by *Noda bi-Yehudah* in support

of his contention that killing an animal is not a prohibited form
of *tza'ar ba'alei hayyim* is, however, rebutted by the 19th-
century scholar R. Joseph Saul Nathanson, *Teshuvot Sho'el u-
Meshiv, Mahadura Tinyana*, III, no. 65. *Sho'el u-Meshiv* notes
that the white mules in the home of R. Judah the Prince were
regarded as posing a threat to human life. Ostensibly, all prohibitions, including both the prohibition against *tza'ar ba'alei
hayyim* and the precept "thou shalt not wantonly destroy,"
may be ignored in order to eliminate danger to life. However,
observes *Sho'el u-Meshiv*, the danger could not have been of a
significant magnitude since Rabbi Judah had already kept the
mules in his custody for a significant period of time without
the animals' having manifested aggressive behavior. Hence,
since no actual danger threatened, "wanton destruction" could
not be sanctioned. However, argues *Sho'el u-Meshiv*, pain
may be inflicted upon animals in order to alleviate human suffering of a comparable magnitude. Therefore, the transitory
pain attendant upon the swift death of an animal would have
been justified in order to eliminate even an improbable threat
to human life. Hamstringing the mules would, however, have
resulted in ongoing suffering on the part of the animals and
could not be sanctioned because the suffering caused them
would have been disproportionate to the human anguish alleviated thereby.[23] Accordingly, concludes *Sho'el u-Meshiv*, it
may be inferred that causing the death of an animal is justifiable only if necessary to alleviate human pain, even if such pain
is minor in nature, provided that no "wanton destruction" is
involved. However, it cannot be inferred that causing the
death of an animal is excluded from categorization as *tza'ar
ba'alei hayyim*. According to *Sho'el u-Meshiv*, the exchange
between R. Phinehas and R. Judah serves only to support the
conclusion that animals may be killed when necessary for human welfare but it does not yield the conclusion that killing
animals is excluded from the prohibition against *tza'ar ba'alei
hayyim*.

A 20th-century scholar, R. Yechiel Ya'akov Weinberg, *Se-*

ridei Esh, III, no. 7,[24] cites a statement of the *Gemara*, *Avodah Zarah* 13b, in support of the position that putting an animal to death does not constitute a forbidden form of *tza'ar ba'alei hayyim*. The discussion of the *Gemara* centers upon the problem presented by an animal that has been sanctified during the period following the destruction of the Temple. Since the animal cannot be used for its intended purpose and it is also forbidden to derive benefit from such an animal or to make use of it in any way, it can only serve as a vehicle for transgression. Its elimination, if halakhically permitted, would clearly be desirable. The *Gemara* queries, "Why can it not be made a *gistera*?" That is, why can it not simply be killed by cutting it in half? It is evident from the question, argues *Seridei Esh*, that destroying an animal does not involve the prohibition of *tza'ar ba'alei hayyim*. This argument, however, is not as compelling as it might appear. As will be shown, according to almost all authorities, *tza'ar ba'alei hayyim* is permitted when designed to serve a human need. *Noda bi-Yehudah, Mahudara Kamma, Yoreh De'ah*, nos. 82 and 83, contends that elimination of a potential source of transgression constitutes such a need. Hence rendering the animal a *gistera* might be sanctioned not because causing the death of an animal is uniformly permitted as not involving an infraction of strictures against *tza'ar ba'alei hayyim* but because even though it does involve a form of *tza'ar ba'alei hayyim*, causing an animal pain is permitted when designed to serve a human need. The query "Why can it not be made a *gistera*?" serves to establish that one of two principles is correct: Either the killing of an animal is excluded from the prohibition against *tza'ar ba'alei hayyim* or *tza'ar ba'alei hayyim* is permitted when designed to serve a human need. Accordingly, this source does serve to establish the principle that killing an animal for a purpose designed to serve a human need does not entail transgression of strictures against *tza'ar ba'alei hayyim*.[25]

Both *Seridei Esh* and R. Judah Leib Graubart, *Teshuvot Havalim ba-Ne'imim*, I, no. 43, sec. 4, demonstrate that *Tosafot* maintains that killing *per se* does not constitute an act of *tza'ar ba'alei hayyim*. The *Gemara, Baba Batra*, 20a, indicates that considerations of *tza'ar ba'alei hayyim* prohibit the severing of a limb from a living animal to be used to feed dogs. Yet *Tosafot* states that the entire living animal may indeed be cast before dogs, which will then prey upon it. Thus, *Tosafot* apparently maintains that although a limb may not be torn from a living animal, nevertheless, causing the death of the animal in a similar manner does not involve transgression of the prohibition against *tza'ar ba'alei hayyim*.[26] *Teshuvot Avodat ha-Gershuni*, R. Meir Fischels, quoted by *Teshuvot Noda bi-Yehuda, Mahadura Kamma, Yoreh De'ah*, no. 82, and *Havalim ba-Ne'imim* also cite the comment of *Tosafot, Sanhedrin* 80a, in which *Tosafot* remarks that withholding food and drink from an animal constitutes *tza'ar ba'alei hayyim* but that causing its death by use of a hatchet does not.[27]

However, the exclusion of killing animals from the prohibition of *tza'ar ba'alei hayyim* is not recognized by all authorities. Although his comments are not cited in this context by latter-day authorities, Maimonides apparently maintains that the killing of an animal, in and of itself, constitutes a form of *tza'ar ba'alei hayyim*. Maimonides, in his *Guide of the Perplexed*, Book III, chapter 17, states:

> Divine Providence extends to every man individually but the condition of the individual being of other living creatures is undoubtedly the same as has been stated by Aristotle. On that account it is allowed, even commanded, to kill animals; we are permitted to use them according to our pleasure. . . . There is a rule laid down by our Sages that it is directly prohibited in the Torah to cause pain to an animal based on the words: "Wherefore hast thou smitten thine ass?" (Numbers 22:32). But the object of this rule is to make us perfect; that we should not assume cruel habits; and that we should not uselessly cause pain to others; that, on the contrary, we should be prepared to show pity and mercy to all living

creatures, except when necessity demands the contrary: "When thy soul longest to eat flesh" (Deuteronomy 12:20).[28] We should not kill animals for the purpose of practicing cruelty or for the purpose of sport.[29]

Maimonides' comments regarding unnecessary killing of animals, especially as they single out for censure the killing of animals for sport, stand in sharp contrast to the position of *Noda bi-Yehudah*, particularly as formulated in *Mahadura Tinyana, Yoreh De'ah*, no. 10, in which *Noda bi-Yehudah* addresses the question of the permissibility of engaging in hunting as a pastime.[30] Although *Noda bi-Yehudah* is severely critical of those who engage in this activity on the grounds that hunting is both frivolous and dangerous, he explicitly states that it cannot be proscribed as a form of *tza'ar ba'alei hayyim* because, in his opinion, putting animals to death is not encompassed within the scope of that prohibition. A similar statement attributed to R. Joseph ibn Migas (known as Ri Migash) is quoted in *Shitah Mekubetzet, Baba Batra* 20a. In contrast to the earlier cited comments of *Tosafot*, Ri Migash states that the slaughter of a domestic animal in order to feed its flesh to dogs constitutes no less a form of *tza'ar ba'alei hayyim* than tearing a limb from an animal while it is still alive. Ri Migash apparently maintains that, although animals may be utilized in a usual and customary manner in order to satisfy human needs, they may not be subjected to pain and discomfort in conjunction with a use that is not usual. Ri Migash contends that, since it is not customary to slaughter animals for dogfood, such slaughter, even if performed in the ritual manner, "is also *tza'ar ba'alei hayyim* for it is killing and not ritual slaughter."[31]

In a similar vein, *Sefer Ha-Hinnukh*, no. 451, explains that the rationale underlying the commandment concerning ritual slaughter is the consideration of *tza'ar ba'alei hayyim* and, for that reason, it is forbidden to slaughter an animal "even with a knife which is notched." Thus, *Sefer Ha-Hinnukh* clearly maintains that killing animals other than in the ritually prescribed manner is a form of *tza'ar ba'alei hayyim*. Similarly, Rabbenu

Nissim, *Hullin* 18b, states that killing an animal by crushing its vertebrae rather than by severing the trachea and esophagus constitutes *tza'ar ba'alei hayuim*.[32]

Latter-day authorities who maintain that putting an animal to death constitutes a form of *tza'ar ba'alei hayyim* include R. Joel Sirkes, *Bayit Hadash, Yoreh De'ah* 116, s.v. *mashkin*; R. Jacob Emden, *She'ilat Ya'avetz*, I, no. 110; R. Jacob Reischer, *Teshuvot Shevut Ya'akov*, III, no. 71; R. Eliyahu Klatzkin, *Teshuvot Imrei Shefer*, no. 34; and R. Moshe Yonah Zweig, *Ohel Mosheh*, I, no. 32.

She'ilat Ya'avetz questions whether *tza'ar ba'alei hayyim* applies to all living creatures, including insects and the like, or is limited to beasts of burden and domestic animals.[33] Presumably, if lower animals are excluded, it is on the basis of the rationale that they lack highly developed nervous systems and hence do not experience pain in a manner comparable to mammals and vertebrates. *She'ilat Ya'avetz* concludes that it is permissible to kill harmless insects because they are excluded from the prohibition concerning *tza'ar ba'alei hayyim*. The clear inference to be drawn from these comments is that, with regard to vertebrates, *She'ilat Ya'avetz* maintains that killing *per se* constitutes a prohibited form of *tza'ar ba'alei hayyim*.

Echoing the earlier cited statements of Ri Migash, *Imrei Shefer* forbids the slaughter of animals for purposes of feeding dogs and adds the explanatory comment that it is forbidden to cause pain to an animal for the benefit of another animal. In this regard, the constraint *vis-à-vis* imposition of pain upon animals is identical to that concerning causing human suffering. No pain may be imposed upon a human, even for the benefit of a fellow human, other than upon the consent of the person who suffers the pain. Since animals lack the capacity to grant consent, pain may not be imposed upon an animal for the benefit of another member of the animal kingdom.

Tza'ar Ba'alei Hayyim *for Human Benefit*

Jewish law, at least in its normative formulation, sanctions the infliction of pain upon animals when the act causing pain is designed to further a legitimate human purpose. This is evident from two rulings recorded in *Shulhan Arukh*. Rema, *Shulhan Arukh, Yoreh De'ah* 24:8, rules that prior to slaughtering sheep, the wool covering the area where the throat is to be slit should be removed in order to enable the act of slaughter in the prescribed manner. *Shakh, Yoreh De'ah* 24:8, extends the same requirement to the slaughter of fowl and requires that the feathers be plucked from the throats of fowl prior to slaughter. Rema, *Shulhan Arukh, Even ha-Ezer* 5:14, states even more explicitly:

> Anything which is necessary in order to effect a cure or for other matters does not entail [a violation] of the prohibition against *tza'ar ba'alei hayyim*. Therefore, it is permitted to pluck feathers from geese and there is no concern on account of *tza'ar ba'alei hayyim*. But nevertheless people refrain [from doing so] because it constitutes cruelty.

This ruling, cited in the name of *Issur ve-Heter* 59:36, is supported by the comments of *Tosafot, Baba Metzi'a* 32b.[34] *Tosafot* poses the following question: The *Gemara, Avodah Zarah* 11a, declares that in conjunction with the funeral rites of a monarch, it is permitted to sever the tendons of the horse upon which the king rode. This practice is permitted despite its source in pagan rituals because it is intended as an act of homage to the deceased king. If *tza'ar ba'alei hayyim* involves a biblical infraction, queries *Tosafot*, why may the animal be mutilated in this manner? *Tosafot* answers that such a practice is permitted "in honor of king[s] and prince[s] just as 'thou shalt not wantonly destroy' (Deuteronomy 20:19) is abrogated for the sake of their honor." Insofar as the prohibition concerning "wanton destruction" is concerned, *Tosafot's* comment is clear. The prohibition against "wanton destruction" is not suspended or abrogated for the sake of royal honor; rather, Scripture forbids only wanton destruction of fruit trees and, by extension, of other objects of value as well. Scripture does not forbid enjoyment of consumables because such use does not constitute "destruction." Similarly, "destruction" that serves a legitimate purpose is not proscribed because it is not wanton or "destructive" in nature. "Destruction" for purposes of rendering homage to a deceased monarch is a legitimate use of property and hence is not forbidden. *Tosafot* apparently regards *tza'ar ba'alei hayyim* in a similar light, that is, as forbidden only when wanton in nature,[35] but permissible when designed to achieve a legitimate goal.[36] Hence, declares *Tosafot*, mutilation of the royal steed in conjunction with the funeral of a monarch is permitted even though the animal experiences pain because it serves to fulfill a legitimate purpose. In accordance with this position, Rema rules that *tza'ar ba'alei hayyim* is permissible for purposes of healing or for any other legitimate purpose.[37]

Among early authorities, the permissibility of *tza'ar ba'alei hayyim* for human benefit is explicitly accepted by Rambam, *Avodah Zarah* 13b, who states that the "slaughter and causing of pain to animals is permissible for the need of man." A similar view can be inferred from the comments of Rabbenu Nissim of Gerondi, cited by *Nemukei Yosef*, *Baba Metzi'a* 32b. The *Gemara* explicitly exempts scholars and others for whom such activity would be unseemly and undignified from the obligation of assisting in the unloading of a burden from an overladen animal. *Nemukei Yosef* questions why it is that considerations of human dignity are permitted to supercede biblical obligations regarding the welfare of animals. In resolving this difficulty, *Nemukei Yosef* quotes the comments of Rabbenu Nissim, who states that "since *tza'ar ba'alei hayyim* is permitted for the use of humans[38] *a fortiori* [it is permitted] for their honor."[39] Another early authority, Ritva, *Shabbat* 154b, maintains that *tza'ar ba'alei hayyim* is permitted even for financial reasons, as is evident from his statement that "for the purpose of [man's] service and preservation of his money [*tza'ar ba'alei hayyim*] is certainly permitted."

Terumat ha-Deshen, Pesakim u-Ketavim, no. 105, regards the permissibility of causing suffering to animals for the benefit of mankind to be inherent in the biblical dispensation granting man the right to use animals for his needs.[40] R. Moses Sofer,

Hagahot Hatam Sofer, Baba Metzi'a 32b,[41] cites the divine declaration to Adam and Eve, "and have dominion over the fish of the sea, and over the fowl of the air, and over every living thing that creepeth upon the earth" (Genesis 1:28)[42] as establishing man's absolute and unlimited mastery over the animal kingdom.[43] R. Judah Lieb Graubart, *Havalim ba-Ne'imim*, I, no. 43, sec. 3, advances an identical argument on the basis of Genesis 9:1–2: "And God blessed Noah and his sons. . . . And the fear of you and the dread of you shall be upon every beast of the earth, and upon every fowl of the air, and upon all wherewith the ground teemeth, and upon all the fishes of the sea: into your hand are they delivered."

Terumat ha-Deshen, Pesakim u-Ketavim, no. 105, and R. Elijah of Vilna, *Bi'ur ha-Gra, Even ha-Ezer* 5:40, cite a number of talmudic sources as the basis of Rema's ruling. Leviticus 22:24 serves to establish a prohibition against the emasculation of animals. The *Gemara, Shabbat* 110b, regards removal of a rooster's comb as causing the rooster to become sterile but nevertheless permits the practice because it does not involve excision of a sexual organ.[44] This procedure is permissible despite the fact that it obviously causes pain. The attendant pain, argues *Bi'ur ha-Gra*, does not render the procedure impermissible because it is designed to promote a human benefit. Moreover, the *Gemara, Haggigah* 14b, tentatively considers the possibility that Scripture forbids only the emasculation of members of those species of animals that may be offered as sacrifices, an inference that might be drawn from the context of Leviticus 22:24. Since castration is necessarily accompanied by pain, this possibility could be entertained only if it is accepted as an antecedent premise that *tza'ar ba'alei hayyim* is not forbidden when necessary to achieve a beneficial result. Furthermore, these scholars indicate that placing a heavy load upon a beast of burden, an act that is clearly sanctioned by the *Gemara, Baba Metzi'a* 32b, is in itself a form of *tza'ar ba'alei hayyim* and is permitted only because the prohibition does not apply in situations in which the act is undertaken for human benefit.[45]

A 20th-century halakhist, R. Ya'akov Breisch, *Helkat Ya'akov*, I, no. 30, sec. 6, seeks to find further support for this position in *Taz's* understanding of a discussion recorded in the *Gemara, Hullin* 28a. In the household of Rava, the skin on the throat of a dove was found to have been pierced and bleeding. The question confronting Rava was whether or not the dove might yet be slaughtered and eaten. A perforation or anomaly of either the trachea or the esophagus would have rendered the bird unfit. Since the outer skin had been pierced, there was reason to suspect that the trachea or the esophagus or both might have been damaged as well. Those organs could not be examined satisfactorily after slaughter because a perforation or anomaly might have been present at the site of the incision made by the slaughterer's knife and would not be discernible subsequent to slaughter. Moreover, since the esophagus is pink in color, it is not possible to examine any part of it prior to slaughter because a drop of blood might possibly be lodged at the site of the perforation and cover a miniscule hole or (according to *Tosafot*) the reddish color of the esophagus itself might render a perforation or an anomaly indiscernible. Rava's son Rav Yosef counseled that the trachea, which is white, be examined prior to slaughter and, since ritual slaughter of fowl (as distinct from four-legged animals) requires the severance of either the trachea or the esophagus but not necessarily of both, care be taken not to pierce the esophagus. Rav Yosef further directed that, subsequent to slaughtering the bird, the esophagus be removed and examined along its inner surface, which is white.

This narrative serves as the basis of the normative rule to be applied in similar situations in which an animal has experienced a trauma in the area to be incised in the act of slaughter. The problem arising in such instances is that the site at which the trachea is to be severed must be examined prior to slaughter. If, as must be presumed to be the case, the tear in the skin covering the trachea is small, such an examination is impossible. *Taz, Yoreh De'ah* 33:11, indicates that the tear in the skin of the throat must be enlarged in order to examine the trachea. Clearly, enlarging the hole causes pain to the animal. It must be presumed that this procedure is sanctioned only because it is necessary to confirm that the bird is fit for consumption. Accordingly, this ruling would support the thesis that *tza'ar ba'alei hayyim* is permissible when necessary for human welfare. *Helkat Ya'akov* agrees that subsequent to Rema's ruling, there is no question that the procedure described by *Taz* is permissible. However, he points out that the talmudic discussion cited by *Taz* cannot be adduced as the basis of this ruling concerning *tza'ar ba'alei hayyim*. That discussion could well be understood as permitting a procedure of this nature in the rare circumstances in which the requisite visual examination of the trachea can be undertaken without further elongation of the already existing cut.

   Teshuvot Shevut Ya'akov, III, no. 71,[46] and *Teshuvot Rav Pe'alim*, I, *Yoreh De'ah*, no. 1, find support for Rema's ruling in the *Mishnah, Avodah Zarah* 13b. It is forbidden to sell a solitary white chicken to an idolator for fear that he may intend to offer the bird as a pagan sacrifice. However, since a mutilated bird would not be used for idolatrous purposes, the *Mishnah* permits the seller to render the chicken unfit for sacrificial use by removing a digit from its foot prior to sale. Here, too, such a procedure necessarily entails pain to the chicken. Accordingly, argue *Shevut Ya'akov* and *Rav Pe'alim*, such a practice could be permitted only because it is prompted by legitimate commercial need. The procedure sanctioned by the *Mishnah* serves as a paradigm establishing the general principle that *tza'ar ba'alei hayyim* is permissible when necessary to satisfy a human need.[47]

   Although Rema's ruling is accepted by virtually all latter-day authorities, it appears that his position is rejected by at least one early authority. The authors of the commentary of *Tosafot* on *Avodah Zarah* 11a pose the same question with regard to the mutilation of the royal steed as raised in the commentary of *Tosafot* on *Baba Metzi'a* 22b. However, in their commentary on *Avodah Zarah*, the authors of *Tosafot* resolve the problem in an entirely different manner.[48] But, since the problem is completely dispelled on the premise that *tza'ar ba'alei hayyim* is permissible for human benefit, *Tosafot*'s failure to resolve the problem in that manner in the commentary on *Avodah Zarah* presumably reflects the fact that the authors of the commentary of the *Tosafot* on that tractate (in disagreement with the view of the authors of *Tosafot* on *Baba Metzi'a*) regard *tza'ar ba'alei hayyim* as not permissible even when designed to promote human benefit.[49]

A somewhat modified position is espoused by R. Joseph Teumim, *Pri Megadim, Orah Hayyim, Mishbetzot Zahav,* 468:2. *Pri Megadim* reports that his advice was sought by an individual who maintained exotic birds in his garden and was fearful that they might take flight. The interlocutor sought a ruling with regard to the propriety of breaking "a small bone in their wings" in order to render them incapable of flight and prevent financial loss to their keeper. *Pri Megadim*'s response was negative for, in his opinion, "*tza'ar ba'alei hayyim*, other than in place of great need, is forbidden." Apparently, *Pri Megadim* distinguishes between ordinary "need" or "benefit" and "great need" and sanctions *tza'ar ba'alei hayyim* only in the latter situation. In a similar vein, *Teshuvot Avodat ha-Gershuni*, no. 13, quotes a certain R. Tevel the physician as declaring that *tza'ar ba'alei hayyim* cannot be sanctioned for purposes of realizing "a small profit."

There is also some controversy regarding the nature of the need or benefit that is deemed to warrant causing pain to animals. *Issur ve-Heter he-Arukh* 59:36, cites a version of *Tosafot* that differs from the published texts. *Issur ve-Heter he-Arukh* states that in declaring that *tza'ar ba'alei hayyim* "if it is efficacious for some matter is permissible," *Tosafot* intends to permit *tza'ar ba'alei hayyim* only for therapeutic purposes, including procedures necessary for the treatment of even non–life-threatening maladies.[50] Thus, *Issur ve-Heter* apparently regards *tza'ar ba'alei hayyim* designed to serve other needs, for example, financial profit, as improper and forbidden.[51]

Among latter-day authorities, R. Yitzchak Dov Bamberger is quoted by R. Jacob Ettlinger, *Teshuvot Binyan Zion*, no. 108, as asserting that Rema permits *tza'ar ba'alei hayyim* "only when there is need for medical purposes even for a patient who is not dangerously ill but we have not found that he permitted *tza'ar ba'alei hayyim* for financial profit."[52] This interpretation of Rema is difficult to sustain for two reasons: (1) Rema, *Shulhan Arukh, Even ha-Ezer* 5:14, rules that "anything which is necessary in order to effect a cure *or for other matter* does not entail [a violation] of the prohibition against *tza'ar ba'alei hayyim*." (2) Rema, *Shulhan Arukh, Yoreh De'ah* 24:8, indicates that plucking feathers from a live bird is permissible as a matter of normative law. The feathers plucked in this manner are designed for use as quills. No one has suggested that the procedure is permitted only if the quill is needed by a physician to write a prescription; indeed, such an interpretation could not be sustained, since Rema's caveat regarding the nonacceptability of such practices does not apply to procedures required by reason of medical need.[53] Nevertheless, R. Moshe Yonah Zweig, *Ohel Mosheh*, I, no. 32, sec. 11, cites Rabbi Bamberger's position as meriting serious consideration.[54] Rabbi Ettlinger himself, however, distinguishes between "great pain" and "minor pain" and permits minor pain for other "definite" benefits as well.[55] R. Eliyahu Klatzkin, *Teshuvot Imrei Shefer*, no. 34, sec. 1, adopts an intermediate position in stating that Rema intended to permit *tza'ar ba'alei hayyim* for medical purposes or for purposes of similar importance and necessity but not simply for the purpose of financial gain. *Imrei Shefer* does not indicate what these purposes of similar necessity might be. In support of the position that *tza'ar ba'alei hayyim* may not be sanctioned for financial gain, *Teshuvot Imrei Shefer*, no. 34, sec. 1, cites the statement of the *Gemara, Baba Batra* 20a. The *Gemara* forbids the severing of a limb from a live animal in order to feed it to dogs because of considerations of *tza'ar ba'alei hayyim. Imrei Shefer* notes that if the limb were to be fed to the dogs, their master would benefit financially in not having to provide other food on their behalf. Evidently, then, monetary gain is not sufficient to obviate the prohibition concerning *tza'ar ba'alei hayyim.*[56]

However, the majority of rabbinic authorities regard financial gain as a legitimate "need" or "benefit" which, at least as a matter of law, may be fostered even at the expense of *tza'ar ba'alei hayyim.* The comments of a number of authorities who espouse this view have been cited earlier. Other authorities who permit *tza'ar ba'alei hayyim* for monetary advantage include R. Moses Sofer, *Hagahot Hatam Sofer, Baba Metzi'a* 32b,[57] who remarks that the prohibition does not apply when the act is performed "for the benefit of human beings, their honor or financial benefit."[58] An identical position is adopted by *Teshuvot Avodat ha-Gershuni*, no. 13; *Teshuvot Noda bi-Yehudah, Mahadura Tinyana, Yoreh De'ah*, no. 10, *s.v. ve-amnam*;[59] *Teshuvot Panim Me'irot*, I, no. 75; *Teshuvot Pri Yitzhak*, I, no. 24; and *Teshuvot Yad Eliyahu, Ketavim* 3:5.[60] *Pri Hadash, Yoreh De'ah* 53:7, permits severing a broken wing from a bird so that the jagged edge will not perforate an internal organ and thereby render the bird nonkosher and hence unfit for consumption. According to *Pri Hadash, tza'ar ba'alei hayyim* is warranted under such circumstances because of potential financial loss. Among contemporary authorities, a similar view is expressed by R. Yetzchak aja'akov Weisz, *Teshuvot Minhat Yitzhak*, vi, ms. 145.

4. Morality Beyond the Requirements of Law

Despite his ruling that plucking feathers from a live bird for use as quills is permitted as a matter of law, Rema adds the comment that people refrain from doing so because of the inherent cruelty involved in this practice.[61] The immediate source of both this caveat and of the normative ruling regarding the plucking of feathers is the 15th-century rabbinic decisor R. Israel Isserlein, *Terumat ha-Deshen, Pesakim u-Ketavim*, no. 105. *Terumat ha-Deshen*, however, elaborates somewhat and presents a talmudic source for the popular renunciation of this practice. *Terumat ha-Deshen* states, "and perhaps the reason is that people do not wish to act with the trait of cruelty *vis-à-vis* creatures for they fear lest they receive punishment for that, as we find in chapter *Ha-Po'alim* with regard to our holy teacher."[62] It is particularly noteworthy that *Terumat ha-Deshen* suggests the possibility of divine punishment for cruelty toward animals even in a situation in which no infraction of normative law is involved.[63]

The talmudic source cited by *Terumat ha-Deshen* is an anecdote concerning R. Judah the Prince related in the *Gemara, Baba Metzi'a* 85a.[64] R. Judah suffered excruciating pain for many years until suddenly the pain subsided. In the following narrative, the *Gemara* explains both why R. Judah experienced suffering and why the suffering was ultimately alleviated:

> A calf, when it was being taken to slaughter, went and hung its head under Rabbi [Judah]'s cloak and cried. He said to it, "Go, for this wast thou created." [In heaven] they said, "Since he has no mercy, let suffering come upon him." . . . One day Rabbi [Judah]'s maidservant was sweeping the house; some young weasels were lying there and she was sweeping them away. Rabbi [Judah] said to her, "Let them be; it is written 'And His tender mercies are over all His works' (Psalms 145:9)." [In heaven] they said, "Since he is compassionate, let us be compassionate to him."

Reflected in this account, and in the halakhic principle derived therefrom, is the distinction between normative law and ethical conduct above and beyond the requirements of law (*lifnim me-shurat ha-din*).[65] In its normative law, Judaism codifies standards applicable to everyone and makes no demands that are beyond the capacity of the common man; but at the same time, Jewish teaching recognizes that, ideally, man must aspire to a higher level of conduct. That higher standard is posited as a moral desideratum, although a norm that is not

enforceable by human courts. Not every person succeeds in
reaching a degree of moral excellence such that he perceives
the need and obligation to conduct himself in accordance with
that higher standard. Those who do attain such a level of moral
perfection are obliged, at least in the eyes of Heaven, to
conduct themselves in accordance with that higher standard.
No human court can inquire into the degree of moral perfection attained by a particular individual and, hence, such a court
cannot apply varying standards to different people. The heav-
enly court, however, *is* in a position to do so and, accordingly,
will punish a person who does not comport himself in accordance with the degree of moral perfection he has attained.
Thus, the *Gemara, Baba Kamma* 50a, cites the verse "And it
shall be very tempestuous about Him" (Psalms 50:3) and, in a
play on the Hebrew word "*sa'arah*," which connotes both
"tempestuous" and "hair," it declares that "the Holy One,
blessed be He, is particular with those around Him even with
regard to matters as light as a single hair."

R. Yechiel Ya'akov Weinberg, *Seridei Esh*, III, no. 7,
hastens to point out that Rema's cautionary statement with regard to normatively permitted forms of *tza'ar ba'alei hayyim*
should not be construed as applicable to medical experimentation. In a short comment, *Seridei Esh* rejects the application
of Rema's remarks to medical experimentation for what really
are three distinct reasons: (1) Moral stringencies beyond the
requirements of law are personal in nature; a person may accept stringencies of piety for himself but may not impose them
upon others. (2) Elimination of pain and suffering of human
beings takes precedence over considerations of animal pain.
(3) The concern for avoiding causing pain to animals, even
when it is halakhically permitted to cause such pain, is ger-
mane only at the cost of foregoing benefit to an individual but
not when benefit may accrue to the public at large. The last
point is supported by the fact that no hesitation is expressed
with regard to inflicting pain upon animals for the sake of "the
honor of kings," which is tantamount to the honor of the entire
community, as evidenced by the earlier cited statement of the

Gemara, Avodah Zarah 11a, which sanctions hamstringing the steed of the deceased monarch.

Seridei Esh's comments are in opposition to the view expressed by *Helkat Ya'akov*, I, no. 30, sec. 6, to the effect that although medical experimentation upon animals is certainly permissible as a matter of law,[66] nevertheless, in accordance with Rema's caveat, it is proper to refrain from inflicting pain upon animals even for such purposes "as a matter of piety to preserve [oneself] from the trait of cruelty." More recently, a member of the Supreme Rabbinical Court of Israel, R. Eliezer Waldenberg, *Tzitz Eli'ezer*, XIV, no. 68, found no difficulty in supporting medical experimentation upon animals but urged that pain be minimized insofar as possible.

In one of the earliest responsa that specifically address the question of animal experimentation, *Shevut Ya'akov*, III, no. 71, draws yet another distinction between plucking feathers, which is eschewed as a form of cruelty, and certain types of medical experimentation. *Shevut Ya'akov* was asked whether the toxicity of certain medications might be tested by feeding them to dogs or cats. *Shevut Ya'akov* replies in the affirmative and states that feeding a possibly poisonous substance to an animal is not comparable to plucking the feathers of a goose. In the latter case, the pain is caused directly and is immediately perceived with the plucking of each feather. On the other hand, the pain caused an animal as a result of imbibing a poisonous substance is neither direct nor immediate and hence, rules *Shevut Ya'akov*, there is no reason to refrain from such experimentation "even as an act of piety." The cogency of this distinction lies in the recognition that, according to Rema, the concern with regard to *tza'ar ba'alei hayyim* in cases in which a human need exists is not with regard to the welfare of the animal but with regard to the possible moral degeneration of the human agent who may acquire traits of cruelty as a result of performing acts that are objectively cruel even when warranted by the attendant circumstances. Apparently, *Shevut Ya'akov* feels that the danger of developing a cruel disposition exists only when the human act is the immediate and proximate cause of perceivable pain, not when the act is not immediately associated with the pain experienced by the animal. Quite obviously, *Shevut Ya'akov's* distinction does not apply to forms of medical experimentation in which the pain is immediately attendant upon the procedure performed, *e.g.*, unanesthetized vivisection, while the criteria formulated by *Seridei Esh* apply to such situations as well.

It should, however, be noted that the foregoing analysis of the consideration underlying the practice of refraining from plucking feathers from a live animal is not at all obvious. As has been noted earlier, *Termumat ha-Deshen*, who is the source of Rema's remarks, declares that this practice is eschewed because of fear of punishment for causing pain to animals even when it is entirely permissible, as evidenced in the narrative concerning R. Judah and the calf recorded in the Gemara, *Baba Metzi'a* 85a. Ostensibly, the concern reflected in that report is for the welfare of the animal. However, R. Judah Leib Zirelson, *Ma'arkhei Lev*, no. 110, interprets that narrative in a manner entirely compatible with what appears to be the premise underlying the distinction formulated by *Shevut Ya'akov*. *Ma'arkhei Lev* asserts that it is inconceivable that R. Judah was punished for allowing the calf to be slaughtered for its meat. Rather, declares *Ma'arkhei Lev*, he was punished for his outburst, "Go, for this wast thou created." That sharp remark betrayed a lack of sensitivity inappropriate for a person of R. Judah's moral stature. Thus R. Judah was punished for his own lack of sensitivity rather than for the suffering caused to the calf.[67]

Ma'arkhei Lev himself draws a much broader distinction between the conduct frowned upon by Rema and other uses to which animals may be put without breach of even the "trait of piety" commended by Rema. According to *Ma'arkhei Lev*, the crucial factor is the element of necessity. Quills may be removed from dead fowl as readily as from live ones. Hence, plucking feathers from a live bird is an entirely unnecessary act of cruelty, even though the act itself serves a human purpose. According to *Ma'arkhei Lev*, in any situation in which there exists a need that cannot otherwise be satisfied, it is not improper to cause discomfort to animals, and refraining from doing so does not even constitute an act of piety. R. Judah was punished, asserts *Ma'arkhei Lev*, because his sharp and impulsive remark was entirely gratuitous. In support of this thesis *Ma'arkhei Lev* cites a ruling recorded in *Shulhan Arukh*, *Orah Hayyim*, 362:5. On the Sabbath it is permissible to carry objects only within an enclosed area. *Shulhan Arukh* rules that an enclosure may be formed by stationing animals in a manner such that they constitute a "wall," but only on the condition that the animals are bound so that they remain immobile. Animals forced to remain in a stationary position for the duration of an entire Sabbath day certainly experience discomfort. Nevertheless, none of the commentaries on *Shulhan Arukh* indicate that, in light of Rema's caveat regarding plucking feathers from a live fowl, the practice of utilizing animals for fashioning a "wall" should be eschewed.[68] The reason that they fail to do so, argues *Ma'arkhei Lev*, lies in the distinction that must be drawn between a use of animals essential for achieving a purpose pertaining to human welfare and one which, while it serves a purpose, is nevertheless not absolutely necessary in order to achieve the desired end.[69]

5. Conclusions

Jewish law clearly forbids any act that causes pain or discomfort to an animal unless such act is designed to satisfy a legitimate human need. All authorities agree that hunting as a sport is forbidden. Although many authorities maintain that it is not forbidden to engage in activities that cause pain to animals in situations in which such practices yield financial benefits, there is significant authority for the position that animal pain may be sanctioned only for medical purposes, including direct therapeutic benefit, medical experimentation of potential therapeutic value, and training medical personnel.[70] A *fortiori*, those who eschew this position would not sanction painful procedures for the purpose of testing or perfecting cosmetics. An even larger body of authority refuses to sanction inflicting pain on animals when the desired benefit can be acquired in an alternative manner. Even when the undertaking is designed to promote human welfare, there is greater justification for causing the swift and painless death of an animal than for subjecting it to procedures that cause suffering.

Judaism recognizes moral imperatives that establish standards more stringent than the standard of conduct imposed by law. According to the view of most authorities, those moral imperatives should prompt man to renounce cruelty to animals even when the contemplated procedure would serve to promote human welfare.

Medical experimentation designed to produce therapeutic benefit to mankind constitutes an exception to this principle[71] and is endorsed by virtually all rabbinic authorities. Nevertheless, as stated by R. Eliezer Waldenberg, *Tzitz Eli'ezer*, XIV, no. 68, sec. 7, it is no more than proper that, whenever possible, such experimentation be conducted in such a manner that any unnecessary pain is avoided and, when appropriate, the animal subject should be anesthetized.

Notes

1. Arthur Schopenhauer, *Die Beiden Grundprobleme der Ethik* (Frankfurt a.m., 1841), pp. 243–244. For an English translation, see Arthur Schopenhauer, *The Basis of Morality*, translated by Arthur B. Bullock (London, G. Allen & Unwin Ltd., 1915), p. 218. See also Arthur Schopenhauer, *The World As Will and Representation*, translated by E. F. J. Payne (New York, Dover Publications, 1957), II, p. 645.

2. The obligation of *imitatio Dei* is derived from the verse "and thou shalt walk in His ways" (Deuteronomy 28:9). See Maimonides, *Hilkhot De'ot* 1:5–6.

3. It is told of the hasidic master, R. Zusya of Anapole, that, saddened by the sight of caged birds, he would purchase them from their owners in order to set them free. He informed his disciples that he regarded this to be a form of "ransoming prisoners," which constitutes a moral imperative. See also narratives concerning R. Eliyahu

Lapian recounted by Aaron Soraski, *Marbitzei Torah u-Musar* (Brooklyn, 1977), IV, 165, and R. Abraham Isaiah Karelitz (*Hazon Ish*) by R. Shlomoh Cohen, *Pe'er ha-Dor* (Bnei Brak, 1966), I, 175.

    4. See Me'iri, *Baba Metzi'a* 33a, and *Sefer ha-Hinnukh*, no. 596. The purpose of other biblical laws pertaining to animals is less clear-cut. The prohibition against plowing with animals of different species, recorded in Deuteronomy 22:10, is understood by *Sefer ha-Hinnukh*, no. 550 and by *Da'at Zekenim me-Ba'alei ha-Tosafot* and *Ba'al ha-Turim* in their respective commentaries on Deuteronomy 22:10 as rooted in considerations of prevention of cruelty to animals. But it is understood in an entirely different manner by Maimonides, *Guide of the Perplexed*, Book III, chapter 49, as well as by Nahmanides in his commentary on Deuteronomy 22:10. However, Maimonides, *Guide*, Book III, chapter 48, regards the prohibition against slaughtering an animal and its young on the same day (recorded in Leviticus 22:28) as a measure designed to prevent the slaughter of the offspring in the presence of its parent. The underlying concern is to spare the mother the anguish of seeing her young killed before her eyes, "for in these cases animals feel very great pain, there being no difference regarding this pain between man and the other animals. For the love and the tenderness of a mother for her child is not consequent upon reason, but upon the activity of the imaginative faculty, which is found in most animals just as it is found in man." Here, Maimonides speaks of concerns for the welfare of the animal rather than for the moral character of the human agent; see below, notes 14 and 15 and accompanying text. This interpretation is reflected in the comments of R. Bahya ben Asher, Leviticus 22:28, and in part in *Sefer ha-Hinnukh*, no. 294. *Sefer ha-Hinnukh* regards the commandment prohibiting the slaughter of an animal and its young on the same day as designed both to spare the parent from anguish and as a conservation measure. See also Abarbanel's *Commentary on the Bible*, Leviticus 22:28. Maimonides' analysis of the rationale underlying this precept is rejected by Nachmanides in his *Commentary on the Bible*, Deuteronomy 22:6. According to Nachmanides, the concern is not to avoid causing pain to the animal but to purge man of callousness, cruelty, and savagery.

    The *Gemara, Baba Metzi'a* 32a, declares that assistance in unloading a burden from an animal is mandated by reason of *tza'ar ba'alei hayyim* but that the obligation to assist in loading the burden upon the animal is not independently mandated by reason of *tza'ar* ba'alei hayyim. However, Ritva, cited by *Shitah Mekubetzet, Baba Metzi'a* 31a, *s.v. aval te'inah*, asserts that the commandment requiring a person to render assistance to another individual who is engaged in loading an animal is predicated, at least in part, upon considerations of *tza'ar ba'alei hayyim*, that is, a single person engaged in this task is likely to cause additional discomfort to the animal by applying the full force of his body weight during the loading, whereas when assisted by another, there is no need for him to apply such pressure.

Sefer ha-Hinnukh, no. 186, is of the opinion that the prohibition against the slaughter of sanctified animals outside the Temple precincts is rooted in considerations of *tza'ar ba'alei hayyim*. According to *Sefer ha-Hinnukh*, such slaughter is forbidden because it serves no purpose. See note 29.

Neither the prohibition against mating animals of different species (Leviticus 19:19) nor the prohibition against emasculation of animals (Leviticus 22:24) is understood by classical rabbinic scholars as rooted in considerations of animal welfare. For a discussion of animal welfare as a possible rationale underlying other commandments, see R. Joel Schwartz, *Ve-Rahamav al Kol Ma'asav* (Jerusalem, 1984), pp. 11–16.

5. The requirement that the parent bird be released before the young are taken and the concomitant prohibition against taking both the parent and the young together, recorded in Deuteronomy 22:6–7, quite obviously have the effect of sparing the parent from anguish. However, the *Mishnah, Berakhot* 33b, does not view this desideratum, laudable as it may be, as the underlying purpose of the commandment. *Cf.*, however, Maimonides, *Guide*, Book III, chapter 48; Nahmanides, *Commentary on the Bible*, Deuteronomy 22:6; and *Sefer ha-Hinnukh*, no. 545.

6. See *Berakhot* 41a and *Gittin* 62a. See also Maimonides, *Hilkhot Avadim* 9:8; *Magen Avraham, Orah Hayyim* 167:18; R. Meir of Rothenberg, *Teshuvot Maharam ben Barukh he-Hadashot*, no. 302; R. Jacob Reisher, *Teshuvot Shevut Ya'akov*, II, no. 13; *Hayyei Adam* 45:1; and R. Joel Schwartz, *Va-Rahamav al Kol Ma'asav*, pp. 59–62. R. Jacob Emden, *She'ilat Ya'avetz*, I, no. 17, rules that there is no absolute requirement to feed a dog or a cat before eating oneself, since these animals sustain themselves on table scraps and forage for food, but that it is nevertheless proper to feed them first in order "to acquire the trait of compassion." *Magen Avraham, Orah Hay-*

yim 324:7, declares that providing food for any animal, including animals belonging to other people and ownerless animals, constitutes a *mitzvah*. See also R. Simeon ben Zemah Duran, *Teshuvot Tashbatz*, III, no. 293; R. Jacob Ettlinger, *Teshuvot Binyan Zion*, no. 103; and R. Eiliyahu Klatzkin, *Teshuvot Imrei Shefer*, no. 34, sec. 1. *Cf.* R. Moser Sofer, *Teshuvot Hatam Safer, Yoreh De'ah*, no. 314, *s.v. ve-la'asot*, and no. 318, *s.v. ve-hineh.*

7. Similarly, Scripture records that Laban gave straw to the camels and only afterward did he provide food for Abraham's servant. See Genesis 24:32–33 and *Sefer ha-Hinnukh* (ed. Reuben Margulies, Jerusalem, 1957), no. 531. *Cf.* R. Joel Schwartz, *Ve-Rahamav al kol Ma'asav*, p. 60, note 4.

8. The same authority, *Sefer ha-Hinnukh*, no. 540, asserts that the obligation to come to the assistance of an animal that has fallen applies equally with regard to assisting a person who is overladen. See also Maimonides, *Sefer ha-Mitzvot, mitzvot aseh*, no. 203, and *Mitzvot la ta'aseh*, no. 270. This is also the position of R. Solomon ben Adret, *Teshuvot ha-Rashba*, I, nos. 252, 256, and 257. *Cf.*, however, R. David ibn Zimra, *Teshuvot ha-Radbaz*, I, no. 728, and R. Ya'ir Chaim Bachrach, *Teshuvot Havot Ya'ir*, no. 191.

9. For a full analysis, see commentary of Rabbenu Nissim, *ad locum*, and R. Joseph Babad, *Minhat Hinnukh*, no. 80.

10. Whether *tza'ar ba'alei hayyim* is prohibited by virtue of biblical or rabbinical law is of no significance insofar as the normative regulations prohibiting overt acts of cruelty *vis-à-vis* animals are concerned. There are, however, a number of distinctions (most of which are currently of relatively minor impact) with regard to the duty to intervene in order to relieve or prevent animal suffering. The most obvious distinctions are those posited by the *Gemara, Baba Metzi'a* 33a: "'[If thou seest the ass of him that hateth thee lying under its burden]' 'lying' [just now], but not an animal which habitually lies down [under its burden]; 'lying,' but not standing." The *Gemara* then queries, "If you say that [relieving the suffering of an animal] is biblically [enjoined] what does it matter whether it was lying [this once only], habitually lay down, or was standing?" and concludes that such distinctions are cogent only if *tza'ar ba'alei hayyim* is the subject of rabbinic enactment but that such exclusions from the duty to relieve animals from pain cannot be entertained if *tza'ar ba'alei hayyim* is a

matter of biblical law. Indeed, it is Maimonides' failure to make such distinctions which, in part, prompts *Kesef Mishneh, Hilkhot Rotzeah* 13:9, to conclude that Maimonides maintains that *tza'ar ba'alei hayyim* is biblically enjoined. On the basis of the discussion recorded in *Baba Metzi'a* 33a, *Minhat Hinnukh*, no. 80, concludes that intervention to rescue an animal from pain is mandated only if *tza'ar ba'alei hayyim* is forbidden by biblical law; if *tza'ar ba'alei hayyim* is the subject of rabbinical decree, such legislation only prohibits acts of cruelty but does not command intervention. See below, note 11. See also Mahari Perla, commentary on *Sefer ha-Mitzvot* of R. Sa'adya Ga'on, *aseh* 24, *s.v. ve-adayan tzarikh.* (However, *cf.* R. Moses Sofer, *Teshuvot Hatam Sofer, Yoreh De'ah*, no. 314, *s.v. ve-la'asot*, and no. 318, *s.v. ve-hineh*, who apparently maintains that the obligation to rescue an animal from pain is limited to one's own animals. See also *Teshuvot Hatam Sofer, Hoshen Mishpat, no. 185, s.v. ma-she-katavta me-Rabad.* Thus *Hatam Sofer* maintains that, although an overt act of cruelty toward any animal is forbidden, one may allow an ownerless animal to starve. See, however, R. Ezekiel Landau, *Teshuvot Noda bi-Yehudah, Mahadura Kamma, Yoreh De'ah*, nos. 81–83, who fails to draw a distinction of this nature. See also *Kitzur Shulhan Arukh* 191:1 and sources cited by R. Eliyahu Kaltzkin, *Teshuvot Imeri Shefer*, no. 34, sec. 1.) Another distinction is found in the application of certain Sabbath restrictions. If it is accepted that obligations with regard to *tza'ar ba'alei hayyim* are biblical in origin, a non-Jew may be requested to perform acts of labor on the Sabbath, *e.g.*, milking a cow, in order to relieve the animal's discomfort, and certain specific rabbinically proscribed acts may also be performed even by a Jew in order to alleviate the animal's pain. But no suspension of Sabbath restrictions is countenanced if duties with regard to *tza'ar ba'alei hayyim* are the product of rabbinic enactment. See Ritva, *Baba Metzi'a* 32b, as well as Rosh, *Baba Metzi'a* 2:29 and *Shabbat* 18:3; see also *Magen Avraham, Orah Hayyim* 305:11, and *Korban Netanel, Shabbat* 18:3, sec. 50. (Compare, however, *Teshuvot Rav Pe'alim*, I, *Yoreh De'ah*, no. 1, who maintains that such actions are permitted only when the life of the animal is endangered. Failure to milk a cow, he asserts, endangers the health of the animal.) There is some controversy with regard to whether a non-Jew may be directed to perform a rabbinically proscribed act; see *Encyclopedia Talmudit*, II, 45. According to the authorities, who adopt a permissive position with regard to this question, such a procedure would be permissible if it were accepted that regulations concerning *tza'ar ba'alei hayyim* are rabbinical in nature. (In this context the citation of *Pilpula Harifta, Baba Metzi'a* 2:29, by R. Zev Metzger in his survey, "Nisuyim Refu'iyim be-Ba'alei Hayyim," *Ha-Refu'ah le-Or ha-Halakhah*, vol. II [Jerusalem, 5743], part 3, p. 11, appears to be inaccurate.) See also note 52.

11. It is the virtually unanimous opinion of rabbinic decisors that obligations with regard to *tza'ar ba'alei hayyim* are biblical in nature. See Rif, *Shabbat* 128b; *Sefer ha-Hinnukh*, nos. 450 and 451; Rosh, *Baba Metzi'a* 2:29 and *Shabbat* 3:18; *Nemukei Yosef, Baba Metzi'a* 32b; Me'iri, *Baba Metzi'a* 32b; *Shita Mekubetzet, Baba Metzi'a* 33a; *Sefer Yere'im*, no. 267 *Sefer Hasidim* (ed. Reuben Margulies), no. 666; Rema, *Hoshen Mishpat* 272:9, *Levush, Orah Hayyim* 305:18; and *Magen Avraham, Orah Hayyim* 305:11.

Maimonides, both in his *Commentary on the Mishnah, Beitzah* 3:4, and in the *Guide*, Book III, chapter 17, affirms that the prohibition against *tza'ar ba'alei hayyim* is biblical in origin. There is some dispute regarding the proper understanding of the position adopted by Maimonides in his *Mishneh Torah*. Although in *Hilkhot Shabbat* 25:26 he appears to espouse the identical position, the language employed in *Hilkhot Rotze'ah* 13:9 is somewhat ambiguous. Nevertheless, *Kesef Mishneh, ad locum*, understands even the latter source as consistent with the view that the prohibition against *tza'ar ba'alei hayyim* is biblical in nature. However, *Pnei Yehoshu'a, Baba Metzi'a* 32b, and R. Elijah of Vilna, both in his *Hagahot ha-Gra al ha-Rosh, Baba Metzi'a* chapter 2, sec. 29:1, and in his *Bi'ur ha-Gra, Hoshen Mishpat* 272:11, understanding Maimonides' ruling in *Hilkhot Rotze'ah* as reflecting the view that these strictures are rabbinic in nature. See also *Minhat Hinnukh*, no. 80.

Pri Megadim, Orah Hayyim, Eshel Avrahm 308:68, and R. Meir Simchah ha-Kohen of Dvinsk, *Or Same'ah, Hilkhot Shabbat* 25:36, both resolve any apparent contradiction in Maimonides' rulings by asserting that in *Hilkhot Shabbat* Maimonides' intention is only to affirm the biblical nature of the obligation concerning the requirement that animals be permitted to rest on the Sabbath in order to prevent their suffering on that day. In comments that are at variance with his own previously cited thesis, *Or Same'ah, Hilkhot Rotze'ah*

13:9, offers a novel analysis of Maimonides' position. *Or Same'ah* here asserts that Maimonides affirms the biblical nature of strictures against *tza'ar ba'alei hayyim* but that he distinguishes between practicing cruelty toward animals, which is forbidden, and intervention in an overt manner to spare an animal from discomfort. According to these comments of *Or Same'ah*, Maimonides maintains that such intervention is not mandated. According to *Or Same'ah*, Maimonides reasons that there is no prohibition against causing discomfort to an animal in order to satisfy a human need; similarly, there is no requirement that a person be discomforted in order to promote the welfare of an animal.

Mordekhai, *Baba Metzi'a* 2:263, rules that *tza'ar ba'alei hayyim* is biblically enjoined, but in his work on *Avodah Zarah* 1:799 the same authority rules that such strictures are rabbinical in nature. *Hiddushei Anshei Shem, Baba Metzi'a*, sec. 20, endeavors to resolve the contradiction by asserting that, according to Mordekhai, "grave pain" (*tza'ar gadol*) involves a biblical prohibition, whereas "minor pain" (*tza'ar mu'at*) involves only a rabbinic injunction. It is noteworthy that, according to the *Hiddushei Anshei Shem*, causing an animal to die of starvation involves only "minor pain," whereas killing an animal in an overt manner is categorized as entailing "grave pain." (However, see R. Jacob Ettlinger, *Teshuvot Binyan Zion*, no. 108, who states that "perhaps" causing an animal to die of starvation entails "grave pain.") Quite independently, *Nimukei Yosef, Baba Metzi'a* 32b, draws a similar distinction between "grave pain" and "minor pain" without in any way referring to Maimonides' statements. According to *Nemukei Yosef*, "minor pain" is the subject of rabbinic injunction, while "grave pain" is biblically proscribed. See also Ritva, *Avodah Zarah* 11a.

As will be shown below, a latter-day authority, R. Jacob Ettlinger, *Teshuvot Binyan Zion*, no. 108, permits causing an animal "grave pain" only for purposes of human medical needs but permits "minor pain" even for lesser reasons, at least insofar as normative law is concerned.

12. See also Rabad, quoted in *Shitah Mekubetzet, Baba Metzi'a* 32b, *s.v. teda*, and *Luvush, Orah Hayyim* 305:18. If obligations concerning *tza'ar ba'alei hayyim* are derived from the commandment concerning "unloading," it would certainly seem to follow that this obligation is not limited to a prohibition against cruelty but includes a

positive obligation to intervene in order to rescue an animal from pain. See R. Joel Schwartz, *Ve-Rahamov al Kol Ma'asav*, p. 43, note 3 and *cf.* note 10.

13. See note 43.

14. See also *Minhat Hinnukh*, no. 80.

15. It must, however, be noted that, even with regard to rights enjoyed by humans, the emphasis in Jewish law is upon the notion of "duty" rather than "right." Thus, satisfaction of a debt is actionable, not primarily as enforcement of the creditor's right, but as a means of compelling fulfillment of the religio-moral obligation of the debtor. In all matters of jurisprudence, the emphasis is upon prevention of moral degeneration attendant upon the misappropriation of property belonging to another rather than upon satisfaction of the claim of the rightful owner. In adjudicating claims between litigants, the *Bet Din* acts, as is its duty, primarily to compel fulfillment of a religio-moral duty rather than to redress a wrong. See Moshe Silberg, "Law and Morals in Jewish Jurisprudence," *Harvard Law Review*, LXXV (1961–1962), 306–331. Similarly, proper behavior *vis-à-vis* animals would be compelled by the court as the fulfillment of a religious obligation.

16. See also Nahmanides' comments in his *Commentary on the Bible*, Deuteronomy 22:6.

17. Indeed, *shehitah* is the most humane method of slaughter known to man. The procedure involves a transverse cut in the throat of the animal with an extremely sharp and smooth knife. Because of the sharpness of the knife and the paucity of sensory cutaneous nerve endings in the skin covering the throat, the incision itself causes no pain. The incision severs the carotid arteries as well as the jugular veins. The resultant massive loss of blood causes the animal to become unconscious in a matter of seconds. There is ample clinical evidence confirming the total absence of pain to the animal as a result of *shehitah*. This has long been recognized by scientists of international repute. In view of recurring and misinformed attacks upon *shehitah*, it is instructive to cite a portion of a detailed clarifying statement by Dr. Leonard Hill, Professor of Physiology, University of London, and Director of Applied Physiology, National Institute for Medical Research, which appeared in *Lancet*, CCV (1923), p. 1328 and was reprinted in Solomon David Sassoon, *A Critical Study of Electrical Stunning and The Jewish Method of Slaughter (Shechita)*, 3rd ed.,

(London, Letchworth, 1955), pp. 4–6 (hereafter referred to as Sassoon, *A Critical Study*). Dr. Hill writes:

> It is generally assumed by laymen that the shooting is much
> more humane than the older methods. They suppose that the
> cutting of the throat is a most painful operation, and that strug-
> gling movements are necessarily a sign of pain. Educated in the
> false ideas and statements of writers of romance, they are easily
> led astray by agitators having no knowledge of physiological
> science, nor surgical experience. Now the surgeon knows that
> sudden big injuries are not felt at the time of their infliction.
> He knows, moreover, that structures beneath the skin, apart
> from sensory nerves, are insensitive to the knife. It is well
> known that men injured in battle—severely and perhaps fa-
> tally—often fight on unaware that they are wounded until they
> see the blood or become exhausted. At most the wounded feel
> a dull sensation of a blow and numbness in the injured part.
> Pain comes later when a wound becomes septic and inflamed.
> The merciful insensitiveness of man to severe injury was im-
> pressed upon me, when I was a young house surgeon, by two
> cases—one of a man with his pelvis crushed between the buff-
> ers of a train. Conscious, although collapsed, he was able to tell
> me that he had felt no pain; shortly afterwards he died of shock.
> A similar case was that of a man impaled by the shaft of an iron
> railing through falling out of a window.
>
>   In defending the Jewish method of slaughter from unjust
> attack, the distinguished surgeon Mr. T. H. Openshaw stated
> that several cases of throat-cutting, which surviving from their
> injury had come under his care at the London Hospital, were
> questioned by him. Not one of these had felt the cut when it
> was made. When a very sharp knife is used to cut the healthy
> (not inflamed) skin, very little pain is felt—even by a man who
> is expecting the cut—particularly so in parts, such as the back,
> which are not so trained to delicate sensibility as the finger-
> tips. Horses standing loose in a stall are bled from the jugular
> vein for the obtaining of anti-diphtheritic serum; they continue
> during the operation to eat placidly at the manger. Sensitive as
> the horse is to the sting of a fly, or whip, or prick of a spur, it
> takes no notice of the cut of a sharp knife. The skin has been
> evolved sensitive only to those things which concern it in the
> natural struggle for existence, and deep structures, apart from
> sensory nerves, protected as they are by the skin, are wholly

insensitive to touch. The touch of whip or spur is like the sting
of a fly, and is therefore felt by the horse, which must protect
himself against a natural enemy; on the other hand, the cut of a
sharp knife is not a natural stimulus and is unfelt.

Of these facts laymen are, as a rule, wholly ignorant. As to
the duration of consciousness after the cutting of the throat, I
can cite an experiment made by myself some years ago when,
together with Mr. Openshaw, I defended the Jewish method of
slaughter. I anaesthetized a calf and inserted a tube in the pe-
ripheral end of the carotid artery—that is, in the end connected with the arteries supplying the brain. It must be borne in
mind that the vertebral arteries do not also supply the brain of
cattle but end in the muscles of the head. The tube placed in
the artery was filled with a strong saline solution to prevent
clotting of the blood, and connected with a mercurial man-
ometer arranged so as to record (on a revolving drum) the blood
pressure. The animal's neck was then cut with a sharp knife so
as to divide the great blood-vessels at one stroke. The man-
ometer recorded an instant fall of blood pressure which reached
zero in a second or two, showing that the circulation in the
great brain has ceased. Now we know by human experience
that such sudden cessation of the circulation by depriving the
brain of oxygen instantly abolishes consciousness, whether
produced by pressure on the brain or by heart failure, or by
occlusion of the great blood-vessels of the neck. An old medical
writer tells of a beggar in Paris who had a large hole in his skull
covered with skin. He sat in the street and for a coin allowed a
person to press upon his brain, when he fell asleep. The moment the pressure was withdrawn he became conscious again.
The very word carotid betokens sleep. Mountebanks used to
compress these arteries in a goat and make the animal fall
down unconscious or spring up again at their will. The garroter
by compressing these arteries by a grip from behind rendered
his victim unconscious while he robbed him of his watch and
money. A schoolboy playing at hanging has lost consciousness
through the sudden compression of these arteries and had died
in consequence. This unhappy accident has been repeated
through a general ignorance of the danger.

Two facts are, then, indisputably established: (1) that a big
injury, such as throat-cutting, is not felt at the moment of infliction; (2) that the cutting of the big arteries in the throat in-

stantly arrests the circulation in the great brain and abolishes consciousness.

See also Leonard Hill, "The Jewish Method of Slaughter: A Rejoinder to the Dutchess of Hamilton," *The English Review* (June 1923), pp. 604–607, reprinted in Sassoon, *A Critical Study*, pp. 36–38. Further statements confirming the painless nature of *shehitah* by Lord Horder, F.A.C.P., and Sir C. P. Lovatt Eveans, Emeritus Professor of Physiology, London University, are included in Sassoon, *A Critical Study*, pp. 38–39. See also Solomon David Sassoon, *Supplement to the Booklet Entitled: A Critical Study of Electrical Stunning and the Jewish Method of Slaughter (Shechita)* (London, Letchworth, 1956).

Both the absence of pain as a result of the incision and the almost instantaneous loss of consciousness subsequent to *shehitah* are confirmed in a report prepared in 1963 by L. I. Nangeroni and P. D. Kennett of the Department of Physiology, New York State Veterinary College, Cornell University, Ithaca, New York, titled "An Electroencephalographic Study of the Effect of Shechita Slaughter on Cortical Function in Ruminants." The primary significance of this study lies in the clinical investigation of changes in function that occur in the cerebral cortex following the act of *shehitah*. The investigators utilized an electroencephalograph in order to determine the precise moment at which the animal consciously ceases to perceive pain and other environmental stimuli. Recordings were taken with sheep, calves, and goats as subjects. In the rams tested, the time that elapsed subsequent to making the incision until the cerebral cortex lapsed into a state of complete unconsciousness ranged from 3.3 to 6.2 seconds. In calves it was found that consciousness appeared to be poor by the time that 4.0 seconds had elapsed after the cut, and complete unconsciousness, in which the animal could not perceive stimuli of any kind, became manifest between 4.4 and 6.9 seconds. Of two goats tested, one became unconscious 5 seconds after slaughter; in the case of the second goat, the electroencephalogram was obscured, and hence it was impossible to determine the exact time at which unconsciousness was reached.

Electroencephalographic evidence serves to determine the precise moment at which the animal becomes unconscious and conclusively establishes the time beyond which it is manifestly impossible for the animal to experience pain. In the animals examined this ranged from 3.3 to 6.9 seconds following the incision. However, this does not mean that the animals experienced pain during the few seconds prior to becoming unconscious. Indeed, there is no way to interpret an electroencephalogram to determine whether or not pain is actually being experienced by an animal. It can only serve to establish that the animal is, in fact, unconscious and hence no longer capable of experiencing pain. With regard to the possibility of the animal's feeling pain in conjunction with the incision before consciousness is lost, the report states:

> As anyone who has slit a finger on a page of a magazine knows, the pain from such a cut comes not during the actual cutting, but afterwards when the edges of the cut are rubbed or pressed together and the nerve endings in the skin are stimulated. The edges of the cut neck cannot be thus brought together after Shechita simply because of the animal's hanging position (p. 17).

See also I. M. Levinger, "Physiological and General Medical Aspects of Shechita," in *Shechita*, edited by Michael L. and Eli Munk (Jerusalem, 1976), pp. 160–185.

18. See also Nahmanides, *Commentary on the Bible*, Deuteronomy 22:6, and R. Joseph Albo, *Book of Principles*, Book III, chapter 15. An identical view is expressed by Philo, *De Virtutibus*, 141.

19. This point is made by *Pri Megadim* with regard to ritual slaughter in particular. See the concluding section of *Pri Megadim's* introduction to *Hilkhot Shehitah*.

20. See *Taz, Yoreh De'ah* 116:6 and *Taz, Yoreh De'ah* 117:4. See also note 60.

21. The identical position is reiterated by the same author in *Teshuvot Noda bi-Yehudah, Mahadura Tinyana, Yorah De'ah*, nos. 10 and 13. In the latter responsum *Noda bi-Yehudah* rules that, although *tza'ar ba'alei hayyim* is permitted when necessary to serve a human need, nevertheless, when the option is available, it is preferable to sacrifice the animal rather than to perform a painful procedure upon a living animal. *Noda bi-Yehudah* presumably reasons that, since killing an animal involves no transgression of *tza'ar ba'alei hayyim*, there is no dispensation to cause pain when the same need can be met by killing the animal.

22. A similar position is espoused by *Sefer ha-Eshkol*, III, *Hilkhot Shehitah*, no. 10; *Teshuvot Bet Ya'akov*, no. 42; R. Yonatan Eibeschutz, *Kreti u-Pleti* 57:9 and *Gilyon Maharsha, Yoreh De'ah* 117:4. *Cf.* R. Eliezer Waldenberg, *Tzitz Eli'ezer*, XIV, no. 68, sec. 4.

23. A similar analysis of the considerations underlying the exchange between R. Phinehas and R. Judah was advanced earlier by *Terumat ha-Deshen, Pesakim u-Ketuvim*, no. 105. See also R. Yitzchak Blaser, *Teshuvot Pri Yitzhak*, I, no. 24, who offers an even more comprehensive analysis in a similar vein.

24. This responsum was addressed to R. Ya'akov Breisch and was first published in the latter's responsa collection, *Helkat Ya'akov*, I, no. 31.

25. Similarly, the *Gemara*, Hullin 85b, permits putting an animal to death by means other than ritual slaughter when the intent is not to use the animal's meat for consumption but its blood is required for some other purpose. That source also serves to establish either that *tza'ar ba'alei hayyim* is permitted when designed for human welfare or that putting an animal to death is excluded from the prohibition against *tza'ar ba'alei hayyim*.

R. Moses Sofer, *Teshuvot Hatam Sofer, Yoreh De'ah*, no. 103, citing *Avodah Zarah* 13b, permits killing a sickly animal by means other than ritual slaughter. It is, however, not possible to determine whether *Hatam Sofer* sanctions this practice because he espouses the position that putting an animal to death is excluded from strictures prohibiting *tza'ar ba'alei hayyim* or because the pain inflicted is designed to serve a human need, *viz.*, to prevent the loss that would accrue to the animal's owner if it were to become carrion and its meat no longer salable. This point seems to have been missed by R. Zev Metzger, "Nisuyim Refu'iyim be-Ba'alei Hayyim," *Ha-Refu'ah le-Or ha-Halakhah*, vol. II, part 3, p. 31. See also notes 57 and 60.

26. See also *Tosafot, Hullin* 2a, *s.v. shema. Tosafot* apparently permits killing an animal by means of ritual slaughter in order to feed its meat to dogs. *Cf.* above, note 25, and below, note 53 and accompanying text.

27. *Cf.*, however, *Sho'el u-Meshiv, Mahadura Tinyana*, III, no. 65, who refutes this evidence, claiming that *Tosafot* merely asserts that when *tza'ar ba'alei hayyim* is warranted it must be minimized insofar as possible.

28. The immediately following verse, "then thou shalt kill of thy herd and of thy flock . . . and thou shalt eat within thy gates" (Deuteronomy 12:21), serves to sanction ritual slaughter for purposes of food. Since, in context, the reference in Deuteronomy 12:20 is to rit-

ual slaughter, it is clear that Maimonides regards even the painless mode of ritual slaughter, when undertaken other than for purposes of food, as forbidden by reason of *tza'ar ba'alei hayyim*. However, Maimonides would certainly regard ritual slaughter undertaken to satisfy other legitimate human needs as tantamount to slaughter for purposes of food. Ritual slaughter other than for purposes of food is clearly permitted, as evidenced by the statement of the *Gemara*, *Hullin* 85b, to the effect that R. Hiyya slaughtered a bird in the prescribed manner because he sought to use its blood to destroy worms that had infested his flax. See *Sefer Hasidim* (ed. Reuben Margulies), no. 667. Moreover, when the blood of an animal is necessary for some beneficial purpose, the *Gemara*, *Hullin* 85b, permits putting an animal to death even by means other than ritual slaughter in order to conserve its blood. The comments of Rashi, *Shabbat* 75a, *s.v. shohet*, indicate that, under any circumstances, when an animal is killed for human benefit other than for food, it is not necessary to put it to death by means of ritual slaughter. Cf. Rashi, *Hullin* 27b, *s.v. hayyev le-khasot*.

29. See also *Sefer ha-Hinnukh*, no. 186, who explains that the slaughter of sanctified animals outside the Temple precincts, even though the act is performed in the ritually prescribed manner, is forbidden because no purpose is served by it. *Sefer ha-Hinnukh* comments that wanton killing of animals is tantamount to "shedding blood."

30. For other sources prohibiting hunting, see *Va-Yikra Rabbah* 13:3; Rashi, *Avodah Zarah* 18b, *s.v. kenigyon*; *Teshuvot Mahari Brona*, no. 71; *Teshuvot Maharam of Rothenberg*, no. 27; Rema, *Shulhan Arukh*, *Orah Hayyim* 316:2; *Teshuvot Shemesh Tzedakah*, *Yoreh De'ah*, nos. 18 and 57; *Giv'at Sha'ul*, *Parshat Va-Yeshev*, pp. 87–88; *Pahad Yitzchak*, *s.v. Tzeidah*; *Teshuvot Toldot Ya'akov*, *Yoreh De'ah*, no. 33; and *Darkei Teshuvah*, *Yoreh De'ah* 117:44.

31. See also *Teshuvot Imrei Shefer*, no. 34, sec. 1; R. Yechiel Ya'akov Weinberg, *Seridei Esh*, III, no. 7; R. Ya'akov Breisch, *Teshuvot Helkat Ya'akov*, I, no. 31, sec. 4; and R. Moshe Yonah Zweig, *Ohel Mosheh*, I, no. 32. See also R. Jacob Reischer, *Teshuvot Shevut Ya'akov*, II, no. 110, who declares that an "unusual" practice involving pain is prohibited, particularly when designed for only "a minor benefit." Cf. *Teshuvot Rav Pe'alim*, I, *Yoreh De'ah*, no. 1.

32. See *Havalim ba-Ne'imim*, I, no. 43, sec. 4. This also appears to be the position of *Teshuvot ha-Ge'onim* (ed. Abraham E. Harkavi), no. 375.

33. *Havalim ba-Ne'imim*, I, no. 43, sec. 6, quotes *She'ilat Ya'avetz*'s comments as cited by a secondary source, *Bet Efrayim, Yoreh De'ah* 117. That source quotes *She'ilat Ya'avetz* as stating that *tza'ar ba'alei hayyim* applies only to "work animals." *Havalim ba-Ne'imim* cites a ruling of *Sefer Hasidim* (ed. Reuben Margulies), no. 44, which forbids pulling the ears of a cat and states that this position contradicts the view of *She'ilat Ya'avetz*. In point of fact, *She'ilat Ya'avetz* explicitly states "and perhaps even dog[s] and cat[s] are included [in the prohibition] since they also are domesticated and perform work." A more significant contradiction to the position of *She'ilat Ya'avetz* is found by *Havalim ba-Ne'imim* in the comments of *Shevut Ya'akov*, III, no. 71. *Shevut Ya'akov* demonstrates that *tza'ar ba'alei hayyim* is permitted for the benefit of human beings on the basis of the *Gemara, Shabbat* 77b. The *Gemara* observes that God did not create a single thing without purpose and gives specific examples of the utility of seemingly useless creatures: the fly is crushed and applied to the bite of a hornet's sting; the mosquito is crushed and used as a remedy for a serpent's bite; a crushed spider is used as a remedy for a scorpion's bite; and various serpents are boiled to a pulp and rubbed in at the site of an eruption. *Shevut Ya'akov* adduces that dictum as proof that *tza'ar ba'alei hayyim* is permissible for human welfare. *Havalim ba-Ne'imim* points out that *Shevut Ya'akov*'s argument is cogent only if, in contradiction to *She'ilat Ya'avetz*'s position, he assumes that considerations of *tza'ar ba'alei hayyim* apply to all creatures, including serpents and insects. See also note 46.

34. *Cf.*, however, R. Elijah of Vilna, *Bi'ur ha-Gra, Even ha-Ezer* 5:40, and the comments of R. Jacob Breisch, *Teshuvot Helkat Ya'akov*, I, no. 30, secs. 2–3, as well as Shmuel, Moshe Mordecai and Eleazar Shulsinger, *Mishmar ha-Leviyim* (Zikron Me'ir, 5740), no. 20. See also R. Yechiel Ya'akov Weinberg, *Seridei Esh*, III, no. 7, and *Helkat Ya'akov*, I, no. 31, secs. 1–3.

R. Judah Leib Zirelson, *Ma'arkhei Lev*, no. 110, finds a biblical source for this ruling:

> And Samson went and caught three hundred foxes and took torches and turned tail to tail and put a torch in the midst between every two tails. And when he had set the torches on fire,

he let them go into the standing corn of the Philistines and burn up both the shucks and the standing corn and also the oliveyards (Judges 15:4–5).

Ma'arkhei Lev argues that inflicting severe pain on the foxes was sanctioned only because it served a human need and hence the general principle can be traced to these verses. R. Jacob Breisch, *Teshuvot Helkat Ya'akov*, I, no. 30, sec. 5, cogently rebuts this argument on the grounds that Samson was involved in a defensive war against the Philistines and, in fact, his own life was endangered. Hence Judges 15:4–5 serves only to establish that *tza'ar ba'alei hayyim* is permitted when human life is endangered but not necessarily for the sake of a lesser purpose.

35. *Cf. Teshuvot Mareh Yehezkel*, no. 59, who expresses amazement at Rema's ruling in querying, "from whence is it derived that violation of the biblical prohibition of *tza'ar ba'alei hayyim* may be sanctioned to effect a cure or for human benefit?" In light of *Tosafot*'s comments to the effect that the prohibition does not encompass such contingencies, *Mareh Yehezkel*'s incredulity is misplaced.

36. See note 50.

37. See R. Abraham Hafuta, *No'am*, IV (5721), 223f. *Piskei Tosafot, Avodah Zarah* 1:11, in what is apparently a précis of *Tosafot, Baba Metzi'a* 32b (or the précis of a different manuscript of *Tosafot* on *Avodah Zarah*), states that *tza'ar ba'alei hayyim* is forbidden only when the pain caused to the animal yields "no profit" (*beli revah*).

38. *Cf.*, however, *Teshuvot Imrei Shefer*, no. 34, sec. 11, who endeavors to ascribe a different import to the words of Rabbenu Nissim.

39. *Nemukei Yosef* cites Nehmanides as resolving this difficulty in an entirely different manner. Nahmanides asserts that the "commandment concerning honor of the Torah takes precedence over considerations of *tza'ar ba'alei hayyim*." The readily apparent explanation of Nahmanides' failure to advance an analysis similar to that offered by Rabbenu Nissim is that he does not sanction *tza'ar ba'alei hayyim* for the purpose of satisfying a human need. However, that position is rejected by Nahmanides' own remarks in his commentary on *Avodah Zarah* 13b.

40. This concept is echoed in Psalms 8:7–9, which says of man:

Thou hast made him to have dominion over the works of Thy
hands; Thou hast put all things under his feet. Sheep and oxen,
all of them, yea, and the beast of the field. The fowl of the air,
and the fish of the sea; whatsoever passeth through the paths of
the seas.

As evidenced by numerous biblical verses, it is clear that man is
granted license to utilize animals as beasts of burden, for agricultural
purposes, as a means of transportation, and the like. Judaism also accepts the view that animals were created for the benefit of mankind.
Thus, the Gemara, *Berakhot* 6b, reports: R. Eleazar said, "The Holy
One, blessed be He, declared, 'The whole world in its entirety was
not created other than on behalf of this [human species].'" Even
more explicit is the statement of R. Simeon ben Eleazar, *Kiddushin*
82b, declaring ". . . they [animals] were not created other than to
serve me." This view is not contradicted by the position espoused by
Maimonides in a celebrated dispute with Sa'adya Ga'on in which
Maimonides denies the homocentric nature of the universe. Sa'adya,
The Book of Beliefs and Opinions, Treatise IV, introduction, asserts
that man is the intended and ultimate purpose of creation; Maimonides, *Guide*, Book III, chapter 13, challenges this view, pointing
out that the human species has no need for a great part of the cosmos.
Maimonides maintains that all parts of the world are equally intended
by the divine will but acknowledges that certain beings were created
for the service of others. Thus, in Maimonides' view, there is no contradiction in acknowledging that service to other species is the instrumental purpose of some creatures while still affirming their own existence as the final cause of those creatures.

41. See also *Teshuvot Hatam Sofer*, *Hoshen Mishpat*, no. 185,
s.v. ma-she-katavata me-Rabad; *cf.*, however, *Teshuvot Hatam Sofer*,
Yoreh De'ah, no. 314, *s.v. amnam*; and *Teshuvot Imrei Shefer* no. 34,
sec. 2.

42. *Terumat ha-Deshen* rules that, as a matter of law, it is permissible to cause pain to animals even for the esthetic pleasure of
man, and, accordingly, he permits clipping the ears and tail of a dog
"in order to beautify it." *Cf.*, however, *Sefer Hasidim* (ed. *Mekitzei
Nirdamin*), no. 589, who forbids any attempt to effect a "change" in
correcting a congenital anomaly in limb or organ of an animal on
grounds that such a procedure constitutes a violation of the prohibition against *tza'ar ba'alei hayyim*. In an even more general state-

ment, *Da'at Kedoshim, Yoreh De'ah* 24:12, declares that acts that cause discomfort to animals are permissible in order to satisfy "any desire of man even if his desire in this regard is not in accordance with the weighing of need or benefit but only a desire without a proper reason." The same authority permits such procedures even if there is only the mere possibility that the need or desire may be satisfied thereby. See also *Da'at Kedoshim, Yoreh De'ah* 23:28. A similar view is expressed by *Ezer me-Kodesh, Even ha-Ezer* 5:14. *Cf.*, however, note 66.

43. *Cf.*, however, *Sefer Hasidim* (ed. Reuben Margulies), no. 666, who applies Genesis 1:28 in a radically different manner. *Sefer Hasidim* remarks that Adam was forbidden to eat the flesh of animals but was granted dominion over them, whereas the sons of Noah were permitted to eat the flesh of animals but were not granted dominion over them. According to *Sefer Hasidim*, it is because the sons of Noah were not granted dominion over animals that the angel chastized Balaam in demanding: "Wherefore has thou smitten thine ass these three times?" (Numbers 22:32). As pointed out by R. Reuben Margulies in his commentary of *Sefer Hasidim, Mekor Hesed* 666:7, *Sefer Hasidim* obviously maintains that Noachides are forbidden to engage in acts involving *tza'ar ba'alei hayyim*. As indicated earlier, Maimonides also cites Numbers 22:32 as the source of the prohibition against *tza'ar ba'alei hayyim*. Hence there is some reason to assume that Maimonides also maintains that *tza'ar ba'alei hayyim* is prohibited to Noahides. *Teshuvot Imrei Shefer*, no. 34, secs. 2 and 8, also suggests that Noahides may be bound by strictures concerning *tza'ar ba'alei hayyim* which, in his opinion, may be encompassed in the prohibition contained in the Noahide Code concerning eating a limb torn from a living animal. See, however, *Pri Megadim, Orah Hayyim, Mishbetzot Zahav* 467:2, and R. Shalom Modecai Schwadron, *Teshuvot Maharsham*, III, no. 364, who apparently maintain that non-Jews are not bound by strictures concerning *tza'ar ba'alei hayyim*. See also *Toldot Ya'akov Yoreh De'ah*, no. 33.

44. See Rema, *Even ha-Ezer* 5:13. *Cf. Bi'ur has-Gra, Even ha-Ezer* 5:31, and R. Jacob Emden, *She'ilat Ya'avetz*, I, no. 111.

45. For a rebuttal of the evidence yielded by these sources, see R. Yitzchak Dov Bamberger, *Teshuvot Yad ha-Levi*, I, *Yoreh De'ah*, no. 196, and *Teshuvot Imrei Shefer*, no. 34, sec. 10.

46. *Shevut Ya'akov* also adduces proof that *tza'ar ba'alei hayyim* is permitted, at least for medical purposes, on the basis of the statement of the *Gemara, Shabbat* 77b, that various insects were created so that, when crushed, they might be used as remedies for various bites and that serpents were created so that they might be boiled and used as a cure for eruptions; see note 33. As additional evidence, he cites the statement of the *Gemara, Shabbat* 109b, advising that if one is bitten by a snake, "he should procure an embryo of a white ass, tear it open, and be made to sit upon it." A further source that may be cited is the statement of the *Gemara, Shabbat* 110b, which advises *inter alia* that in treating jaundice "let him take a speckled swine, tear it open and apply it to his heart." However, these sources fail to demonstrate that *tza'ar ba'alei hayyim* is permitted for medical purposes if the killing of animals is excluded from the prohibition; see notes 21 through 25 and accompanying text.

47. See, however, R. Yechiel Ya'akov Weinberg, *Seridei Esh*, III, no. 7, and *Helkat Ya'akov*, III, no. 31, sec. 4. Rabbi Weinberg argues that this source cannot serve as a basis for Rema's ruling, since "perhaps" such practices are condoned only for the purpose of preventing idolatrous activities. *Cf.* Nahmanides, *Avodah Zarah* 13b. In his analysis of the *Gemara*'s citation of the verse "and their horses shall you hough (*et suseihem te'aker*)" (Judges 1:6), Nahmanides equates abrogation of idolatrous practices with other human needs. See also *Teshuvot Imrei Shefer*, no. 34, sec. 9, who endeavors to show that *tza'ar ba'alei hayyim* was permitted in the case of the white chicken sold to an idolator only to spare the animal from even greater pain. The same authority, *Teshuvot Imrei Shefer*, no. 34, sec. 14, also suggests that this procedure is permitted only when performed in a manner that does not entail pain; see note 52. A similar explanation is advanced by *Havalim ba-Ne'imim*, I, no. 43, sec. 3.

48. *Tosafot, Avodah Zarah* 11a, states that *tza'ar ba'alei hayyim* is permitted "in honor of the king which is the honor of all of Israel, and the honor of the multitude takes precedence over *tza'ar ba'alei hayyim*." See also *Teshuvot Noda bi-Yehudah, Mahadura Tinyana, Yorah De'ah*, no. 10.

49. See also the comments of Nahmanides cited in note 39. *Teshuvot Rema Panu*, no. 102, forbids placing a bird upon the eggs of another species in order to hatch them because of concern for *tza'ar ba'alei hayyim*. This ruling is also recorded in *Kitzur Shulhan Arukh*

191:4. Ostensibly, this authority maintains that *tza'ar ba'alei hayyim* is prohibited even when designed for general human benefit or, minimally, when undertaken for financial profit; however, see below, note 58. *Cf.* R. Shimon ben Zemah Duran, *Tashbatz*, II, no. 58, cited by *Pithei Teshuvah*, *Yoreh De'ah* 297:1, who maintains that this procedure causes no discomfort to the bird.

50. See commentary of *Zev Zakhar*, sec. 17, on *Issur ve-Heter*, *ad loc*. *Zev Zakhar* points out that an entirely different inference should be drawn from the published text to *Tosafot*, *Avodah Zarah* 11a, *viz.*, that *tza'ar ba'alei hayyim* is permissible only for the sake of "the king's honor which is the honor of the multitude." *Cf.* also *Teshuvot Imrei Shefer*, no. 34, sec. 9. (It should be noted, however, that experimentation designed to benefit the public at large is to be regarded as undertaken for the sake of "the honor of the multitude"; see R. Abraham Hafuta, *No'am*, IV [1961], 224.) *Teshuvot Noda bi-Yehudah*, *Mahadura Tinyana*, *Yoreh De'ah*, no. 10, assumes that *Issur ve-Heter* cites *Piskei Tosafot* rather than *Tosafot*. The phraseology employed by *Piskei Tosafot* is "there is no prohibition of *tza'ar ba'alei hayyim* other than if he derives no '*revah*.'" The term "*revah*" is somewhat ambiguous and has the connotation of either "profit" or "benefit."

51. See *Or Gadol*, *Shabbat* 24:1, who endeavors to demonstrate that the permissibility of *tza'ar ba'alei hayyim* in order to prevent financial loss is the subject of dispute among early authorities. According to *Or Gadol*, Rashi permits *tza'ar ba'alei hayyim* in such circumstances, while Nahmanides and Rashba maintain that *tza'ar ba'alei hayyim* is forbidden when undertaken solely to avoid financial loss.

52. Evidence in support of the position that *tza'ar ba'alei hayyim* is permitted for financial gain adduced from the statement of the *Mishnah*, *Avodah Zarah* 13b, permitting the removal of a digit from the foot of a chicken is dismissed by *Binyan Zion*. *Binyan Zion* argues that, in declaring this practice to be permissible, the *Mishnah* adopts the position that *tza'ar ba'alei hayyim* is prohibited only by virtue of rabbinic decree, but that, in accordance with the accepted opinion that *tza'ar ba'alei hayyim* is biblically proscribed, dispensation for such acts does not exist. *Havalim ba-Ne'imim*, I, no. 43, sec. 3, offers the explanation that the *Mishnah* intends to permit the removal of a digit "only by utilization of a drug which does not entail pain to the

chicken." See also *Teshuvot Imrei Shefer*, no. 34, sec. 14, and *Nahal Eshkol, Hilkhot Avodah Zarah* 45:6. Painless amputation by means of a drug was known in the days of the *Talmud*; see *Baba Kamma* 85a and Rashi, *ad loc.*, *s.v. bein sam le-sayif.* Presumably, reference is to use of a local anesthetic that was known in the days of the *Talmud*; see *Imrei Shefer*, no. 34, sec. 15.

53. Rabbi Bamberger's letter to *Binyan Zion* has now been published in *Teshuvot Yad ha-Levi*, I, *Yoreh De'ah*, no. 196. Upon examination of his comments, it is evident that Rabbi Bamberger does not attempt to interpret Rema's comments but rather expresses disagreement with *Terumat ha-Deshen*.

54. See also *Teshuvot Toldot Ya'akov, Yoreh De'ah*, no. 33, and *Apei Zutri, Even ha-Ezer* 5:25. *Cf.*, however, R. Eliezer Waldenberg, *Tzitz Eli'ezer*, XIV, no. 68, sec. 5.

55. See note 11. In support of his position, *Binyan Zion* cites the statement of the *Gemara, Bekhorot* 36b, countenancing infliction of a blemish upon an entire flock of animals in order to circumvent the requirement that every tenth animal be offered as a sacrifice. For a rebuttal of that argument, see *Teshuvot Imrei Shefer*, no. 34, sec. 2.

56. The identical source was adduced earlier by R. Yitzchak Dov Bamberger, *Teshuvot Yad ha-Levi*, I, *Yoreh De'ah*, no. 196, as evidence that *tza'ar ba'alei hayyim* is not permitted for the sake of financial gain.

57. See also *Teshuvot Hatam Sofer, Hoshen Mishpat*, no. 185, *s.v. ma-she-katavta me-Rabad. Cf.*, however, *Teshuvot Hatam Sofer, Yoreh De'ah*, no. 314, *s.v. amnam*, and *Teshuvot Imrei Shefer*, no. 34, sec. 2.

58. *Teshuvot Rav Pe'alim*, I, *Yoreh De'ah*, no. 1, rules that *tza'ar ba'alei hayyim* is permitted when designed for human benefit, but only if the desired benefit cannot be achieved in another manner. *Rav Pe'alim* cites *Teshuvot Rema Panu*, no. 102, who forbids placing a bird upon eggs of another species in order to hatch them. Since *Rav Pe'alim* assumes that *tza'ar ba'alei hayyim* is permitted even for the purpose of financial profit, he declares that the ruling of *Teshuvot Rema Panu* applies only in situations in which a bird of the same species is available. See also *Kitzur Shulhan Arukh* 191:4 and *Pithei Teshuvah, Yoreh De'ah* 293:1.

59. *Cf. Teshuvot Noda bi-Yehudah, Mahadura Kamma, Yoreh De'ah*, no. 83.

60. There are also a number of authorities whose comments yield the conclusion that either *tza'ar ba'alei hayyim* is permissible for purposes of financial gain or that putting an animal to death involves no infraction of the prohibition against *tza'ar ba'alei hayyim. Taz, Yoreh De'ah* 117:4, reports that he was asked by a person engaged in the sale of hides whether it is permissible to kill an animal by means other than ritual slaughter because the hide of an animal slaughtered in the ritual manner commands a lower price. The *Gemara, Hullin* 85b, indicates that when the blood of an animal is required for a beneficial purpose, the animal may be put to death by means other than ritual slaughter. See *Shulhan Arukh, Yoreh De'ah* 28:18 and *Derishah, Yoreh De'ah* 28:6. Similarly, *Taz, Yoreh De'ah* 116:6, quotes *Yam shel Shlomoh, Baba Kamma* 10:37, to the effect that one who owns a dog that causes damage or destroys food may poison the dog even though it presents no danger to human beings and that the destruction of the animal involves no prohibition of *tza'ar ba'alei hayyim.* See also *Teshuvot Hatam Sofer, Yoreh De'ah*, no. 103, cited earlier in note 25.

61. See R. Jacob Emden, *She'ilat Ya'avetz*, I, no. 110, who reports that the renowned kabbalist R. Isaac Luria, known as the *Ari ha-Kadosh*, directed his disciples not to kill "even a louse." *She'ilat Ya'avetz* states that this directive was based upon "trait of piety and upon [kabbalistic] mystery." An opposing view is adopted by *Sefer Hasidim* (ed. Reuben Margulies), no. 831:

> There were two people. One did not want to burn the flies. His friend said to him, "'Be not righteous overmuch'" (Ecclesiastes 7:16). "Better to burn the flies so that they shall not fall into the food and drink. [Then] one who swallows them will sin. Therefore it is written 'Be not righteous overmuch.'"

62. However, *cf. She'ilat Ya'avetz*, I, no. 110, who asserts that "perhaps" the calf was the incarnation of a human soul and that this fact was known to R. Judah.

63. *Cf.*, however, *Teshuvot Imrei Shefer*, no. 34, sec. 10, who asserts that *Terumat ha-Deshen* seeks to establish a normative halakhic principle, "for if the matter were permitted there would be no suspicion of punishment."

64. R. Nathan Zevi Friedman, *No'am*, V (1962), 190, seeks another talmudic source for Rema's comment and, in doing so, apparently overlooks the fact that *Terumat ha-Deshen* himself cites *Baba Metzi'a* 85a as his source.

65. A somewhat parallel although less clearly developed concept may be found in Aristotle's notion of "superhuman virtue," which he defines as "a kind of heroic and divine excellence." See *Nicomachean Ethics*, Book VII, 1145a. However the concepts are dissimilar in that Aristotle's superhuman virtue appears to be essentially unobtainable, and indeed Aristotle presents no imperative for seeking its attainment, whereas in Jewish teaching all people may, and indeed should, aspire to act *lifnim me-shurat ha-din*. Also, for Aristotle, superhuman virtue is a quality of character from which certain modes of conduct flow. There is no indication that Aristotle ascribes any moral value to an act that merely mimics the conduct of one who has acquired this quality of character. In Jewish teaching, the act itself is deemed meritorious.

66. The sole rabbinic authority to express reservations with regard to the permissibility of animal experimentation as a matter of normative law is *Imrei Shefer*, no. 34, sec. 16. *Imrei Shefer* declares that "it is not clear" that *tza'ar ba'alei hayyim* is permitted "for the purpose of tests and experiments." *Imrei Shefer* readily acknowledges that *tza'ar ba'alei hayyim* is clearly permitted for therapeutic purposes but distinguishes between therapeutic procedures of demonstrated value and experimentation undertaken on the mere possibility that "perhaps there will emerge from this benefit through medical science." (It may be noted that *Teshuvot Noda bi-Yehudah, Mahadura Kamma, Yoreh De'ah*, no. 83, similarly suggests that *tza'ar ba'alei hayyim* may not be permissible when undertaken to avoid possible but uncertain transgression. *Noda bi-Yehudah* himself, however, concludes that, at least in some circumstances, *tza'ar ba'alei hayyim* is permissible in order to eliminate the potential for transgression.) *Imrei Shefer* concludes that "we cannot conclusively determine whether, in accordance with the precepts of our holy Torah, license is granted to Jewish physicians to engage in those tests on the bodies of living creatures." As has been noted earlier, *Da'at Kedoshim, Yoreh De'ah* 24:12, explicitly affirms that the concept of benefit to man includes even "possible benefit." See above, note 42.

The distinction drawn by *Imrei Shefer* between *tza'ar ba'alei hayyim* designed for direct therapeutic benefit and experimentation for the general advancement of medical knowledge is, in effect, an application of a principle of Jewish law first enunciated by *Noda bi-Yehudah, Mahadura Tinyana, Yoreh De'ah*, no. 210, in a classic responsum regarding postmortem examinations. *Noda bi-Yehudah* states definitively that the suspension of virtually any biblical prohibition is warranted in face of an already present danger, or, in rabbinical terminology, in the case of a *holeh le-faneinu* (literally "a patient in front of us"). The concept of a *holeh le-faneinu* is, roughly speaking, the halakhic equivalent of "a clear and *present* danger." Prohibitions are suspended for the purpose of saving an endangered life, but not in anticipation of a purely hypothetical eventuality. Accordingly, *Noda bi-Yehudah* rules that performance of an autopsy is warranted in order to obtain specific information of value in the treatment of another similarly afflicted patient, but not in the vague hope that some potentially life-saving knowledge may be gained in the process of the postmortem examination. *Imrei Shefer* appears to apply the same principle to experimentation upon animals.

67. *Cf.* Maharsha, *Baba Metzi'a* 85a, and *Teshuvot Imrei Shefer*, no. 34, secs. 10 and 12, who offer explanations for the censure of R. Judah that differ from that advanced by *Ma'arkhei Lev* but that are entirely consistent with the conclusion reached by *Ma'arkhei Lev*.

68. See, however, R. Chaim Pelaggi, *Ruah Hayyim*, no. 630, who cites this ruling as evidence that *tza'ar ba'alei hayyim* is permitted "for the purpose of a *mitzvah*." A similar view was expressed earlier by *Shiltei Gibborim, Avodah Zarah* 1:21, and *Knesset ha-Gedolah, Hoshen Mishpat* 240:6. See also *Sedei Hemed, Ma'arekhet ha-Tzadi*, no. 1, who maintains that the treatment of the scapegoat sent into the wilderness and destroyed in conjunction with the sacrificial ritual of *Yom Kippur* serves as a paradigm permitting *tza'ar ba'alei hayyim* for the purpose of fulfilling any *mitzvah*. The difficulty raised by *Ma'arkhei Lev* is readily resolved if, as may be assumed, it is recognized that Rema's caveat does not apply to *tza'ar ba'alei hayyim* in a matter pertaining to a *mitzvah*.

69. The analysis of Rema's position as presented by *Ma'arkhei Lev* seems to be at variance with that of *Taz, Even ha-Ezer* 5:11. *Taz* remarks that, in accordance with Rema's caveat, it is improper to re-

move the comb of a rooster. However, since the presumed sterilization does serve a need that cannot be achieved in another manner,
according to *Ma'arkhei Lev*'s analysis, removal of the comb should be
sanctioned even according to Rema.

70. This does not apply to painful procedures performed on living animals by students enrolled in laboratory courses as part of their
general education. It should be stressed that even those authorities
who sanction the infliction of pain upon animals for the benefit of human beings do so only when the benefit is practical in nature, but not
when the pain is inflicted merely for the satisfaction of intellectual
curiosity. Thus, even according to those authorities, only experiments directly related to the development of a specific skill necessary
for fulfillment of the student's professional or vocational goal may be
sanctioned. Nevertheless, in this writer's opinion, students directed
to perform such procedures as part of the course requirements for
earning an academic degree may do so according to the opinion of
those authorities who sanction *tza'ar ba'alei hayyim* for financial gain
or for the fulfillment of a human need because earning a degree leads
directly to economic gain. However, since acquisition of theoretical
knowledge for its own sake and perfection of skills that are not intended for applied use do not constitute such a need, it is improper
for educators to impose such requirements upon students for general
educational purposes. Castration, spaying, and sterilization of living animals are forbidden by biblical law. Accordingly, Jewish students and practitioners may not perform such acts even in situations
in which considerations of *tza'ar ba'alei hayyim* do not pertain.
Whether such acts are also prohibited to Noahides is the subject of
some controversy both among the Tanna'im and among rabbinic decisors; see *Encyclopedia Talmudit*, III, 356.

71. Israel-Michael Rabbinowicz, *La médécine du Thalmud* (Paris,
1880), p. 56, note 1, and p. 57, note 1, cites therapeutic procedures
performed upon animals that are reported by the *Gemara*, *Hullin*
57b, as evidence that vivisection was performed by the Sages of the
Mishnah. See, however, *Teshuvot Imrei Shefer*, no. 84, sec. 16, who
refutes this contention in arguing that those procedures were undertaken to correct injuries sustained in accidents or the like.

4 The Place of Animals in Creation: A Christian View [1]

Andrew Linzey

> It [creation] exists for God's glory, that is to say, it has a meaning and worth beyond its meaning and worth as seen from the point of view of human utility. It is in this sense that we can say that it has intrinsic value. To imagine that God has created the whole universe solely for man's use and pleasure is a mark of folly.

These words come from the Report of a Working Group set up in 1971 by the then Archbishop of Canterbury "to investigate the relevance of Christian doctrine to the problems of man in his environment." [2] The Report's affirmation of the "intrinsic" value of creation is so traditional that it may be interpreted as theologically unexceptional. It is, after all, quite central to Christian doctrine that the creation made by God is good. But could it be that this affirmation, commonly held by Judaism and Islam as well as Christianity, has implications for our moral treatment of animals that have hitherto largely been unseen? In what follows I hope to indicate something of the minimum that can be deduced from this insight from a Christian perspective and to consider how morally significant that minimum might be.

To begin with, it is important to see how it is that the affirmation of the intrinsic value of the world is inseparable from the Christian doctrine of God. It is not sufficient to say that the creation made by God must necessarily be good. It is

important to indicate *how* the goodness of creation is constituted and *how* the creativity of God is related in Christian
doctrine to his further works of incarnation, reconciliation,
and redemption.

1. God the Creator

God can be defined in classical terms as "infinite, self-
existent, incorporeal, eternal, immutable, impassible, simple,
perfect, omniscient and omnipotent."[3] He is the source of all
being, life, energy, and movement—everything. He brings
into being another reality that is objectively distinct from himself. God does not need creation. The created world exists
both as a manifestation of his love and his intention to manifest his love within it. The created order is dependent upon
God not only for its creation but also for its continued existence. Everything that exists therefore does so in a relationship with the creator to which it belongs. From this straightforward statement, the value of creation may be perceived by
implication in the following ways:

(i)   It has its origin with God, who is by definition holy
      and perfect. Because it is ontologically distinct from
      him, creation occupies a separate sphere of existence
      and possesses its own separate identity.
(ii) It cannot exist and continue to exist without God's ex-
      press approval and will. It cannot within the limits of
      divine purpose be other than it is or cease to be with-
      out him.
(iii) It exists meaningfully, that is, with purpose, insofar
      as its creator confers purpose upon it.
(iv) It exists within a relationship of grace, that is, an
      unconditional beneficent attitude on the part of the
      creator.

Viewed against this larger backdrop we see that the creation and its order, character, and design, insofar as they reflect
the creator's intention, must be valuable to him. The question
must inevitably be raised as to how far the creation as we now

see it faithfully reflects the designs of the creator. Classical
Christian theism teaches the fallenness of human nature, a
state that in principle affects at least the whole of the created
world. As Eric Mascall writes, "Like a microscopic crack in a
china vase, it [i.e., our fall from grace] initiated a process of
disintegration and corruption whose consequence spread far
beyond the area of their origin and affected the whole subsequent history of the human race and of the material realm."[4]
This means that any reading off from the created world to the
realm of moral imperatives must be highly suspect at best. For
the laws of nature, operative in this fallen world, may not be
the absolute or initially chosen laws of God. This does not
mean that Christians cannot learn from nature or marvel at it,
only that we cannot assume that the creation as we now know
it is a textbook of moral reference. The fallenness of creation
aside, however, the doctrine of creation maintains the intention of God to create all things good and so that all things must
be valuable to him.

2. God Incarnate

The doctrine of the incarnation may be taken as affirming, in the classical formulation of Chalcedon, that the Second
Person of the Trinity took human flesh at a particular moment
in history.[5] Much that is affirmed in the doctrine of creation is
necessary for this affirmation to make sense:

  (i)   There must be an objective reality, distinct from God
        himself, with which God can have a providential
        relationship.
 (ii)   This objective reality must be such that God can par-
        ticipate within it and do so in such a way that this
        purpose may be fulfilled.
(iii)   This objective reality, presupposed by the incarna-
        tion, must be such that the divine presence can incar-
        nate itself within it.

Point three requires some elaboration. The incarnation
must presuppose that creation is open to God and that human

creation in particular is compatible with the being of God so defined. The incarnation must therefore imply that the world is acceptable and valuable to him and that it is the appropriate medium for his self-revelation. As Mascall writes: "By their very dependence upon God, finite beings are inherently open to him; an absolutely autonomous and incapsulated finite entity would be a contradiction in terms. A created universe . . . is necessarily not only a finite but an open one."[6] In other words, unlike some other world religions the incarnation presupposes what can be called a high doctrine of matter. Material substance, that is, flesh and blood, which is what humans share in particular with much of the animal kingdom, is the pivot of God's redeeming purposes.

It is often suggested that the incarnation underlines the special value of humans in creation. And there can be little doubt of this. But it is a mistake to assume that the incarnation does not also reinforce the value of matter and living beings in particular. There is a long tradition of Byzantine theology that emphasizes the interconnectedness of humans and creation and also of creation and incarnation.[7] As Brian Horne explains: "The Jesus who is crucified is also the Logos of God: through him all things come into being, in him all things are 'summed up,' and by him all things are sanctified by the presence of the Spirit. In taking man to himself, he takes all nature to himself."[8] Whatever the special role and significance of man within creation, the incarnation needs to be seen as the "yes" of God the creator to what is created. It is not a *necessary* implication that the incarnation is the sole affirmation of the worth of humankind. The incarnation can only take place within a world that is valuable and purposeful, for it is the *same Logos* who becomes incarnate who is also the *Logos* through whom all things come to be.[9]

3. God the Reconciler

I shall not be concerned here with the various theories of atonement (propitiation, substitution, ransom, and so forth) but with the idea presupposed by the doctrine (about which there is scarce dispute) that Christ reconciled fallen creation to God the Father by his life and (especially) his death. Again I shall not explore the precise grounds for affirming the fallen nature of creation. Many theories have been expounded but no one explanation has found complete assent within the Christian tradition.[10]

The striking point here is that the act of reconciliation must, logically, include *all* that is fallen, *all* that was previously unreconciled. Does this involve the nonhuman creation? The answer we give to this question will depend in turn upon the further question of whether animals and plants are already reconciled to God by their act of creation or whether in some moral sense they are capable of falling or being influenced by the fall of other beings from divine grace. Christian theology has normally been reluctant to relate the reconciling work of Christ to animals because they are not seen as capable of sin in the traditional sense. But because they are affected by human sin, is it possible that they might be freed from its consequences by the power of the cross? Though theologians have often doubted this, Paul Tillich, for example, sees the possibility of incarnation and reconciliation in nonhuman worlds. He writes: "Incarnation is unique for the special group in which it happens, but it is not unique in the sense that other singular incarnations for other unique worlds are excluded. Man cannot claim," argues Tillich, "that the infinite has entered the finite to overcome its existential estrangement in mankind alone."[11]

This point seems to be supported by a working party report set up by the Board for Social Responsibility of the Church of England in 1970. It concluded: "Both the sufferings of animals and the sufferings of Christ could lead to cynicism if considered in isolation. But in the context of Easter and Pentecost the suffering of Christ takes on new meaning and this new meaning gives point to the groaning and travailing of all creation."[12] There seem to be three possibilities, all of which are compatible with orthodox Christian belief: (1) that animals are not capable of sin or estrangement and therefore not capable of being included in the saving work of Christ; (2) that if they have sinned or fallen from grace it may be possible for the Son of God to become incarnate in their nature in order to reconcile them, or (3) that "by becoming incarnate in one rational species, the Son of God has *ipso facto* become the redeemer of all."[13]

My preference, as will be seen, is for option three, but I propose to leave this question generally open. For its resolution in no way affects what is certainly implied in the affirmation of the atonement. From "God so loved the world" we may logically deduce that it exists as a valuable entity in his sight. No less than with the doctrine of the incarnation, then, we are again led inescapably to the notion that creation has value. God, so Christians affirm, is determined to bind himself to creation in order to save it from the worst possibilities (largely, though not exclusively, represented by man) of self-destructiveness.

4. God the Redeemer

The doctrines of reconciliation and redemption are, of course, essentially different sides of the same activity of God. One may be taken as pointing to the work of Christ in obedience to God the Father in history, the other to the consummation of this work at the end of time. For among all orthodox theologians there is both the affirmation of what has been done up to the present and what needs to be done in the future to fulfill his purposes.

It is at this point, when we are asked to affirm the world-transforming nature of redemption, that we see clearly the significance and worth of all creation. For nothing that God has made can be omitted in the moment of completion. Christians may be questioning and agnostic as to the precise details of this hope, but it cannot but follow from a God who creates, incarnates, and reconciles that *everything* will be made new. The Archbishop's Working Group concludes:

To speak thus of the restoration of all things involves the whole creation and not mankind alone. On any interpretation of the classical Christian teaching about the resurrection of the body, it is difficult to see how man's bodily life can enter into eternity . . . without in some sense involving that world in which we have rejoiced and of which the human body is a part. Nothing which God has made will ultimately be lost. All the splendour of the natural world and the creative achievements of man, however transitory and easily destructible they may appear, have eternal significance.[14]

It must also follow that each and every hurt and harm in creation (both human and animal, insofar as each is capable of being hurt or harmed) will be made good, and that all the suffering of the present time is not worth comparing to the glory as yet unrevealed.[15] The orthodox theologian Keith Ward makes this point emphatically:

If it is necessary that each sentient being must have the possibility of achieving an overwhelming good, then it is clear that there must be some form of life after earthly death. Despite the many pointers to the existence of God, theism would be falsified if physical death was the end, for then there could be no justification for the existence of this world. However, if one supposes that every sentient being has an endless existence, which offers the prospect of supreme happiness, it is surely true that the sorrows and troubles of this life will seem very small by comparison. Immortality, for animals as well as humans, is a necessary condition of any acceptable theodicy; that necessity, together with all the other arguments for God, is one of the main reasons for believing in immortality.[16]

Not all Christians will go as far as Ward,[17] though it cannot be overlooked that some form of eternal life for animals has found serious advocates within Christianity.[18] Whatever the precise ramifications, one simple point needs to be stressed. It is inconsistent with the thrust of all the previous doctrine considered that what has been made, sustained, and loved will not be completed according to the Father's purposes. From this perspective, whatever the precise spiritual status of animals in redemption, God needs to be seen as both the source and the destiny of all created things.

I would not want to argue that the particular way in which I have presented these central doctrines would be agreeable to all Christians. But I hope I have shown enough for it to be clear that the appeal to the value of creation can be supported by orthodox Christian belief and indeed, that these doctrines taken together require such an affirmation. It will be seen that I have not based this conclusion on any particular strand within the biblical tradition, or upon exegesis of particular texts, or on one or more characterizations of theological work. Rather, in taking the nexus of doctrines together, each one relating to and informing the other, we are on much surer grounds, I judge, in claiming to interpret accurately mainstream Christian orthodoxy.

5. Moral Implications

But the central question is: If we accept such a theological notion of the worth of creation, what follows from it and what are the moral implications in particular? There are, I suggest, four implications of direct moral relevance:

(i)   If creation has value to God, then it should possess value to human beings.

(ii) The theological value of creation thus elaborated should be seen to be distinct from man's estimation of his own value and utility as this may be variously defined from time to time.

(iii) The theological purpose of creation should also be seen to be distinct from man's estimation of the purpose and significance of creation.

(iv) If creation has value and should have value for human
      beings, it should follow that man cannot claim a right
      to absolute value within creation.

This first point may appear elementary, and in one sense
it is, but it has immense significance. The affirmation of the
value of creation is first and foremost an affirmation of its
worth to God. The claiming of value for creation is not some
kind of more sophisticated moral judgment; it is perception
of worth that stems from what Christians believe to be true
about the nature and work of God. It is not some kind of op-
tional possibility for those who are Christians; it is inseparable
from the confesson of God as creator, incarnate, and redeemer.
In accepting this implication, however, we are not committed
to the view that all creation has the same or equal value. It is
still possible (and I think desirable) within the general perception of the value of creation that we should distinguish between, say, the value of stones and the value of sentient beings. Again how we interpret the value of respective parts of
creation subsequently is a matter of discernment and judgment. How we should articulate the respective value of different life forms within the range of inter-related theological
themes is a question I hope to raise shortly. At this point, I
want to suggest that there is *prima facie* an obligation to value
the creation that God so values.

I am not suggesting in point two that God's estimation of
the value of creation and man's own evaluation may not sometimes agree or overlap; indeed it would be a poor theology that
held the two at a permanent distance. But whatever conver-
gence there may be, it is a mistake to refuse the distinction.
Man cannot simply take as God's view his own evaluation of
himself in the cosmos. So much in the Christian tradition testifies to this distinction in the case of the individual's estimate
of his value in relation to his fellow man that it only makes
sense to insist upon this same principle of distinction here.
Because of this, it must also follow that man cannot claim to be

the only measure of good as regards his fellow creatures. In many cases they have their own individual lives, their own needs, and their own patterns of behavior. Of course human interests are morally important, but they cannot claim to be the only morally important interests.

Regarding point three, the same must be said about the notion of purpose, which often underlies claims about the nature of value. As the Archbishop's Report indicates, "It (creation) has meaning and worth beyond its meaning and worth from the point of view of human utility."[19] This point is unaffected by how far and how much can be known in theological terms about the purpose of God in his mysterious activity of sustaining creation. What has to be held onto is the distinction between God's purposes and man's purposes. Again we may hope and believe that they meet and converge, but we cannot always resolve the tension in our favor with assurance. The knowledge of God as presupposed in Christian doctrine, even the *saving* knowledge of God in orthodoxy, is not such that we can claim a knowledge of his purpose in all things. This point is aptly made by Karl Barth: "We do not know what particular attitude God may have to them (non-human creatures), and therefore what might be their decisive particularity within the cosmos. . . . We can and must accept them as our fellow-creatures with all due regard for the mystery in which God has veiled them."[20] This point is certainly not new. Christians have often wondered why it is that we do not know more theologically about the life and status of animals. For myself, I am inclined to believe that we can know by implication a great deal more than Barth suggests,[21] but whatever view is held, it must also be appreciated that there can be no straightforward deduction from silence to human *gnosis*, even when man's vital interests are at stake.

The fourth point may be seen as a simple underlining of the previous three, except in one regard. It is sometimes claimed that the traditional affirmation of the special place of humans in creation is such that it resolves any consideration of the value of other life forms in our favor. But even if we accept a hierarchy of valuable beings in God's sight, as some Christians have traditionally posited, it does not follow that either we must ascribe absolute value to humans or absolutely none to animals. We may say that certain forms of life have less value to God than man's value and man may (and often does) judge according to the hierarchy of values he perceives. But it cannot be claimed that creation is of little or no account. This simple point cannot be stressed too strongly, because in a rush to affirm the truth of one aspect of Christian doctrine it is only too easy to lose sight of another. Human beings cannot affirm their own value within the created order without at the same time affirming the value of all created beings. This is not an independent value judgment; it is an implication deeply embedded in the nature of the affirmation itself. This point is made even more strongly by the *Animals and Ethics* Working Party report convened by the Dean of Westminster in 1977:

> On a theistic understanding of creation, such as the Christian entertains, it is a mistake to suppose that all animal life exists only to serve human kind; or that the world was made exclusively for man's benefit. Man's estimate of his own welfare should not be the only guideline in determining his relationship with other species. In terms of this theistic understanding man is custodian of the universe he inhabits with no absolute rights over it. [22]

6. Countertheories

At this stage I want to anticipate three major objections to the position I have advanced so far.

The first objection does not deny that creation has value and that generally humans should treat it as valuable but maintains that human life and well-being have such incomparably greater value to God that it is right for human beings to exercise dominion over animals, human needs always having priority.

In resisting this objection let me make plain that I do not

oppose the view that humans have central value and significance to God in the created order. I am inclined to think that
what is involved in this centrality of value is far more complex
than is often supposed by its advocates and that some statements of man's value in relation to animals have been exaggerated and foolish.[23] But I think it must be deduced from all the
central Christian doctrines we have surveyed that man is cen-
trally important. The real difficulty with this objection is its
linking of our central importance with the concept of dominion as found in Genesis 1:28. It is now commonly held by ex-
egetes that although dominion involves the exercise of power,
it is an exercise that must be subordinate to the moral purposes of God. It cannot be sufficient interpretation (as has
often been thought in the past) to suggest that the gift of
power involves no limit or responsibility. The notion of dominion is part of early kingship theology in which humans are
understood to be God's moral agent in creation and responsible and accountable to him.[24] Those who doubt this need to
look again at the first creation saga in Genesis (1:1–2:4a). For
man's dominion as originally described contains no right even
to kill for food (v. 29); no right of capital punishment; and no
right of death as the first saga originally understood the moral
relationship between man and animals.

Karl Barth is not to be gainsaid on this point: "Whether
or not we find it practicable and desirable, the diet assigned to
men and beasts by God the Creator is vegetarian."[25] Such a
peaceful view of man in creation is reinforced by the second
creation saga (2:4b–end), which describes man as necessary
for the tilling and flourishing of the earth (2:5). Hence part of
man's responsibility is actually to look after creation and be the
agent of its care and cultivation. These views of humans in
creation must not of course overlook the fact that the subsequent tradition does indeed justify man in using creation and
in particular animals for his own needs and purposes. But it
also needs to be appreciated that much in this tradition is
unclear if not ambiguous. Even though, for example, Genesis
9:3 sanctions meat-eating—a concession, some have argued,

to man's sinfulness[26]—it is not given without qualification and limit. For "you shall not eat flesh with its life, that is its blood" (9:4). Thus even within the tradition that justifies omnivorousness, there is the qualification that this may only be done so long as the very life (*nephesh*) of the animal is not appropriated by man. I would not want to deny, however, that it is the Judaic and Christian view that humans can use creation to some degree for their own purposes. Clearly the very picture of man as the gardener in the second saga presupposes cultivation and, thus, agriculture. But what cannot, I think, be gleaned from the Jewish tradition is that man's needs should *always* have priority over those of creation. This is the central point. It is not that man should not use creation, but *the degree and extent* to which this is taken are crucial. Hugh Montefiore underlines this point:

> Once it is believed that men hold their dominion over all nature as stewards and trustees for God, then immediately they are confronted by an inalienable duty towards and concern for their total environment, present and future; and this duty towards environment does not merely include their fellow-men, but all nature and all life.[27]

The second line of objection does not deny either that creation has value or that it has value to humankind; it denies that a proper theological distinction can be drawn between the life of brutes and the life of vegetables and therefore argues that man's needs should always have priority over animals as well as over vegetables.

I think this argument has some kind of force. It must follow from Christian doctrine that *all* creation, whether animate or inanimate, stone, vegetable, or mammal, has value to God and therefore some kind of claim upon us. Perhaps it is true that some moralists in the animal field have tended to exclude nonanimal life as proper objects of value.[28] It is also clear in the creation saga that there is no clear distinction of status between many forms of life. We are not told of the respective values of plants, birds, fish, and mammals. While this is true, it must not be overlooked that within the circles of creation envisaged in Genesis 1, the order of creation moves inexorably toward greater relationship with man. It is true, of course, that man, made in the image of God, stands at the very center, but animals in particular are created on the same day, the sixth (1:24 f). Fish and birds (as well as by implication animals) are the recipients of a special blessing, by which we may judge that they are authorized to be and to reproduce themselves (1:22). It is to these living, creeping, swimming, and flying creatures that God gives the gift of land, territory, food, and sustenance. They stand together with humankind not only as the object of blessing but also as especially pronounced "good" creation (1:25). Again in the second creation saga, although animals are not the required "helpmeet" or partner of man, they are nevertheless brought to him and by the naming of them he exercises a special relationship of power and also responsibility (2:19).

But there is even stronger theological ground for holding that animals have especial value to God. This must be presupposed by the election of "every living creature that is with you" (9:10) within the covenant relationship with man. The covenant to which the Old Testament testifies is a living relationship with God whereby their lives and future are guaranteed by him. "I will remember my covenant which is between me and you and every living creature of all flesh" (9:15). Although it would probably be going too far to suggest that animal and human life are made inseparable by this act, it is no understatement to see the two as fundamentally bound by this divine relationship. This can be seen from the fact that animals are seen as sharing with man his own burden and judgment before the Lord (*e.g.*, Isaiah 50:2; Jeremiah 7:20). Moreover, this covenant relationship implied a moral bond between man and beast—a profound responsibility on man's part to care as best as he could for animals in the present time. Hence, for example, the humanitarian provisions of Hebrew law (*e.g.*, Exodus 23:4–5; Deuteronomy 25:4; 22:6–7; Exodus 23:10). As Anthony Phillips writes: "While the Old Testament recognises that this is not an ideal world, and makes concessions until the messianic kingdom comes, it remains man's duty to do all in his power to reverence animal life."[29] Given this fundamental closeness between animals and humans, it is not possible to claim some kind of absolute priority for man in the ethical sphere. Of course each situation must be weighed carefully and some choices in man's favor are right and just. But what we begin to see in the Deuteronomic tradition, for example, is some due recognition of the claims of animals that necessarily constrains the otherwise free hand of humans.

The third line of objection does not deny that creation has value, even that there are circles of closer proximity to humans within creation, but maintains that it is right that the lower creation should serve the higher creation, as is witnessed in the sacrificial tradition of the Old Testament.

At first sight this objection has considerable force. Is it not true that to some degree the Old Testament sanctions the use of animals in ways that are instrumental to the spiritual welfare of man? Does not God as revealed by the Old Testament require sacrifices of animals to appease his wrath and judgment? "Then Noah built an altar to the Lord, and took of every animal and of every clean bird, and offered burnt offerings on the altar. And when the Lord smelled the pleasing odour, the Lord said in his heart, 'I will never again curse the ground because of man . . . neither will I ever again destroy every living creature as I have done'" (Genesis 8:20–22). If this *is* indeed taken to be the real meaning of animal sacrifice, then there can be little doubt about the low value of animals so envisaged. But is this the right interpretation? How could it be that a God who out of his love creates animals would delight in their gratuitous destruction? Unsatisfied with this interpretation, many scholars have questioned its theological basis. Mascall, for example, writes that

> there has . . . been a tendency, which has had the most
> unfortunate consequences, to assume that the essence of

sacrifice consists in the destruction of some valuable object, preferably a living one, in order to honour or to
propitiate a deity, a destruction which in the case of an
animal victim, will involve its slaying. . . . It has obtained a firm foothold even in the Christian Church and
has provided the guiding concept for many doctrines of
the Atonement.

Reviewing early scholarship, Mascall continues: "It is therefore a matter for deep satisfaction that in recent years there
has come to the fore a wider and more positive notion of sacrifice which, while finding a real place for the insights of what
might be called the established view, altogether avoids its
weaknesses."[30] This work, principally by Eugene Masure and
R. K. Yerkes, has insisted that the basic significance of sacrifice
is not the destruction of the creature but its offering to God.
Writes Masure, the substance of sacrifice

is . . . the return of the creature to him who has made it
for himself so that it may find its end and therefore its
happiness in him and for his glory. . . . Sacrifice is the
movement or action by which we try to bring ourselves
to God, our end, to find our true beatitude in our union
with him. *To sacrifice a thing is to lead it to its end.*[31]

The crucial point here is that far from reinforcing the low
value of the sacrificial victim, the ritual actually (though I accept in practice paradoxically) underlines the value of the animal slain and also its acceptance and transformation by God.
"Even here," Mascall explains, "there is no suggestion that
God is glorified by the destruction of his creature, for if it
could be literally destroyed there would be nothing left for
him to accept and transform."[32] In short, therefore, the tradition of sacrifice is best seen as the freeing of animal life to be
with God, an acknowledgment that it (as with all creatures) belongs not to humans but to God and that God is able to accept
and transform its life. Puzzling though this interpretation may
be, it is the one most consistent with the other biblical threads

concerning the value of animal life and our responsibility for it. Even in the Genesis passage recently recalled, the sacrifice of animals led to the resolve to secure the value of human *and* animal life more firmly (8 : 20–22).

Within the Jewish tradition, however, the practice of animal sacrifice and its efficacy did not pass without question and protest. "What to me is the multitude of your sacrifices?" says the Lord in the book of Isaiah. "I have had enough of burnt offerings of rams, and the fat of fed beasts. . . . I will not listen; your hands are full of blood. Wash yourselves; make yourselves clean; remove the evil of your doings from before my eyes; cease to do evil." (1 : 11 f, *cf.* Psalm 50 : 7 f) Very few if any Christians would find the practice of animal sacrifice acceptable at this present time. This is not because they would wish to deny its historical importance or because they would necessarily find any interpretation of the practice indefensible, but because they believe that the sacrificial tradition has reached its ultimate point and climax in the sacrifice of Christ. He, Jesus Christ, in the true sense of offering, acceptance, and transformation, is our sacrificial victim that leads us to God.[33] It is through him, and not through the sacrifices of animals, that we are able to find ourselves in our Father's presence.

It is this point more than any other that needs to transform the Christian understanding not only of sacrifice but of our relationship with the order of creation itself. It is here that we reach a distinctive Christian interpretation. Many theologians have laid great stress upon the transformation of the notion of sacrifice in Christ, but few if any have drawn out its radical implications for our relationship with animals. For what is involved in the life of Christ is both a different order and nature of sacrifice.

In the first place, the inner logic of the sacrifice of Christ is not the sacrifice of the lower to the higher but the higher to the lower. The power of God is expressed in the notion of "lordship," but the nature of this lordship in the incarnation involves humility, the surrender of absolute power, self-costly loving, a preparedness to suffer, and active compassion toward the weak and helpless. Many strands in the New Testament speak of the humility, the *katabasis*, of God in taking flesh and experiencing for the sake of love the weakness and frailty of the creature (*e.g.*, Mark 8:31 f; John 13:2 f; 2 Corinthians 8:9). Second, the nature of the sacrifice is not simply that of blood (though Good Friday is real enough) but of life and love. It is pre-eminently the sacrifice of God's love for us wrought mysteriously in the acts of incarnation and atonement.

If this is true, then it must follow that the nature of man's dominion or lordship has to be quite different from what we take it to be at present. The question we must ask is: If the omnipotence and power of God are actually expressed in the form of loving condescension toward humans, should we not take this attitude as the model by which we should express ourselves toward the nonhuman world? If, as Christians have traditionally affirmed, in Christ God was truly reconciling the world to himself through the power of his love, should not our exercise of power toward creation be shaped and motivated by this example? This Christologically based notion of love in action is so central to orthodox formulations and indeed is cited so often as an exemplar for our relations with our fellow humans that we may be perplexed to know why it has taken Christians so long to see the force of this example as a model for their relationship with the natural world. We may put the matter like this: Under the dispensation of the Old Covenant it was clear that God allowed man rights to use creation, even though the precise limits of these prerogatives were interpreted ambiguously and differently. But it is not at all clear, as defined under the New Covenant, that man has these same rights and can use his power with the same confidence. For if full weight is given to the moral exemplar of Christ, then it can be validly held that the unique moral capacities of humans demand of them a loving and costly relationship with the natural world. In other words, it could be that our distinctive contribution within the purposes of God the creator is to make actual and real his loving design within it.[34]

7. Use of Animals in Science

We are now in a position where we can confront our question directly: Practically and morally, how should the insight of the worth of creation and of animals in particular help to shape and determine our use of them in science? I think three broad conclusions should be reached:

(i) *Animals are not expendable for humans.* I mean by this that animals must not be viewed simply as raw materials for our designs, no matter how morally laudable. Animals are not things. They are not simply objects of man's use or pleasure. They cannot be used in such a way without infringing on the right of their creator, whose will is such that they should exist as they are within their own terms and limits of existence. Whenever man takes to himself the use of animals, he incurs great responsibility. I do not conclude that animals may *never* be used in any way that betters humankind. There are a variety of ways in which man can live in a symbiotic relationship with animals that benefits both parties. But that is surely the point. When animals are used so that their own lives are enhanced, supported, or protected in some way, the motivation is often more than simple human self-seeking. What is not justifiable is the intention to so use and take over the natural life of animals that its reward for humans is seen as its only reason for existing. The doctrine of creation will not allow us unrestricted and unrestrained use of the animal world for human purposes.

In the interdependent creation where, to the naked eye, each species appears to make its way at the expense of others, and where the apparent needs of humans and animals can conflict, our moral uncertainty is likely to be great. I do not wish to evade this point and suppose that conflicts do not occur and that the resolution of them is an easy matter. In this sense it must be clear that neither humans nor animals can possess absolute rights. But, on the other hand, to cause animals avoidable injury, either through death, deprivation, or suffering, must be seen as morally wrong. This at least should, I judge, be the moral norm. I do not say that realizing this norm will be easy, or that it will not require us to make some real sacrifices, or that individuals should not be free to exercise their own consciences within a framework of law. But I hold that we need fresh conviction and moral energy to realize this norm, socially and individually, as a recognition of the value of animals and therefore their moral claim upon us. As Stephen Clark puts it, "This at least cannot be true, that it is proper to be the cause of avoidable ill." [35]

The question may be asked, however, whether it is a *necessary* implication of the doctrine of creation and the value of life presupposed by it that harming creation is, when avoidable, wrong? Is it not possible to admire creation as if it were a work of art, for its aesthetic value, without subscribing to a theory of moral limits? Such a view misses the point that humans have responsibility for animals in a way that simply does not pertain to works of art. Animals are valuable *in themselves* by virtue of their creation by God. It is not just that injury to animals reinforces a low view of their value (though it certainly does that) but that it is a practical denial of their intrinsic value. Animals belong to God in a way that makes their significance and value more fundamental even than human artistic creations—inspiring though the latter may be.

(ii) *Animals are not instrumental to humans.* I mean by this that animals must not be viewed simply as a means to human ends, no matter how morally laudable. Animals are not laboratory tools. Their purpose for existing is not simply to serve the human species. They do not simply exist in some utilitarian relationship to humans whereby they can be seen as fodder for furthering human purposes of life enhancement or enjoyment or happiness. The doctrine of creation stands in opposition to all such wholly anthropocentric notions. Man, as we have indicated, cannot claim to be the total measure of good as regards other living creatures. Again this is not to deny that man may sometimes use animals for his purposes so long as these purposes are consonant with the theological good of the individual creatures themselves. What he cannot do is assume that his purposes of betterment are always God's purposes. He cannot take his needs as always absolute and primary.

I do not want to oversimplify what is clearly a complex area of man's relationship with animals. In many areas we do not know the precise significance and purpose of living beings. Through ignorance we may do enormous damage; through inactivity we may precipitate adverse conditions for many living beings; and we may often have to judge on what we take to be insufficient or largely intuitional evidence. The effects of what we do to animals in terms of their long-term conditions of life or survival may not be clear to us. All this needs to be granted. But where we have the will and the freedom to do so, it must be wrong to subordinate animal life to human purposes without any regard for the intrinsic value of animals. We need to remind ourselves that in theological terms man's use of animals has the nature of trust; we are accountable to God. Animals do not belong to us.

The use of animals for experimentation poses another considerable problem for Christian moralists. For how are we to evaluate the routinized and institutionalized use of millions of animals, bred, reared, and destroyed for experimental purposes annually? Even if some use of animals for experimental purposes were justified, how in turn could this justify the whole institutionalized subjugation of animal life for human purposes on such a vast scale? It is not only the scale but the intention behind such enormous institutional activity that must make us question the disregard for animals implicit in such trade and business. I think there is an important distinction to be drawn between individual use of animals sometimes prompted by necessity and the subjugation of animals on a huge scale on the assumption that they can be used solely for human ends. It is not clear to me that the value of animals, as understood from the perspective of Christian doctrine, can be subordinated, as many scientists appear to believe, at each and every point to some human good, whether it is imagined, hy-

pothetical, or real. Christian moral theology can never be
happy with ethical thinking given over entirely to human-
centered utilitarian calculation. Some element of calculating
the good as we see it is inevitable in moral evaluation, but
when that evaluation is dominated by the supposed absolute
good of humankind, theological insights are only too easily
pushed aside in favor of some supposed common sense hu-
manitarianism.

One further point in this vein needs to be noted. Although
the benefits of knowledge gained through much animal experimentation are indeed great (and much anti-experiment propa-
ganda has been sadly misleading on this point I fear), it is by
no means clear to me that it can qualify, even in terms of a
utilitarian calculus, to be the absolute good. Raising an issue of
this kind invites the charge of insensitivity to human sickness
and the appalling effects of disease upon human beings, but it
has to be disputed whether knowledge, even such beneficial
knowledge that can save or prolong human life, has priority
over all other kinds. Knowledge of ourselves as moral and spiritual beings is also a moral good. It matters as much that we
have knowledge of our ultimate life and destiny and indeed of
our moral relationship with the natural world as it does that
we have knowledge that will prevent death and alleviate pain.
The scientific attempt to absolutize beneficial scientific knowledge over all other forms of knowledge may be regarded as no
less excessive than previous theological attempts to fill that
category. As Patrick Corbett writes:

> The intellectual founders of the modern world, men like
> Bacon and Descartes, correctly interpreting the scien-
> tific and technological revolution which has eventually
> produced the industrial societies in which we now live,
> laid great emphasis on what may be called analytical or
> conceptual intelligence, the kind of intelligence which
> works experience up into explicit concepts and tested
> propositions, as opposed to the imaginative intelligence
> displayed, for example, by cats, mothers and poets. In a

sense they were right to do so; the development of analytical intelligence is a wonderful and admirable thing
and its practical application has yielded many wonderful
and admirable results. But we are now coming to realise
in many different ways that the emphasis laid upon it in
Western thought has been exaggerated. No matter how
fascinating it is in itself and how gratifying the power it
gives us, to let it dominate our vision of the world is to
lose sight of ourselves. The things that make life valuable—love, friendship, strength, dexterity, imagination,
peace of mind—owe little to analytical intelligence and
are often undermined by intensive cultivation of it.[36]

(iii) *Animals are not to be sacrificed for humans.* I mean
by this that animals must not be seen as lesser beings which
while valuable can be traded in for some kind of greater advantage to humans. The historical language of sacrifice is doubly
inappropriate when applied to laboratory animals. In the first
place, as we have seen from a theological perspective, sacrifice
takes place as an offering to God, not man. It is a practice that
does not involve the destruction of a being but its liberation
and transformation. It can be justified in retrospect on that
strict understanding alone. Second, the specifically Christian
view of sacrifice must necessarily preclude any offering to God
that is not freely given. The sacrifice of Christ was not a propitiation demanded of Christ by an angry God who sought to
override the wishes of his Son. On the contrary, it was the free
offering to God the Father in the cause of love for his
creatures. It is the sacrifice of love freely given, and not the
sacrifice of blood required, that is the distinctly Christian
understanding of this matter. In this sense to speak as some
scientists still do of "sacrificing" animals for human well-being
is erroneous if not slightly disingenuous. If we are to speak of
sacrifice at all in this context it must be the sacrifice of man
who, in accordance with the moral will of God, freely foregoes
immediate gains for the sake of others. It is for this reason that
we may say that it is the special if not distinctive contribution

of Christian theology to ask whether in fact there are not ills
that humans should be prepared to bear rather than inflict
them on animals. Once again, this point has added force when
we ask what exemplar, what illustration, and what model of
authority Christians may take to themselves to guide their
rightful use of animals. If the lordship of God over us is in
principle the same kind of lordship that we should exercise
over animals, and if, as Christians believe, this lordship is revealed in Christ as the way of self-costly loving, humility, and
compassion, then we can have no theological right to claim absolute rights over animals even when our own good purposes
are at stake.

It is for this reason especially that the direction of this
paper moves inexorably against the legalization of experimental procedures on animals. I cannot persuade myself that
the *institutionalization* of this practice is compatible with the
moral norm I have outlined.[37] This norm is already enshrined
in a principle concerning experimentation on human subjects.
Article 1.5 of the Declaration of Helsinki adopted by the
World Medical Assembly in 1964 (and revised by the same
body in 1975) reads: ". . . concern for the interests of the subject (in human experimentation) must always prevail over the
interest of science and society," and article 111.4 (the final provision of the Declaration) reads: "In research on man, the interest of science and society should never take precedence
over considerations related to the well-being of the subject."

This Declaration is in turn a development of the Nuremberg Code of 1947 "which was a by-product of a trial of physicians for having performed cruel experiments on prisoners and
detainees during the Second World War."[38] The Code states as
its first principle: "The voluntary consent of the human subject is absolutely essential." It continues: "The person involved should have the legal capacity to give consent; should
be situated as to be able to exercise free power of choice, without the intervention of any element of force . . . or other ul-
terior form of constraint or coercion."[39]

Animals, of course, cannot give their consent to scientific procedures performed upon them. But this makes the infliction of injury upon them not easier but equally difficult, if not harder, to justify. As Tom Regan explains: "Risks are not morally transferable to those who do not voluntarily choose to take them."[40] If the Helsinki principle is valid, I cannot see any good theological grounds for including humans within its provision and not the other sentient beings which, while arguably less valuable, are objects of special moral responsibility. The subjugation of any being, human, fetal, or animal, to experimental procedures against its own interests must be morally wrong. This principle needs to be enshrined in law for both humans and animals.

I reach this conclusion with some reluctance. This is not because I am in serious doubt about the rightness of the principle, but for three practical reasons. In the first place, the enhanced awareness of the value of creation and of animals in particular is not simply a matter of law. Obedience to law *per se* is a dubious moral good and may not increase real respect for animals. Law *at best* can only prevent the worst and protect the weakest. There needs to be an increased awareness among animal protectionists of the limited value of the law.[41] In the second place, there must be some recognition that some, perhaps many scientists, at least in the United Kingdom, dislike experimenting upon animals, and more importantly, a growing number of them are seeking ways to reduce the number they use or find alternative ways of pursuing the same research. Many scientists are more deeply troubled by the use of animals than absolutist animal literature would suggest. When Hans Ruesch, for example, writes, "Greed, cruelty, ambition, incompetence, vanity, callousness, stupidity, sadism, insanity are the charges that this treatise [his book] levels at the entire practice of vivisection," I can only bewail his lack of charity.[42] I have no desire to be part of unrestrained attacks on science or scientists, even in the cause of moral principles that I share. In the third place, moral absolutism can often spill over into legalism or self-righteousness. Some people enjoy a good moral condemnation the way others enjoy a good dinner. When we reach strongly held principles that are implicitly critical of the actions of our fellow humans, then we always need to look at ourselves and take stock. As for myself, I see no grounds for self-righteousness in this general area of man's treatment of animals. Western society is so bound up with the use and abuse of animals in so many fields of human endeavor that it is impossible for anyone to claim that they are not party, directly or indirectly, to this exploitation either through the products they buy, the food they eat, or the taxes they pay. I agree with Albert Schweitzer that a "good conscience is an invention of the devil."[43]

Nevertheless, having stated these reservations boldly, it is inevitable that it is to the law that we must turn if we are to prevent the routinized and institutionalized abuse of animals in experimentation. The law should defend the interests of those who are weakest in society, and especially those unable to represent themselves in this matter. People, however, must be free to disagree about the appropriate strategy for that end, and the appropriate methods that should be employed in order to advance it, but it is clear that the aim *should be* the end of institutionalized animal experimentation.

I realize that this whole way of approaching the matter may appear strange to many Christians who have been led to believe that the notion of dominion gave humans exclusive rights over the animal world. There is, it is true, a whole tradition of Christian theology that has advanced itself by putting stress upon the uniqueness of man and by separating responsibilities to man from responsibilities to creation.[44] Something in this tradition has value, but much of it we can now see was vitally flawed by its extreme emphasis on the prerogatives of humans without a sufficient appreciation of our responsibility toward creation. I can only plead for an increased appreciation that theological work is in part at least the result of experience and interpretation. At one time and in one place one insight may be pressed to the reduction or exclusion of another; for a time one vital insight may be lost or buried under erroneous interpretation. Theology is ever working toward holding together a range of insights, the full development of which always lies in the future. As one respected theologian recently put it:

> In the past theology has often been slow to respond to new points of insight and sensitivity—though later both its own vision and its own heart have been enlarged by them: to sensitivity, for instance, about the iniquity of slavery and the rights of coloured people. Perhaps the theology of our own age will be convicted of myopia if it does not spend serious reflection upon that new kind of reverence for nature which is appearing among us. The present seems an opportune time for reflection. For the wholly anthropocentric theology of the last 15 or 20 years has clearly run out of inspiration and is degenerating towards triviality. [45]

I want to conclude, therefore, by suggesting that the minimum we have sought to deduce from the concept of the value of creation, considerable though that minimum is, may not be theologically sufficient. It could be that too many moralists in the animal field (myself included), too eager to delineate some minimum moral status for animals in the hope of protecting them from unnecessary ill, have failed to lay before themselves the full positive weight of the value of creation. [46] To recognize the value of creation we have not only to prevent evil but also to promote good. Therefore in each and every situation we must ask what good our presence can bring, and what care, aid, and protection we can offer to the created world. Not just how far or in what circumstance we can prevent the worst possible happening, but rather how we can express in a positive way the very highest moral behavior of which we are capable toward animals. In this regard we must question whether our relationships with animals should be rightly influenced by straightforward utilitarian calculations of the human good presupposed, for example, by animal researchers. It seems to me that we need to be careful lest our own exalted

moral and theological reasoning gives us a basis for the justification of a spirit of moral meanness toward the created world.

Notes

1. I would like to thank Professor Tom Regan of the North Carolina State University, U.S., and Dr. Richard Jurd of the University of
Essex, U.K., for their helpful comments on earlier drafts of this
paper.

2. Hugh Montefiore (ed.), *Man and Nature* (London, Collins,
1975), p. 67. Hereafter referred to as Montefiore, *Man*. Unfortunately, however, the report does not feel it right to "lay down general
principles derived from theological insights" (80 f) and thus does not
consider the question of animal treatment directly. One can only
point out, however, that this procedure has been followed for many
years in moral theology, and many publications of the Board for Social
Responsibility attempt to offer analysis and critique based on theological insight.

3. H. P. Owen, *Concepts of Deity* (London, Macmillan, 1971),
p. 1. For a discussion of these terms, see pp. 4–34.

4. Eric Mascall, *The Importance of Being Human* (London, Oxford University Press, 1959), p. 83. Hereafter referred to as Mascall,
Importance.

5. ". . . in all things like unto us, sin only excepted; begotten of
the Father before ages as to his Godhead, and in the last days, the
Same, for us and for our salvation, of Mary the Virgin *Theotokos* as to
his manhood" from the Council definition, Aloys Grillmeier, *Christ
in Christian Tradition* (Oxford, Mowbrays, 1965), p. 481. This book
gives a useful discussion of the development of Christian doctrine up
to the time of Chalcedon.

6. Eric Mascall, *The Openness of Being* (London, Darton,
Longman and Todd, 1971), p. 146. Mascall also argues that it is the
rationality of man that especially enables him to be open to God in a
rational and personal way, a capacity he judges impossible for other
creatures (p. 148).

7. *E.g.*, "Salvation by means of a flight out of the world, an escape of the spirit from the world, will appear as a limitation or spiri-
tualistic deformation. In reality we are dealing with a way of salvation

which does not tear us out of the world but is rather opened *for* this created world, in the Word become flesh." Vladimir Lossky, *The Vision of God* (London, The Faith Press, 1963), p. 58 (his emphasis).

8. Brian Horne, *A World to Gain: Incarnation and the Hope of Renewal* (London, Darton, Longman and Todd, 1983), p. 55. Hereafter referred to as Horne, *World*. Horne also writes: "My concern is to argue that if there is to be a halt to the destruction of our environment and a restoration of the world of nature, then a change must begin in the Church at a fundamental level. Quite simply, the Church should be less concerned about the salvation of souls and more concerned about the sanctification of life, or, to be more precisely theological, less concerned about 'justification by faith' and more concerned about 're-creation by grace'; and the re-creation will extend to the whole of the natural order. We are not souls to be plucked from matter on the day of our salvation, we are part of a universe which along with us waits for the consummation that has been promised by God in Christ. At the level of doctrine this means the reintegration of the doctrines of creation, incarnation, and atonement. Wholly interdependent, each must be read in terms of others" (p. 53).

9. See, *e.g.*, John 1:3 for the view of Christ as cocreator.

10. For example, Mascall suggests: "Insofar as the evolutionary process may have been distorted before the advent of man, it is reasonable to explain this distortion by the common Christian doctrine that one of the functions which God has committed to the angels is the supervision of the lower creation, so that the defection of certain of the angels has had as one of its consequences a disorganisation of the material world and the dislocation of its functions." Mascall, *Importance*, p. 80.

11. Paul Tillich, *Systematic Theology*, vol. 2, part III (London, SCM Press, 1978), p. 96. Tillich also writes: "If there are non-human 'worlds' in which existential estrangement is not only real—as it is in the whole universe—but in which there is also a type of awareness of this estrangement, such worlds cannot be without the operation of saving power within them . . . the manifestation of saving power in one place implies that saving power operating in all places" (p. 96). It is interesting to note that the kind of awareness Tillich postulates is firmly held by many biologists, *e.g.*, W. H. Thorpe, *Animal Nature and Human Nature* (London, Methuen, 1974), p. 320. See also Tom Regan's *The Case for Animal Rights* (London, Routledge and Kegan

Paul, 1983), pp. 1–82, for a discussion of the philosophical and ethical implications for our treatment of animals. Hereafter referred to as Regan, *Animal Rights*.

12. *Man in His Living Environment* (London: CIO, 1970), p. 65.

13. Mascall, *The Christian Universe* (London, Darton, Longman and Todd, 1966), p. 107. He also writes of a doctrinal "misconception" that "Jesus Christ is of immense significance to human beings, but of no importance whatever to the rest of the universe. This last view is very common today. It interprets Christianity entirely in terms of personal relationships between human beings; it sees great significance in the fact that we are members of the human community but none in the fact that, in our bodily aspects, we are physical objects, parts of the material world" (p. 133).

14. Montefiore, *Man*, p. 63. For a classic treatment of the theme of cosmic redemption, see Alan Galloway's *The Cosmic Christ* (London, Nisbet, 1951).

15. The allusion here, of course, is to Romans 8:18 f. Does v. 19, "For the creation waits with eager longing for the revealing of the sons of God," mean that "on man, thus redeemed, falls some responsibility for the redemption of all creation?" (*Man in His Living Environment*, p. 65). It certainly seems one exegetical possibility.

16. Keith Ward, *Rational Theology and the Creativity of God* (Oxford, Basil Blackwell, 1982), pp. 201–202. Also: "If there is any sentient being which suffers pain, that being—whatever it is and however it is manifested—must find that pain transfigured by greater joy. I am quite agnostic as to how this is to happen; but that it must be asserted to be true follows from the doctrine that God is love, and would not therefore create any being whose sole destiny was to suffer pain." Keith Ward, *The Concept of God* (Oxford, Basil Blackwell, 1974), p. 223.

17. For example, C. F. D. Moule argues "To what, then, is man's true sonship going to lead nature? To some spurious immortality? By no means! The emancipation of nature from its servitude to decay consists, exactly as in the emancipation of an individual from lust, in its material still being used—indeed being used up—but in an overall purpose that is part of God's design." *Man and Nature in the New Testament* (London, The Atholone Press, 1964), p. 14. Hereafter referred to as Moule, *Man and Nature*. But the point that Moule over-

looks is that animals (unlike lust) have intrinsic value and therefore belong to him. Immortality apart, can God leave to one side what is intrinsically valuable to him? Moreover, what if God's "overall purpose" is actually to bring *all* creation into harmony with himself?

18. See Bishop Butler and John Wesley (James Turner, *Reckoning with the Beast* [Baltimore, The John Hopkins University Press, 1980], p. 8). Also C. S. Lewis' theory about tame animals, *The Problem of Pain* (London, Fontana, 1967), pp. 127–28. For a discussion of Lewis' views, see C. E. M. Joad and C. S. Lewis, "The Pains of Animals," *The Month* (February, 1950), pp. 95–104.

19. Montefiore, *Man*, p. 67.

20. Karl Barth, *Church Dogmatics*, vol. III, Part Two (Edinburgh, T and T Clark, 1960), p. 78. Hereafter referred to as Barth, *Church*.

21. I am currently working on a thesis concerning Karl Barth's treatment of the doctrine of creation, and I seek to address myself to this question in that context.

22. Edward Carpenter *et al.*, *Animals and Ethics* (London, Watkins, 1980), p. 6. This report was the result of "A group of biologists, theologians, veterinarians and others concerned with the welfare of animals (who) met during 1977–1979 to prepare an agreed statement on man's relationship with animals which would reflect an ethical approach within a factual context" (p. 5).

23. See my *Animal Rights: A Christian Assessment of Man's Treatment of Animals* (London, SCM Press, 1976), pp. 9–19 and 69–77 in particular (hereafter referred to as Linzey, *Animal Rights*). Also my "Is Anthropocentricity Christian?", *Theology* (January, 1981), pp. 17–21.

24. For example, "in both the Old Testament creation stories we have the picture of man, the ideal king, God's perfect viceregent, under whom nature is fertile and peaceful and all she was meant to be. . . . The 'dominion,' therefore, which man is promised in Genesis 1 is poles apart from the kind of right to egoistical exploitation that it suggests to our ears. It is in essence a perfect obedience to the will of God." See John Austin Baker, "Biblical Attitudes to Nature," in Montefiore, *Man*, pp. 93–94. Hereafter referred to as Baker, "Biblical Attitudes." I am indebted to Baker's essay for many perceptive points.

25. Barth, *Church*, vol. III, Part One, p. 208, though it is worth nothing that Barth does not accept this as a binding commandment (pp. 208–212).

26. "The Old Testament, then, does nothing to justify the charge that it represents an exploitative, humanly egoistical attitude to nature. Although it recognises man's preying on nature as a fact, it characterises that fact as a mark of man's decline from the first perfect intentions of God for him." Baker, "Biblical Attitudes," p. 96.

27. Hugh Montefiore, *Can Man Survive?* (*The Question Mark and Other Essays*), (London, Fontana, 1970), p. 55.

28. R. G. Frey indicates how taking sentiency as a basis for rights or interests leaves non-sentient beings without rights or interests in *Interests and Rights: The Case Against Animals* (Oxford, Clarendon Press, 1980), pp. 28 ff. Frey's point is for discussion only because he doesn't accept the rights or interests of either. But it doesn't follow even if we grant rights to certain beings that the rest are valueless. Stephen Clark makes this clear: "In short, we should recognize . . . that animals and plants and all the creatures and ecologies that variously inhabit the earth have, in a sense, some *right* to our consideration." *The Moral Status of Animals* (Oxford, Clarendon Press, 1977), p. 168. Hereafter referred to as Clark, *Moral Status*.

29. Anthony Phillips, "Respect for Life in the Old Testament," *King's Theological Review* (Autumn, 1983), p. 32. I am indebted to this article, though I am perplexed by the subsequent line: "While animals, like all God's creation, *were made for man*, he must still order that creation in accordance with God's will" (my emphasis, p. 32). I think a fundamental distinction must be drawn between man's dominion over creation and the notion that it was made for him.

30. Mascall, *Corpus Christi* (London, Longmans, 1965), pp. 86–87. Hereafter referred to as Mascall, *Corpus*.

31. Masure cited by Mascall, *Corpus*, p. 92.

32. Mascall, *Corpus*, p. 93.

33. See, for example, the argument of Hebrews 2:14 ff; also Mascall, *Corpus*, pp. 94 ff. Christ's rejection of animal sacrifice may be deduced, *e.g.*, in Mark, by the cleansing of the temple (11:5 f) and the wise reply to the scribe (12:32–35).

34. Moule comes to a similar conclusion: "His [man's] distinctive

contribution to the ecological set-up is meant to be rational and conscious manipulation in accordance with the will of God. It seems to me that such a view is integral with the confession of real incarnation and of new creation in Christ." *Man and Nature*, p. 16. But he appears to overlook that this "manipulation" according to God's will might have a different interpretation in the light of the incarnation. Once again the implication that animals are simply things to be "manipulated" ignores their intrinsic value.

35. Clark, *Moral Status*, Preface.

36. Patrick Corbett, "Postscript," in Stanley and Roslind Godlovitch and John Harris (eds.), *Animals, Men and Morals* (London, Gollancz, 1971), p. 236.

37. This position is substantially unchanged from the one I defended in *Animal Rights*, p. 57: "Whatever we may conjecture about the necessity of some animal experimentation under situations where overriding conditions operate, we should be clear that the legal and social norm should absolutely prohibit all such experimentation." See also Regan's *Animal Rights*, pp. 363–398, which gives the fullest treatment yet of this whole subject and develops similar conclusions.

38. *The Proposed International Guidelines for Biochemical Research Involving Human Subjects* (a joint project of the World Health Organization and Council for Organizations of Medical Sciences), (Geneva, 1982), p. 22, para. 1 f.

39. *Trials of War Criminals Before the Nuremberg Military Tribunals Under Control Council Law No. 10*, vol. 2 (Washington, D.C., U.S. Government Printing Office, 1949), pp. 181 f. I am grateful to Dr. J. M. Finnis of University College, Oxford, for this reference and note 38 above.

40. Regan, *Animal Rights*, p. 377. I am indebted for this and many other perceptive points.

41. I develop this point further in my "Moral Education and Reverence for Life," in D. A. Paterson (ed.), *Humane Education—A Symposium* (Humane Education Council, 1981), pp. 117–125.

42. Hans Ruesch, *Slaughter of the Innocent* (London, Futura Publications, 1979), p. 35. Also my review in *Resurgence* (September–October, 1979), p. 35.

43. Albert Schweitzer, *Civilization and Ethics* (London, Allen and Unwin, 1967), p. 221.

44. Aquinas, Calvin, and Luther are three of the key figures who teach that, individually or collectively, animals are made for man and may be completely subordinate to him. These views certainly had disastrous moral consequences for the animal-man relationship. See, *e.g.*, the brief history in John Passmore's *Man's Responsibility for Nature* (London, Duckworth, 1974), pp. 3–40. It is a matter of continuing debate to what extent the Western Christian tradition is responsible for the current misuse of nature. Horne offers a more favorable interpretation of Aquinas: "The idea of the divine *order*, almost a hierarchy of things in the universe, is central to Thomas Aquinas's understanding of creation. Each thing in the universe occupies its proper place and exists to serve those things that are ranged above it. . . . The proper function of every particle of the created order is ordained by God. On grounds of Thomist theology alone one could argue that the use to which man has put the world in which he lives and has responsibilities is a disruption of God's beneficent ordering of nature." *World*, p. 45 (his emphasis). I think it is right that we should seek the most charitable interpretation of many theologians, even those whose views we may regard as erroneous. Too much critical engagement (including my own) has been infected with a prosecuting zeal at the expense of understanding. I regret to add that much in Peter Singer's *Animal Liberation* (London, Jonathan Cape, 1976), pp. 203–220, exhibits this deficiency. The problem with Aquinas it seems to me is not his notion of an overarching divine order but his oversimplification (we can now judge with hindsight and with the benefit of knowledge simply not at his disposal at the time of writing) of what constitutes this divine order. It is not so obvious to us that the created order as we now know it "serves" the human species in the way postulated.

45. W. H. Vanstone, "On the Being of Nature," *Theology* (July, 1977), p. 283. Vanstone is now a member of the Doctrine Commission of the Church of England.

46. I must add that I now see that my small contribution to the debate (Linzey, *Animal Rights*) was insufficiently theological and far too dismissive of many aspects of the Christian tradition. I hope to remedy this in a future reworking of the book.

5 The Relevance of Animal Experimentation to Roman Catholic Ethical Methodology

James Gaffney

1. The Moral Status of Animals in Roman Catholic Thought

In an amusing chapter of Pierre Daninos' *Le secret du Major Thompson*, a book that, in my day, students of French read at school, the Major's Parisian visitor, having observed with astonishment the civil rights and domestic privileges enjoyed by pets in Britain, summed up his impressions: "*Si les animaux avait un pape, leur Vatican serait à Londres!*"[1]

We may be forcefully reminded by one of the less celebrated biographical details of Pope Pius IX that papist animals would have been wise, at any rate, to establish their pontificate at a distance from the original Vatican. For not only did that extraordinary man publish his famous *Syllabus of Errors*, comprising most of the clichés of modern liberalism, and convoke the first Vatican Council, which defined the dogma of his own infallibility, he also vigorously opposed the founding at Rome of a Society for the Protection of Animals. Apparently what he feared was that the presence of such an organization would foster the theologically erroneous belief (somehow overlooked by the *Syllabus of Errors*) that human beings have duties to animals of other species.

Old and New Testaments

Even had I known about that papal intervention, I doubt that it would have saved me, in childhood, from lapsing into what I then believed to be my first formal heresy, the more ungodly for having occurred in church and while attending to a Scripture reading. Taken from the ninth chapter of St. Paul's First Letter to the Corinthians, it contains the following passage: "It is written in the law of Moses, 'You shall not muzzle an ox when it is treading out the grain.' Is it for oxen that God is concerned? Does he not speak entirely for our sake?" (1 Corinthians 9.9–10).

Having posed these rhetorical questions, Paul proceeds on the assumption that God obviously is not concerned for oxen and certainly does speak entirely for our sake. Accordingly, Paul interprets the text as an allegory, the practical meaning of which affirms the rights not of oxen but of preachers like Paul himself to be paid a suitable wage for their apostolic services. Gratuitous as this interpretation may seem, that it was well on its way to becoming standard even within the first Christian generation is strongly suggested by a passage in the deutero-Pauline First Letter to Timothy: "Let the elders who rule well be considered worthy of a double honor, especially those who labor in preaching and teaching; for the scripture says 'You shall not muzzle an ox when it is treading out the grain,' and 'The laborer deserves his wages'" (1 Timothy, 5.17–18).

What has happened here is that Paul's allegorizing precedent has led to simply equating the Old Testament text about the treading ox with a New Testament saying (found verbatim in Luke 10.7 and slightly altered in Matthew 10.10) about the right of a worker to receive pay. In those Gospels this saying is applied to the right of Jesus' disciples to be supported by the beneficiaries of their ministry, and thus by implication, as in the passage cited from 1 Timothy, to the wage claims of early Christian clergy.

It was a long time before I discovered that, in this matter,

it was not I but Paul who was heretical. For the passage about
the ox was as nonallegorical as everything else in the book of
Deuteronomy, where it is found as part of the law of Moses.
Like certain other passages in that same book, it is plainly intended to be read precisely as a piece of divine legislation
in behalf of animals, despite some inconvenience to human
greed. Thus, for at least one constituent tradition of the Torah,
Paul's assumptions are simply mistaken. It is indeed "for oxen
that God is concerned," and to at least that extent he does "not
speak entirely for our sake." The Mosaic law does envisage
animal interests, does legislate animal rights, and, to that extent, does represent animals as moral objects. One may be reminded that there is nothing very extraordinary about this
way of thinking by the fact that even in the deuteronomic text
of the ten commandments, the injunction to provide a Sabbath
day of rest for one's dependents explicitly includes not only
one's family, servants, and guests but also the domestic animals—"your ox or your ass or any of your cattle" (Deuteronomy 5.14). In the wisdom literature, the underlying moral
finds expression in the unfortunately neglected proverb: "A
righteous man has regard for the life of his beast" (Proverbs
12.10).

Nevertheless, historically, those assumptions of Paul's,
like his tendentious allegorical misinterpretation, won the day
among Christians, effectively depriving them, insofar as they
turned to the Bible for ethical guidance, of any chance of de-
tecting therein the few but clear indications it does contain of
rights (at once moral and legal because constituted by divine
law) conferred upon animals. As a result, Christian ethics,
even at its most biblical, was from the start relentlessly anthropocentric. Its bias in this respect was confirmed by the
typical humanism of Hellenistic culture, and it was subsequently reinforced by a classical tradition whose anthropology
restricted the moral domain to the sphere of rationality in
which, presumably, nonhuman animals had no share.

In the New Testament, and notably in the Sermon on the
Mount, there are no doubt passages that movingly affirm God's

providential care for nonhuman animal life. But what we do
not find is any explicit suggestion, by either doctrine or example, that caring for animals has a place in the following of
Jesus. Pre-Reformation Christianity thus typically overlooked
Old Testament indications concerning the place animals might
occupy in religious morality. And with the medieval system-
atizing of Christian ethics in categories borrowed mainly from
Aristotle, rationality, regarded as the distinguishing characteristic of human animals, was assumed to be the essential qualification of a moral object.

Thomas Aquinas

One can see the result very typically in a passage of
theological ethics in which Thomas Aquinas, applying Aristo-
telian categories to the most fundamental formula of New Testament morality—"Love your neighbor as yourself"—addresses the question of "Whether irrational creatures also are
to be loved out of charity?"[2] Thomas is committed by his
Christianity to the moral conviction that, as Paul expressed it
in his Letter to the Romans, "Love is the fulfilling of the law"
(Romans 13.10). He is also persuaded by his Aristotelianism
to interpret love philosophically as friendship. His question
therefore requires him to decide whether or not one can exercise friendship toward irrational creatures. He finds three reasons for judging that one cannot. First, while friendship means
wanting one's friend's good, irrational creatures "do not properly have a good" because they lack freedom of choice. Second, whereas friendship is based on community of life, irrational creatures cannot have community with "human life,
which is in accordance with reason." Thomas also brings in a
more strictly theological objection, namely, that love is founded
on a community of eternal happiness, "for which an irrational
creature has no capability."[3] Thus, according to the theologian whose influence has certainly exceeded that of any other
among Roman Catholics, irrational creatures, precisely because of their irrationality, cannot be, properly speaking, di-

rect objects of human friendship, or, therefore, of Christian charity wherein the whole of Christian morality is contained. It is noteworthy that, of Thomas' three reasons for attributing this consequence to irrationality, two are still widely accepted, though differently articulated, among Christians and non-Christians alike. His view that irrational creatures cannot exercise free choice and therefore do not properly have a good is a familiar interpretation of the notion that such creatures do not have interests. And his view that they are not qualified for a community based on reason is a familiar interpretation of the notion that they are not social persons. Even Thomas' third argument is often still heard in the form of denying that irrational creatures possess immortal souls, considered a prerequisite for an otherworldly destiny.

I think it is fair to say that these Thomistic theses about irrational creatures represent the main standard assumptions Roman Catholic moralists have typically brought to questions concerning the ethical status of nonhuman animals. In this connection we may need to recall that for Thomas there was no possibility of arguing over whether or not nonhuman animals are, in all cases, irrational creatures. For like all his contemporaries Thomas had adopted the classical definition of a human being as *zoon logikon, animal rationale,* rational animal. Hence the hypothesis of an animal that was both rational and nonhuman could not be a matter for debate or even for thought, for it was simply a contradiction in terms. What is, perhaps, a more promising ground of controversy is the fact that at no point does Thomas suggest that the moral status of irrational creatures might be significantly affected by whether or not they happen to be animals, or, for that matter, whether or not they happen to be alive. This indifference to or presumption against the specific ethical relevance of animality as such has generally characterized Roman Catholic tradition.

Even though, in all that we have considered so far, Thomas Aquinas provides us with no basis whatsoever for paying any kind of ethical attention to irrational creatures, animal or otherwise, he does have something more to say on this subject, in the same context, although not at all emphatically, which provides a real connection between thinking about irrational creatures, animals included, and thinking about Christian morality. In the style of an afterthought he introduces one concession that implies that irrational creatures, although they cannot be direct objects of Christian love (and therefore of Christian morality as he understands it), can be its indirect objects: "Irrational creatures can be loved out of charity as goods that we want for others; insofar as, out of charity, we want to preserve them to the honor of God and utility of human beings."[4] Here Thomas appears to be telling us that we should, after all, be morally concerned about irrational creatures, not for their own sake but for the sake of God and of our human neighbors. With regard to the human neighbors, he refers significantly to the utility of animals. That is, one's charitable disposition toward a human being might naturally and rightly express itself in some degree of care for whatever irrational creatures happen to serve the interests of that human being. Thus, charity toward a human being might obviously prompt us to take care of that person's horse or dog, orchard or garden, or, for that matter, house or car. And the practical implications of that kind of moral argument are extremely far-reaching, easily extending to even such modern concerns as environmental protection legislation. What it could not be extended to is generating any moral concern about irrational creatures that did not find its justification in human expedience. Nor, of course, does it confer any special moral advantage on animals as distinct from other irrational creatures.

Francis of Assisi

Nevertheless, there is another phrase in that afterthought of Thomas' that may serve to enlarge the subject. For he notes that a loving concern to preserve irrational creatures may be motivated not only by "utility of human beings" but also, and in the first place, by "the honor of God." Now that is the kind of phrase that, especially nowadays and in lands as secularized as ours, one is tempted to dismiss as a pious embellishment, devoid of practical implications. But whether or not it would be employed or understood that trivially by a devout Christian friar of 13th century Italy is questionable. And just how questionable it is may strike us most forcefully if we recall the associations most of us have with another devout Christian friar of 13th century Italy, Francis of Assisi, who was still living when Thomas was born. It would contribute nothing to our purpose to try to separate the Francis of history from the Francis of legend. What matters to us rather is that around the mysterious person of this Umbrian saint there developed and still vigorously survives a richly romantic Christian piety, celebrated in every kind of art, that resoundingly answers in its own terms the question Thomas asked: "Whether irrational creatures also are to be loved out of charity?" There is certainly nothing in those Franciscan legends to imply that Francis would have disagreed with anything Thomas said in that question of the *Summa Theologiae*. On the contrary, what we find in the rhapsodic lyrics of the *Cantica delle creature* and the winsome episodes of the *Fioretti* is precisely an exuberant affirmation of the truth so cryptically rendered by that one fragment of a Thomistic afterthought: "Irrational creatures can be loved out of charity . . . insofar as, out of charity, we want to preserve them to the honor of God."[5] That, surely, would be the right theological footnote, if any were appropriate, to a story like "How St. Francis Made Peace Between the People and the Wolf of Gubbio," just as it is the explicit theological refrain of the famous Canticle, beginning with Brother Sun and ending with Sister Death, of which he said, "I want to compose a new praise of the Lord and his creatures, for we daily make use of them and cannot live without them."[6] There can be no way of measuring how much or little the legacy of Francis may have gentled the ruthlessness of Christians in dealing with animals and other non-human creatures, but it does belong to a tradition of religious morals, and it is one of the rare instances in which theology and morality have joined hands and taken wing and carried an extraordinary variety of human hearts and minds aloft with them. And it is pleasant to recall that when the Italian Societies for the Protection of Animals recovered from the initial setback of papal opposition, they were at last blessed by the Church under the patronage, inevitably, of St. Francis of Assisi.

Medieval Christian moral doctrine, as suitably represented by Thomas Aquinas, does not, then, quite justify the assumption that our deeds and dispositions with regard to animals are totally irrelevant to Christian ethics. But it certainly does not descend to particulars, nor, as already noted, does it distinguish the moral relevance of animals from that of other irrational creatures. And, on the whole, these omissions remain typical of Roman Catholic moralists after the Reformation.

Sir Thomas More

However, one interesting and illustrious exception from the Reformation period itself that deserves more notice than it has usually received is the case of another St. Thomas, in life Sir Thomas More. More was, of course, an intensely orthodox Roman Catholic, but one who disliked and largely ignored medieval Scholasticism. He built his own moral culture on an unharmonious combination of monastic asceticism, English jurisprudence, and classical humanism. It is in Book II of *Utopia* that he touches on our subject, and he does so in ways that are strongly suggestive of the rationalistic moralists of the Enlightenment. That the *Utopia* provides the context of these remarks is important, for More's imaginary commonwealth is conceived precisely as a society formed not by Christian revelation but by reason alone. In that sense, the contents of his *Utopia* are not directly a Catholic or a Christian statement. But it is not quite so simple as that, because the *Utopia* does represent something permanently characteristic of both Roman and Anglican Catholicism to which the Continental Protestant Reformation was opposed in many respects. That is, More believed, no less than Aquinas, in a fundamental harmony between the attainments of natural human reason and the deliverances of supernatural divine revelation. Thus the mores of *Utopia* are contrived as an ironic parable for Christians and a reproach to that Christendom whose culture seemed to More in many respects not only subcelestial but subnatural and subrational. It is in this perspective that such a remark as the following ought to be interpreted: "The Utopians feel that slaughtering our fellow creatures gradually destroys the sense of compassion which is the finest sentiment of which our nature is capable."[7] It should be noted here that the point More is making was not entirely lost on Thomas Aquinas. For in his treatment of what seem to be divine statutes protective of animals in the Mosaic law, after establishing a distinction between affections of reason and those of passion, he observes that "if a man's affection be one of reason, it matters not how man behaves to animals."

> But if a man's affection be one of passion, then it is moved also in regard to other animals . . . and since it happens that even irrational animals are sensible to pain, it is possible for the affection of pity to arise in a man with regard to the sufferings of animals. Now it is evident that if a man practices a pitiful affection for animals, he is all the more disposed to take pity in his fellow men.[8]

Unfortunately for animals, Aquinas confined these remarks to a response to an objection that occurs in the least read portion of the *Summa Theologiae* dealing with Jewish ceremonial law, which he considered divinely abrogated. Had the same observations occurred in his moral teachings on cruelty and pity, it might have made quite a difference.

Thomas More invokes the same moral psychology to explain the Utopians' detestation of hunting for sport in a passage that was noticed in the last century by Henry S. Salt in his book *Animals' Rights*.[9]

> Is there any more real pleasure, they [the Utopians] ask,
> when a dog chases a rabbit than there is when a dog
> chases a dog? If what you like is fast running, there's
> plenty of that in both cases. . . . But if what you really
> want is slaughter, if you want to see a living creature
> torn apart under your eyes, then the whole thing is
> wrong.[10]

More's moral objection to such amusement is, of course, strictly humanistic: "[It] results, in the opinion of the Utopians, in a cruel disposition. Or, if he isn't cruel to start with, the hunter quickly becomes so through the constant practice of such bestial pleasures."[11]

Shakespeare reminds us that such ideas were current later in the Renaissance. Thus, in *Cymbeline*, the queen's plan to test slow and painful poisons on "such creatures as we count not worth the hanging—but none human" elicits from her physician the admonition that "your highness shall from this practice but make hard your heart."[12] And in *As You Like It*, the pensive Jaques, lamenting the painful death of a "poor sequester'd stag that from the hunters' aim had ta'en a hurt," reproaches the exiled Duke's followers as "mere usurpers, tyrants, and what's worse, to fright the animals and kill them up."[13]

More unconventionally, More's narrator tells us that among the Utopians, most of whom believe in an afterlife and try to correct the few who do not, are

> some others, in fact no small number of them, who err
> in the opposite direction, in supposing that animals too
> have immortal souls, though not comparable to ours in
> excellence, nor destined to equal felicity. These men are
> not thought to be evil, their opinion is not thought to be
> wholly unreasonable, and so they are not interfered
> with.[14]

That passage would have pleased at least one evangelist of the Enlightenment era, John Wesley, who preached in a famous

sermon that the same opinion is consonant not only with reason but also with faith.[15]

My lengthy discussions of the ideas of Thomas Aquinas,
supplemented by those of Francis of Assisi and Thomas More,
are certainly not intended to suggest that Roman Catholic tradition evidences any strong, unbroken strand of interest in the
moral status of nonhuman animals. They are rather to suggest
that Catholics might have found, as a few still do find among
their acknowledged classics, some stimulation for the rational
and even pious cultivation of such interest. How far Catholic
moral theologians have been from developing such hints may
be drearily indicated by the fact that in most of their books, if
there should occur any index reference to animals, it would
probably lead the reader only to a portion of the treatise on
lust dealing with the sin of bestiality! And in that sordid context to my knowledge compassion for the nonhuman beast is
nowhere explicit.

After the Renaissance and Reformation, Roman Catholicism had little more and nothing new to say about the moral
status of animals. Moral sermonizing by the clergy was largely
influenced by remarkably uniform seminary curricula, dominated on the theoretical side by the teaching of Thomas Aquinas and on the practical side by a body of casuistry designed
for gauging the sinfulness of what penitents told priests about
in sacramental confession. For the latter purpose, sins were
elaborately classified and analyzed, but mistreatment of animals seldom if ever found a place in the resulting catalogs of
misconduct, and the same can be said of moral instructions
contained in popular catechisms.

Nineteenth Century Liberalism

Moreover, as has often been noted, a modern renewal
of interest in animals as proper objects of human morality
arose chiefly within movements of thought characteristic of
liberal social criticism. And since the outstanding movements
of liberal social criticism were closely associated with a secu-

larism and anticlericalism hostile to ecclesiastical power and privilege, Catholic response to them was typically defensive. Catholicism was not in the vanguard of defenders of the rights of man nor of the rights of woman implied therein. Catholicism's predominantly conservative reaction to typical 19th century liberalism was, especially in ultramontane circles, indiscriminately resistant. It is scarcely surprising that 19th century Catholic opposition to so seemingly innocuous a cause as that of animal protection (imported to the Continent from Britain) was led by a pope for whom liberal slogans were part of the devil's idiom. Nor is it surprising that Catholic writers of that period who evinced any interest in that subject typically broached it in tones not of sympathy but of warning. The various humane policies of liberalism tended to be tarred by Catholics with the same brush used upon its prevailingly secular philosophy. Even in the less reactionary Catholic mood of a later period, one finds those warnings regularly reiterated as qualifications of a grudging approval of animal protection. I shall cite an example translated from the Italian Catholic encyclopedia, since the English language counterpart of that multivolume reference work, *The New Catholic Encyclopedia*, maintains total silence on this subject, as do the great Catholic theological encyclopedias in French and German. The fullest and most sympathetic treatment in any comparable religiously oriented encyclopedia in English is that of the *Encyclopedia Judaica*, a reminder that the Hebrew Bible laid foundations on which it was possible and natural to build, even though early Christianity's disinclination to do so had far-reaching effects. Here, in any case, is the typically admonitory passage from *l'Enciclopedia Cattolica*:

> Societies for the protection of animals may be approved insofar as their objective is the elimination of cruelty to beasts. Not, however, insofar as they base their activities, as they sometimes do, on false principles (attributing rights to animals, or cultivating in their regard a saccharine, sentimental sort of love, love easily

withheld from the neighbor, or alleging a duty of charity, which, in the Christian sense of that phrase, cannot
obtain).[16]

It may be noted in passing that the passage contains the
familiar objection to concern for animals—that loving them
detracts from loving one's fellow human beings. No doubt we
have all known crotchety, misanthropic persons who doted on
some pet, but I have never been able to fathom the supposi-
tion of a causal connection such that these people would be
likely to be less crotchety and misanthropic if they were indifferent to their pets. The common objection seems to rest on
the psychologically bizarre premise that each of us has a fixed
capital of kindness, so that whatever is spent on nonhuman
animals is thereby lost to human ones. This is the reverse of
the more plausible assumption, which I have illustrated from
Thomas Aquinas and Thomas More, that pity and cruelty,
whatever their initial objects, tend to become habitual elements of character and to enlarge their scope accordingly.

2. Current Trends

Turning now from history to prognostication, it may be
asked whether or not currently prevailing trends in the way
Roman Catholics argue about ethical matters have any bearing
on a moral re-evaluation of human treatment of animals. I believe they do, in at least four respects. First, there is a strong
insistence on the basic importance of human dignity. Second,
there is a growing bioethical perplexity about life that is ge-
netically human but not actually rational. Third, there is a vig-
orous minority opinion that virtue and vice are the primary
concerns of ethics. And fourth, there is a majority preference
for consequentialist methodology. I shall attempt a (dangerously) brief explanation of the meaning and relevance of each.

Human dignity, traditionally a classical or neoclassical
phrase, has become a prominent feature of Roman Catholic
vocabulary during the past century, and especially since the

Second Vatican Council, where it was repeatedly invoked in support of various social reforms. It is a vague but powerful idea that connotes the unique value of every human being as God's created image, and it relates that value to a unique human function as nature's overlord. Thus, the idea is often introduced by reference to the 8th Psalm.

> Yet thou hast made [man] little less than God,
> and dost crown him with glory and honor.
> Thou hast given him dominion over the works of thy
>   hands;
> thou hast put all things under his feet,
> all sheep and oxen and also the beasts of the field,
> the birds of the air, and the fish of the sea.
>   (Psalms 8.5–8.)

The idea of human dignity in current Roman Catholic usage is thus theologically and not empirically or philosophically grounded. For ethical purposes, it is regarded as that by virtue of which all human beings are in some sense equal, despite their dissimilarities, and collectively superior to all other earthly creatures. On the face of it, this is not a view that spontaneously encourages moral regard for animals. For it to do so depends on how one interprets human "dominion" and the condition of being located under human "feet." A rather ruthless interpretation has certainly been common among Roman Catholics. Although it has become increasingly popular, a defensible alternative of interpreting the human overlord's divinely constituted role as one of benign stewardship, expressed more properly in care than in consumption, is largely absent from Roman Catholic church teaching and preaching and unfamiliar to most of the laity. This pastoral and educational task seems to me crucial, but there are not a few who reject it not as illegitimate but as trivial and therefore as a potential distraction from more urgent matters. I think defenders of animals need to deal with this objection more sensitively and constructively than they have usually done. It is related but not reducible to the more naive objection already noted that animal lovers tend not to love their human neighbors. In both cases a kind of unspoken "law of the conservation of benevolence" seems to be operative.

The appeal to human dignity as the foundation of moral regard is significantly different from the traditional appeal to rationality, and the difference has practical consequences. That human dignity can exist in the absence of rationality is implied in common usage, inasmuch as we often describe and treat as human beings that are, to all appearances, neither reasoning nor capable of reasoning. If we insist on calling a newborn baby rational, we can only mean that reasoning is something which we expect it to become capable of in the course of time. At present its reasoning is not actual but potential, and we tend to extend the term rationality to include such potentiality. But the same could not be said of someone whose central nervous system was so defective that the ability to reason was permanently excluded. Yet, although rationality cannot be meaningfully attributed to such a case, human dignity can be. And since the basis of such attribution is not behavioral but genetic, human dignity is considered to be coextensive with the species *Homo sapiens*, regardless of the condition of any particular specimen. By the same token, the moral status founded upon human dignity is verified merely by identification as a specimen of *H. sapiens*. It is pointless to ask if any nonhuman animals possess human dignity, since the necessary and sufficient condition for possessing it is membership in that species. And it is hard to discuss the alleged necessity and sufficiency of that condition if it is asserted not on the basis of observation or argument but on the basis of divine revelation. Whether or not biblical sayings extolling humanity can reasonably be pressed to such conclusions is, of course, very debatable, though it is not often debated. And there is certainly a need for Roman Catholics to clarify what they mean by human dignity and how they justify their practical understanding of it. At present, the phrase is often employed in very important contexts in an unfortunately incantatory manner. The practical effect of this usage is, on the one hand, to extend the scope of moral concern to all of human life, whether rational or not, and, on the other hand, to inhibit extending such concern beyond human to other animal life. Because that effect simply begs the question of whether or not "speciesism" is a type of unfair moral discrimination, use of the term represents a semantic problem that animal protectionists cannot afford to overlook in contemporary dialogue with Roman Catholicism.

More encouraging to such dialogue is the currently increasing emphasis by some Roman Catholic ethicists on the fundamental importance of moral character or of virtue and vice. This may be dealt with briefly, for we have already seen that a historically important argument against cruelty to animals has been based on the plausible assumption that cruel behavior tends to make one a cruel person, whether the victims of cruelty are human or non-human animals. And to become cruel is precisely to acquire a facility for spontaneously cruel behavior, of which both human and non-human animals are potential victims. The familiarity of this idea, as Kant pointed out, is nicely illustrated by Hogarth's famous series of engravings entitled "The Stages of Cruelty," which begin by depicting children abusing pets and end with a portrayal of murder. Hogarth is, of course, proceeding on an assumption that he expects the viewers of his work to share, namely, that cruelty to animals tends to engender an indiscriminately cruel disposition. Although this is not a scientifically verified assumption and is one that could theoretically be tested by psychological experimentation, it does not seem unreasonable to transfer the burden of proof to those who reject it.

Finally, it may be noted that in recent years Roman Catholic ethicists have shown a strong tendency to favor consequentialism and proportionalism in moral argumentation.[17] What this kind of ethical thinking basically entails is a readiness, within limits, to judge the moral rightness or wrongness of an action by assessing its good and bad consequences and comparing them with the good and bad consequences of alternative ways of acting in identical circumstances. What is seldom made clear or even taken up by Roman Catholic ethicists of consequentialist leanings is just what can and what cannot count, in their system, as significantly good or bad consequences. They explicitly do not intend only morally good and bad consequences, and they seek to make this clear by using such terms as "ontic," "premoral," or "nonmoral" evil for the relevant bad consequences.

Their examples are, to be sure, typically confined to consequences affecting human beings either helpfully or hurtfully. But the relevance of consequences affecting animals is not denied but simply ignored. And there seems to be no systematic reason why animal pain should not, in itself, count for something, as a morally relevant bad consequence of those human activities that avoidably cause it. Given the (artificially) pure alternative of two courses of action, whose results differed only in the fact that one did and the other did not cause animals to suffer, it is scarcely obvious that a consequentialist should regard the choice as morally indifferent. But if it is not to be so regarded, the pain inflicted on animals by human activities must count in consequentialist moral evaluation. The question of how much it is to count for, as weighed against demonstrated or believable human advantages, though difficult to assess, is not negligible.

A possible difficulty concerning this evaluation of animal pain has recently been suggested by the philosopher R. G. Frey in his important book *Interests and Rights*, significantly subtitled *The Case Against Animals*.[18] As it happens, I fully agree with Frey that the notion of rights is ultimately unhelpful to our understanding of the moral (as distinct from the legal) status of animals, or indeed, of human beings. But my agreement does not extend to Frey's subordinate contention that pain is not intrinsically evil. No doubt people mean different things by the phrase "intrinsic evil," but I think the very least one has to imply in calling something intrinsically evil is that it is not desirable on account of anything it is in itself or contains as part of itself, so that, if it should be desired at all, it could only be by virtue of its connection with some good that is not part of itself. It seems to me that this is admirably exemplified by "suffering, distress of body and mind," which is how *The Concise Oxford Dictionary* defines "pain." Under the influence of penitential or ascetic motives it is of course possible, and it may even be thought wise, to desire pain, but only for the sake of something distinct from the pain yet not readily achievable without it. To desire pain for its own sake seems utterly irrational. Not even masochism offers an instance of this, since even a masochist desires pain not for its own sake but for the sake of an abnormally associated pleasure. Frey's demand for a strict proof that "pain is undesirable in itself" may offer a wholesome exercise for analytic philosophers, but to require moral policies to wait upon such attainments seems little short of fanatical. The admonition with which Aristotle introduced the first major treatise on ethics 23 centuries ago remains apposite: "It is the mark of an educated man to look for precision in each class of things just so far as the nature of the subject admits."

It may also be pointed out that Frey has introduced gratuitous confusion by a discussion he introduces with the curious statement that "in Roman Catholic and Anglican orthodoxy . . . though cardinal sins are regarded as intrinsically evil, the mere having of unpleasant sensations is not."[19] The fact is that neither Roman Catholic nor Anglican tradition contains anything whatsoever that could be properly described as orthodox teaching on either of those points. Since Frey proceeds to cite Peter Geach to the effect that "sin and unpleasant sensations are not the same thing,"[20] I suspect that he has confused the distinction between intrinsic and nonintrinsic evil with the altogether different distinction between moral and nonmoral evil. And that, I suppose, is why he goes on belaboring such banalities as "one can sin without inflicting unpleasant sensations," "one can inflict unpleasant sensations without sinning," and "sin is not to be committed merely in order to avoid inflicting pain."[21] These are, certainly, truisms of Christian theological ethics, but they are irrelevant to the question of whether or not pain is an intrinsic evil. As far as I can see,

Frey's argument at this juncture rests squarely upon a not very subtle category mistake.

If theological language is to be invoked, the question for us is not whether or not one can sin without inflicting pain, or can inflict pain without sinning, or may sin to avoid inflicting pain. It is rather whether or not one can sin by inflicting pain, not only on human beings, which every religious moralist takes for granted, but also on animals. Unless we are prepared to assert that it is invariably simply absurd to demand any moral justification for inflicting pain on animals, we have to admit the possibility of such sin. In contemporary Roman Catholic ethics, while consequentialism leads naturally to acknowledging that possibility, at the same time the exclusivist implications of human dignity inhibit following that lead to its remoter conclusions.

I suppose that the earliest truly eloquent expression of moral indignation against unfair discrimination that we have in our language is the passage in which Shylock, in *The Merchant of Venice*, defends as fair vengeance his extracting of the pound of flesh. Why, he asks, has the Christian so habitually abused and despised him?

> What's his reason? I am a Jew! Hath not a Jew eyes?
> Hath not a Jew hands, organs, dimensions, senses, affections, passions? Fed with the same food, hurt with the same weapons, subject to the same diseases, healed by the same means, warmed and cooled by the same winter and summer as a Christian is? If you prick us, do we not bleed? If you tickle us, do we not laugh? If you poison us, do we not die? And if you wrong us, shall we not revenge? If we are like you in the rest, we will resemble you in that. [22]

It may be worth noting that in this savagely righteous denunciation of chronic injustice perpetrated by Christians upon Jews, what Shylock insists upon is not the Jew's humanity but his animality, not his rationality but his organicity and sen-

tiency, and not his capacity to be offended but his susceptibility to bodily hurt. He is thus able to make his moral point
with great effectiveness without even risking his adversaries'
contemptuous dismissal of any claim to human dignity. He
strategically chooses the low ground because on that low
ground even the most virulent anti-Semitism cannot obscure
the justice of his complaint. What for Shylock was the shrewdly
chosen low ground must, I suppose, be considered the high
ground for animals. But I do not see why that should make the
same sort of argument morally unpersuasive when used in
their behalf.

Conclusion

It is clear from the foregoing pages that Roman Catholic moral tradition typically regards animals as means to human ends. Hence, typically Catholics have not withheld moral
approval from any treatment of animals that serves human
ends and that therefore is believed, on other grounds, to be
morally innocent. Accordingly, the use of animals in science
has been presumed by most Catholics to be as legitimate as
the projects they serve. Moral objections by Catholics to painful experimentation with animals have primarily concerned
not the welfare of the animals but of the human beings who
might, through abusing them, contract habits of cruelty that
infect human social behavior. Although a current of tradition
best exemplified in Franciscanism fosters a religious esteem
for animals by way of honoring the Creator in his creatures,
that current remains outside the mainstream of Catholic attitudes. Straightforward claims that animals have moral rights
or constitute direct moral objects are hardly to be found
among Catholic statements that are not consciously revision-
ist. Yet, revisionism exists among Catholics, usually unor-
ganized and often sentimental, but more and more, I think,
reflectively conscientious. Given enlarging ecumenical experience, expanding sympathy with liberal ideologies, and increasing education in undogmatic ethical inquiry, I anticipate

that Catholics' opinions about the treatment of animals, in science and elsewhere, will be progressively less distinguishable from those of their neighbors.

Notes

1. Pierre Daninos, *Le secret du Major Thompson* (Paris, Hachette, 1956), p. 99.

2. Thomas Aquinas, *Summa Theologiae*, IIaIIae, xxv, 3. Hereafter referred to as Aquinas, *Summa*.

3. Aquinas, *Summa*, IIaIIae, xxv, 3.

4. Aquinas, *Summa*, IIaIIae, xxv, 3.

5. Aquinas, *Summa*, IIaIIae, xxv, 3.

6. Anthony Mockler, *Francis of Assisi: The Wandering Years* (Oxford, Phaidon, 1976), p. 254.

7. Thomas More, *Utopia* (New York, Norton, 1975), p. 81. Hereafter referred to as More, *Utopia*.

8. Aquinas, *Summa*, IaIIae, cii, 6.

9. Henry S. Salt, *Animals' Rights Considered in Relation to Social Progress* (Clark Summit, Pa., Society for Animal Rights, 1980), pp. 72–73.

10. More, *Utopia*, p. 58.

11. More, *Utopia*, p. 59.

12. William Shakespeare, *Cymbeline*, Act I, Scene 5.

13. William Shakespeare, *As You Like It*, Act II, Scene 1.

14. More, *Utopia*, p. 81.

15. John Wesley, "The General Deliverance," in *Wesley's Works*, vol. VI (Grand Rapids, Mich., Baker Book House, 1978), pp. 241–252.

16. Kurt Rathe, "Animale," in *Enciclopedia Cattolica*, vol. I (Florence, Sansoni, 1948), col. 1344.

17. For recent discussions of this trend, see John Connery, "Morality of Consequences," in Charles Curran and Richard McCormick (eds.), *Readings in Moral Theology, No. 1* (New York, Paulist, 1979),

and Edward V. Vacek, "Proportionalism: One View of the Debate," *Theological Studies*, 46 (1985), pp. 287–314.

18. R. G. Frey, *Interests and Rights: The Case Against Animals* (Oxford, Clarendon, 1980). Hereafter referred to as Frey, *Interests and Rights*.

19. Frey, *Interests and Rights*, p. 161.

20. Frey, *Interests and Rights*, p. 161. The reference is to Peter Geach, *Providence and Evil* (Cambridge, Cambridge University Press, 1977).

21. Frey, *Interests and Rights*, p. 161.

22. William Shakespeare, *The Merchant of Venice*, Act III, Scene 1.

6 Animal Experimentation: The Muslim Viewpoint

Al-Hafiz B. A. Masri

The question of the use of animals in science cannot be studied in isolation. To appreciate its full implications, it must be addressed against the backdrop of the similarities and differences that exist between humans and the rest of the animated world. How we understand these similarities and differences—indeed, how we answer the question at hand—is greatly influenced by our response to two more fundamental questions:

(i) Can man's claim to being the apex of value in the world be justified?

(ii) If a distinctively religious justification of this claim is offered, what are its moral implications for how humans may treat other forms of life, animals in particular?

For the Islamic approach to these questions, we have three sources of guidance. The original source is the Quran, the holy book revealed to the prophet Muhammad during a period of 22 years, from 610 to 632 C.E. The second source is Hadith or "tradition" in English, an instructional corollary to the Quran based on the sayings and deeds of the Prophet. Hadith is considered in Islamic jurisprudence as an explanatory appendix to the Quranic law. In case these two sources do not lay down a clear-cut statute in a particular case, the

Muslim jurists (*muftis*) refer to the legal assertions based on
precedent, precedents set mainly during the period of the
first four caliphs (from 632 to 656 C.E.). Only in that comparatively rare case when there is no precedent does the mufti
issue a new judicial decree, and even here it must be consonant with the time-honored customary law that is based on
general Muslim practices. To approach the distinctively Islamic answer to the questions before us thus requires that we
refer to each of the authoritative sources mentioned—to the
Quran, to Hadith, and to customary law. The main tenets of
this last source will be summarized further on. To begin with,
we will confine our attention to the teachings of the Quran and
Hadith.

1. Animal Psyches and Communities

The Quran and Hadith instruct us that all species of
animals are "communities" like the human community. In
other words, they are communities in their own right and not
merely in relation to humankind or its values. The exact words
of the Quran are

> There is not an animal on earth
> Nor a bird that flies on its wings,
> But they are communities like you.
> (ch. 6 v. 38.)

According to the learned commentators of the Quran, the
word communities is used here in the sense of genera and animals and birds for all kinds of vertebrates, quadrupeds, mammals, birdlike mammals such as bats, crustaceans, reptiles,
worms, and insects. They all live a life, individual and social,
like the members of the human society.

To define what it means by the "communities of animals,"
the Quran says:

> Allah has created every animal from water:
> Of them there are some that creep on their bellies:

> Some that walk on two legs:
> And some that walk on four.
>
> (ch. 24 v. 45.)

The first category includes all kinds of worms, reptiles, centipedes, insects, and all such creatures. The second category includes birds and human beings; and the third category covers all kinds of mammals. The significant point to note is that, physically, humans have been put in the same bracket as all other creatures.

The following Hadith leaves no ambiguity about the sense in which the Quran uses the word "communities":

> Abu Huraira reported the Prophet Muhammad as telling of an incident that happened to a prophet in the past. This prophet was stung by an ant and, in anger, he ordered the whole of the nest of ants to be burned. At this God reprimanded this prophet in these words: "Because one ant stung you, you have burned a whole community which glorified Me." [1]

One of the reasons why the human and all other species have been classified together throughout the Quran is that even animals possess a psyche. Although their psychic force is of a lower level than that of human beings, there is ample evidence in the Quran to suggest that animals' consciousness is of a higher degree than mere instinct and intuition.

We are told in the Quran that animals have a cognizance of their Creator, and hence they pay their obeisance to him by adoration and worship. Out of the many verses of the Quran on this proposition, a few must suffice here:

> Seest thou not that it is Allah Whose praises are
>   celebrated
> By all beings in the heavens and on earth,
> And by the birds with extended wings?
> Each one knows its own [mode of] prayer and psalm.
> And Allah is aware of what they do.
>
> (ch. 24 v. 41.)

The statement that "Each one knows its own prayer and psalm" is worth noting. The execution of a voluntary act, performed knowingly and intentionally, requires a faculty higher than those of instinct and intuition.

In the event that some may doubt that animals could have such a faculty, the following verse points out that it is human ignorance, not animals, that prevent us from understanding their celebration of God.

> The seven heavens and the earth and all things
>   therein, Declare His glory,
> There is not a thing but celebrates His praise;
> And yet ye mankind! ye understand not
> How do they declare His glory.
>
> (ch. 17 v. 44.)

The following verse tells us how all the elements of nature and all the animal kingdom function in harmony with God's laws; only some humans disobey and so bring affliction on themselves. The Quran dwells on this subject repeatedly to emphasize the point that humans should bring themselves into harmony with nature, as the rest of creation does:

> Seest thou not that unto Allah payeth adoration
> All things that are in the heavens and on earth;
> The sun, the moon, the stars, the hills, the trees, the
>   animals;
> And a large number among mankind?
> But there are many [humans] who do not,
> And deserve chastisement.
>
> (ch. 22 v. 18.)

It is understood that the inanimate elements of nature perform the act of worshipping God without verbal communication by functioning in conformity with the divine ordinances known as the laws of nature.

In the case of animals, however, the Quran teaches that God actually communicates with them, as the following verse shows:

> And your Lord revealed to the bee, saying:
> Make hives in the mountains,
> And in the trees,
> And in [human] habitations.

(ch. 16 v. 68.)

It is anybody's guess what form God's communication with animals takes. We know only that the Quran uses the same Arabic word *Wahi* for God's revelations to all his prophets, including Prophet Muhammad, as well as to the bee. It is obvious that the connotation of God's revelations to his messengers would be different from that of his revelations to animals. But this is too complex a theological subject that cannot be dealt with here. Nevertheless, it proves the basic fact that animals have enough psychic endowment to understand and follow God's messages—a faculty higher than instinct and intuition.

Animals are not inferior to us because they have a different vocal apparatus; nor does the fact that they cannot make articulate speech, like we can, mean that they are "contemptible dumb animals." Science has proved now that they communicate not only with each other but also with humans, at least enough to express their social interests and biological needs. Those of us who enjoy the privilege of a loving and caring relationship with our pets will bear witness to this fact.

With the aid of modern technology, naturalists have made some progress in deciphering bird and animal languages. But, according to the Quranic evidence, humans had acquired this lore as early as the time of King Solomon, son of Prophet David. Perhaps in those times human civilization was nearer to nature than it is today. The Quranic verse runs like this: "And Solomon was David's heir, and he said: / 'O ye people! we have been taught the speech of birds.'" (ch. 27 v. 16.)

2. Man's Place in the Order of Species

Man's superiority over other species does not lie in his physique. As a matter of fact, physically, man is inferior to ani-

mals in many respects. The babbler birds of the Nagib desert
could teach us a lesson or two in family bonds when the elder
brothers and sisters take charge of the fledglings in the arbors;
or we could learn much from the acrobatics of monkeys. What
chance has a human ballerina against the poise and grace of a
flying squirrel's aerial dance?

Imam Ali bin Abi Talib has this to say about animals' ex-
emplary way of life, which is worthy of imitation by humans:
"Be like a bee; anything he eats is clean, anything he drops is
sweet and any branch he sits upon does not break."[2]

The real criterion of man's superiority in Islamic thought
lies in his spiritual volition, called *Taquwah* in the Quran. This
spiritual power bestows on humans a greater measure of balance between their conscious and unconscious minds, thus enabling them to make the best use of their freedom. They are
considered the best of God's creation only because of this difference. Without the proper exercise of this power, our superiority would be groundless.

There are quite a few men and women with beautiful and
strong bodies walking about on this earth who, because of
their lack of willpower, have absolutely no claim of superiority
over animals. The Quran describes such people as originally
"created in the best make" but, because of their lack of discipline, they are "rendered as the lowest of the low" (ch. 95
vv. 4, 5):

> Those who incurred the curse of Allah and His wrath,
> Those some of whom He debased into apes and
>   swine. . . .
>
> (ch. 5 v. 63.)
>
> They are like cattle,—nay, more misguided; for they
>   are heedless
> [of warning.]
>
> (ch. 7 v. 179.)

Man has been endowed with the ability to differentiate
between evil and virtue and to exercise his freedom of choice.

In the words of Hazlitt: "Man is the only animal that is struck with the difference between what things are, and what they ought to be." Animals do not possess this freedom of choice. That is why the Quran characterizes those humans who fall short of this endowment as the "lowest of the low." The following verse emphasizes the point:

> And be not like those who said: "we hear"
> While they did not pay attention;
> The vilest of beasts, in the sight of Allah,
> Are the deaf and the dumb—
> Those who do not comprehend.
>
> (ch. 8 vv. 21, 22.)

The Imam Ali says about such people: "The worldly-minded people are like barking dogs and wild beasts, some of them roar on others, the strong ones eat the weak and the big ones hurt the small."[3] And again, writing of those who misuse their freedom, he says: "A savage and ferocious beast is better than a wicked and tyrant ruler."[4]

Islamic teaching concerning the inter-relation and inter-dependence between human beings and the rest of the animated world is very explicit, consisting of an elaborate code of laws (Shariah). These begin with the dictum that man has been designated the authority as the vicegerent of God on earth. The Quran mentions this repeatedly, but the following verse provides a good example: "He [God] it is who made you vicegerents on earth; / So he who disavows, will bear its consequences." (ch. 35 v. 39.)

While elaborating the responsibilities of this office, the Quran lays great emphasis on the development of godly attributes in man. Compassion, love, mercy, justice, charity—these are among the divine attributes that, as his vicegerent, we are enjoined to acquire as we work to establish his kingdom on earth in harmony with his laws of nature. This kingdom of God is not meant to be only a human domain. God's mercy encompasses all creation, including the animal kingdom. Called to administer justice and grace over the whole of his kingdom, man cannot succeed if he fails to nurture in himself the attributes embodied infinitely in God.

Contrary to certain scientific theories, Islam believes that the divine design of animated nature includes some unalterable factors, providentially created and preserved in the origin of species, to keep species distinct from one another. Territorial, climatic, and other such evolutionary or devolutionary processes may change the ethological characteristics or anatomical structures of these species. In their struggle for existence, animals may learn how to camouflage themselves to distract attention or to deceive by impersonation or manipulation of their environment. However, no species can transgress beyond the distinct orbit that is ordained for it by the divine law, commonly known as predestination or fate. Within the biological world, some things are unalterable.

The religious concept of predestination or fate has played a significant role in determining the Islamic code of human behavior toward animals. According to the Vedic philosophy, all suffering is meted out by Nemesis, the goddess of retribution, for one's misdeeds in the previous existence, and there is nothing one can do to stop the wheel of any creature's fateful Karma. Unfortunately, some of the believers in all the major religions, including Islam, have failed to understand the real import of the theory of predestination taught by all the religions in their respective ways. This lack of understanding has been one of the causes of human indifference toward animal suffering.

According to Islam, the literal interpretation of the theory of predestination is "pre-fixing the fate of some one or some thing" in the sense of determining the capacity, capability, endowment, function, and other faculties. The Quran uses the Arabic word *Taqdir* meaning fate for the fixed orbits of the planetary motions as well as for the inorganic substances and for animated creatures, including human beings. Within those pre-fixed limitations, however, conditions could be changed for the better—for example, suffering could be avoided or lessened by human effort and skill.

A true conception of the Islamic maxim "there is an antidote for every ailment" could become an antidote for the
prevalent apathy and fatalistic resignation not only to the evil
plight of animals but also to much of human suffering.

3. The Teachings of Islam on Animal Welfare

Thus far we have discussed the relative status and importance of animals in nature, their psychic faculties, and
their communicative capacities. We have also elucidated some
of the causes of man's malevolence toward animals and his indifference to their welfare.

The teachings of Islam offer a good deal of guidance for
animal welfare. All the sources of Islamic instruction, especially the Quran, place great emphasis on nature study as a
prelude to a better understanding of life as one homogeneous
organism. The Quran is full of verses exhorting humans to
study nature—the planetary systems, the terrestrial elements,
the fauna and flora on our earth. The real purport of this repeated appeal in the Quran is to give credence to the existence
of the Godhead as the primal originator of the universe. But
the point that concerns us here is that the animal kingdom has
a very prominent place in these citations. There are so many
verses in the Quran on this theme that it is not feasible to
quote them in this paper. The overall approach is to accentu-
ate the importance and utility of all life on earth.[5]

Preservation of Species

Wherever the Quran speaks of creation, it speaks of
creation in pairs. According to the Quran, not only the humans and the fauna but also every kind of flora has been created in male and female sexes. Today we know, on scientific
grounds, that all plants, like animals, possess generative organs. The Quran could not have been more pellucid in expression on this subject more than 14 centuries ago. The following
verses emphasize the salient point that each species has been

conditioned biologically to procreate in order to perpetuate its
kind and, thus, to go on playing its role in the created order:

> [God is] the Originator of the heavens and the earth;
> He has created mates for you from among yourselves,
> And mates of the cattle too,
> Multiplying you thereby.
>
> (ch. 42 v. 11.)

> Glory be to Him Who created all the pairs,
> Of that which the earth grows,
> And of themselves [human beings],
> And of that which they do not know.
>
> (ch. 36 v. 36.)

> [My Lord is He] Who spread out for you
> The earth like a carpet;
> And made for you therein paths;
> And sent down water from the cloud.
> Then thereby We have produced
> Diverse pairs of plants—
> Each distinct from the other.
>
> (ch. 20 v. 53.)

> And We cause florae of every kind
> To grow as spouses.
>
> (ch. 31 v. 10.)

> And it is He who spread out the earth . . .
> And of all fruit He produced therein,
> As spouses of two and two.
>
> (ch. 13 v. 3.)

The story of Noah's ark is well known. The Quran tells it
in chapter 11, verses 36 to 48:

> When the deluge came and the flooding of the whole
> area was imminent, there was the danger that some of
> the species of animals or birds might be exterminated.
> At such a time God's main concern was to save at least

one pair of each species, along with the faithful followers of Noah; and He gave Noah the following instructions:

"Load in the Ark two of all species—
One male and one female of each pair."
(ch. 11 v. 40.)

These observations of the Quran lay down two basic principles: first, that the preservation of species is of paramount importance; second, that the divine scheme of regeneration works through the opposite but complementary forces of Nature not only in animals and plants but also in the inorganic matter. Modern science has discovered that the whole order of nature is functioning according to the law of parity. The Quran refers to this law in the preceding verses.

Animals' Fair Share in Food

In the Islamic view, animals are tenants in common with humans. Let us see now why some humans do not act according to the terms of this partnership.

Man has always been in competition with animals for food, and the problem has been aggravated in the modern world, especially because of human overpopulation.

The Quran tried to allay this fear of man by reassuring him that God is not only the creator but also the nourisher of all that he creates. For human beings, however, the Quran lays down the condition that they will have to work for their sustenance and that their emolument will be proportionate to their labor. The following verse serves as the maxim for this principle:

And that man shall have nothing
But what he strives for.
(ch. 53 v. 39.)

In the next verse, this stipulation is repeated in the words "those who seek," with the additional proviso that God provides according to the needs of the people:

> And [God] bestowed blessings on the earth,
> And measured therein sustenance in due
>   proportion . . . ,
> In accordance [with the needs of] those who seek.
>
> (ch. 41 v. 10.)

The conditions laid down in these two verses for human beings to work for the necessities of life seem to be conveniently ignored by some people. Some of us tend to rely solely on God's beneficence and to just lie down on our backs with our mouths open and wait for the manna from heaven to fall. Others have invented dubious ways and means to get more than their share by as little work as possible. Some of those who do work muscle in and poach on others' preserves.

As for animals, the Quran repeatedly emphasizes the fact that food and other resources of nature are there to be shared equitably with other creatures. Below are just a few of many such verses:

> Then let man look at his food:
> How we pour water in showers,
> Then turn up the earth into furrow-slices,
> And cause cereals to grow therein—
> And grapes and green fodder,
> And olive-trees and palm-trees,
> And luxuriant orchards,
> And fruits and grasses.

Let us stop at this point of the quotation and ask ourselves the question: For what and for whom has this sumptuous meal been laid out? The last line of the verse tells us that all these bounties of nature are as "provision for you as well as for your cattle." (ch. 80 vv. 24–32.)

Again, in the following verse, the bounties of nature are enumerated, with the accent on animals' share in all of them:

> And He [God] it is Who sends the winds
> As glad tidings heralding His mercy;
> And We send down pure water from the clouds,

> That We may give life thereby,
> By watering the parched earth,
> And slake the thirst of those We have created—
> Both the animals and the human beings
> In multitude.
>
> (ch. 25 vv. 48, 49.)

And what is the reason for creating everything, *viz.*, the cosmos as an ordered whole, the dark nights and the bright days, the earth with its immense expanse, shooting forth its moisture and its pastures, and the stable mountains—all this has been created for whom and why? The Quranic answer, again, is "as a provision for you and your cattle." (ch. 28 v. 33.)

> And do they not see?
> That We meander water to a barren land,
> And sprout forth from its crops—
> Whereof their cattle as well as they themselves eat;
> Will they take no notice of it?
>
> (ch. 32 v. 27.)

One could obtain the impression from these verses that they refer only to livestock in whose welfare we have a vested interest. But the message of the Quran, in this context, comprehends the entire animal kingdom, as is made clear in the following verses:

> There is no moving creature on earth,
> But Allah provides for its sustenance.
>
> (ch. 11 v. 6.)

In the words of Moses, as recorded in the Quran:

> Surely the earth belongs to Allah;
> He bequeaths it to whosoever He pleases
> Of His servants.
>
> (ch. 7 v. 128.)

> And the earth!
> He has assigned to (all) living creatures.
>
> (ch. 55 v. 10.)

The Quran has recounted the history of some past nations to show how they fell into error and perished. We come across a pertinent incident that is relevant to our discussion here. The tribe of Samood were the descendants of Noah. Their name is also mentioned in the Ptolemaic records of Alexander's astronomer of the second century. The people of Samood demanded that the Prophet Saleh show them some sign to prove that he was a prophet of God. At that time the tribe was experiencing a dearth of food and water and was, therefore, neglecting its livestock. It was revealed to the Prophet Saleh to single out a she-camel as a symbol and ask his people to give her her fair share of water and fodder. The people of Samood promised to do that, but later killed the camel. As a retribution, the tribe was annihilated (ch. 11 v. 64; ch. 26 vv. 155, 156; ch. 54 vv. 27–31).

This historic incident sets forth the essence of the Quran's teaching on "animal rights." Cruelty to animals is so offensive to God that it is declared as a serious sin, as quoted in two Ahadith in the conclusion of this paper. Cruelty to animals does not end there. It generates sadistic characteristics leading to acts of cruelty against fellow human beings. The last Hadith quoted in this paper elucidates this psychological weakness of human nature.

4. Islamic Laws

Islam's concern for animals goes beyond the prevention of cruelty to them which, logically, is a negative proposition. On the positive side, Islam enjoins us to take responsibility for the welfare of all creatures. In the spirit of the positive philosophy of life, we are to be their active protectors. Even in the case of cruelty, prevention of physical cruelty to animals is not enough; mental cruelty is equally condemned. In the following Hadith, a bird's emotional distress, for example, is called an injury:

> We were on a journey with the apostle of God, who left us for a short space. We saw a hummara [a bird] with its two young, and took the young birds. The hummara

hovered with fluttering wings, and the prophet re-
turned, saying, "Who has injured this bird by taking its
young? Return them to her."[6]

Islam, like most other religions, has laid down a code of
law governing the use of animals for the necessities of our life.
The second source of guidance, mentioned earlier, comprises
specific instructions regarding the treatment of domestic animals, beasts of burden, pets, and other such animals who have
become a part of human society.

The spirit and letter of these laws strongly deprecate all
direct or indirect acts of cruelty to animals, such as:

(i) Subjecting animals to pain, both physical and, as we
have just seen, mental, or killing them for sport, such
as in blood sports and fishing, except for food.
(ii) Killing them for luxuries (for their fur or tusks, for example) or for other inessential by-products, such as
cosmetics.
(iii) Depriving free-born animals and birds of their natural life by enclosing them in zoos, cages, and aquar-
iums, except when this is necessary for their safety
and preservation.
(iv) Breeding animals and birds in confined and unhy-
gienic conditions, an increasingly common practice in
modern farming.
(v) Using snares, leghold traps, and other contraptions
that maim and cause lingering death.
(vi) Finally, using animals in painful, disfiguring, or ter-
minal research or studies in science.

We will discuss this last category more fully below. First, however, a few words about the Islamic traditions and teachings on
animal slaughter and cruelty.

Traditional Slaughter

The Islamic traditional method of slaughter, like that of
Judaism, dispenses with preslaughter stunning. Western ani-

mal welfare workers are at a loss to understand why, in spite of
all the Islamic concern we have seen in the foregoing pages for
animal well-being, the Muslims are adamant in rejecting the
use of preslaughter stunners. Even the apparently convincing
sayings of Prophet Muhammad, as quoted below, are not helpful in resolving the issue:

> Shaddad bin Aus reported God's Messenger as saying:
> "God Who is Blessed and Exalted has declared that
> everything should be done in a good way; so when you
> kill, use a good method, and when you cut an animal's
> throat, you should use a good method; for each of you
> should sharpen his knife and give the animal as little
> pain as possible."[7]

Even a cursory discussion of this subject is beyond the
scope of this paper, especially if the perennial controversy between the vegetarian and the nonvegetarian disciplines is included. In the absence of any central religious authority
within the Islamic community of nations, such as the caliph-
ate, each country's accredited jurists (muftis) decide whether
or not a particular thought or action conforms to the ecclesiastical tenets of the Islamic law (Shariah). The jurispruden-
tial procedure involved in this approach has been explained
earlier. The recent scientific and technological demands for
modulation in our respective conventions are putting pressure
on all religions. Less than half a century ago, no one had even
heard of the stunners and no mufti had ever thought of slaughtering animals by stunning them prior to the use of a sharp
knife. Today, mainly because of intercontinental emigration
and the interlacing of cultures, such problems have become
conspicuous and must be addressed.

The only way to solve the controversial problem of the
use of stunners is to go to each of the major Islamic countries
and demonstrate to the accredited muftis that the use of stunners meets the laws of the Islamic Shariah. If and only if they
are convinced, they will give their written approval of the use
of stunners. Such a jointly issued decree or *fatwah* will go a

very long way in convincing the Muslim population once and for all. The occasionally published opinions of individual Muslim theologians or the *Ulama'a* are not enough to resolve the issue one way or the other. Such opinions become more misleading when they are expressed by people who pose as Muslims when they are not. Many such opinions circulating in the West have been issued by members of a splinter group called *Ahmadics* but generally known as *Mirzaics*. They are a separate cult and have unanimously been declared non-Muslim by the Muslim world.

Animal sacrifice is another issue that is not easy for Westerners to understand or condone. This subject, too, although very relevant to the theme of this book, is beyond the scope of this paper. However, it seems appropriate to explain briefly why and with what provisos this pre-Islamic practice was incorporated in Islam.

From the beginning of the recorded history of religion, man has been offering animal sacrifices at the altars of Deilics. During the early stages of man's spiritual development, it was not uncommon to make human sacrifices. According to the Quranic records, it was through the Prophet Abraham that humans were replaced by animals when Abraham was commanded by God to replace a ram for his son as a sacrifice. The Prophet Moses continued with the sacrifice of animals.

Islam also carried on with this practice, but with a difference. It channeled the whole concept of animal sacrifice into an institution of charity. Instead of burning the meat of the sacrificed animal at the altar or letting it rot, Islam ordered it to be distributed either wholly or partly among the poor. Since then Muslims from all over the world sacrifice animals and distribute the meat among the poor in their neighborhoods. Especially during the Festival of Sacrifice (Idd al-Adha), which the Muslims celebrate annually in commemoration of Prophet Abraham's willingness to sacrifice his son, every Muslim who can afford it is required to offer this animal sacrifice and distribute the meat among the poor, keeping a portion for his own consumption.

Every Muslim is aware of the fact that the sacrifice would lose its intrinsic merit if the meat were allowed to go to waste and did not reach the poor. In chapter 22, verses 28 and 36, the Quran states this proviso very clearly.

It is very unfortunate that much of the meat of animals sacrificed during the festival of Mecca goes to waste. The pilgrims who offer this sacrifice know that this waste nullifies its merit and reduces their offering to a mere ritual, but they seek consolation in the belief that the moral responsibility lies with the government authorities. Many Muslim theologians have drawn the attention of the Meccan authorities to this breach of the spirit of Islamic law. It is to be hoped that some day something will be done about it.[8]

Another relevant point to understand in this respect is that the age-old concepts of atonement for sins or peace-offerings to God by way of animal sacrifices were discredited by Islam. According to verse 37, chapter 22:

> It is not their meat, nor their blood,
> That reaches Allah;
> It is your piety that reaches Him.

Cruelty

Many practices in the West, because they involve cruelty to animals, are not only against the spirit of Islam but also against the teachings of all religions. Factory farming is an example. Perhaps the most distressing aspect of this development is that the so-called underdeveloped and developing countries of the world have begun to emulate their Western models. Better and quicker profits, plus the feeling that "civilized" Western society has given its tacit approval to the intensive rearing of farm animals, are eroding the gentler and more humane methods once the rule in these countries. The same is true in the case of other cruel practices now current in the West. Cruelty to animals seems to export well.

Islam has a number of things to say about the general

treatment of animals. Iman Ali has laid down the following maxim in simple words: "Be kind to pack animals; do not hurt them; and do not load them more than their ability to bear."[9]

The late Maulana Maududi was an internationally honored Muslim theologian of this century and the founder of a movement called *Jama'at-i-Islami*. His views are very pertinent to our subject:

> God has honored man with authority over His countless creatures. . . . This superior position . . . does not mean that God has given him unbridled liberty.
>
> Islam says that all the creation has certain rights upon man. They are: he should not waste them on pointless ventures nor should he unnecessarily hurt or harm them.
>
> We have been forbidden to kill them merely for fun or sport.
>
> Killing an animal by causing continuous pain and injury is considered abominable in Islam.
>
> . . . It does not allow their killing (even of dangerous and venomous animals) by resort to prolonged painful methods.
>
> To catch birds and imprison them in cages without any special purpose is considered abominable.[10]

Maulana Maududi's advice about beasts of burden is the same as that of Imam Ali, quoted above.

In spite of modern mechanization, animals are still very much in use in farming and transport, especially in the rural areas of the East. Their use, and sometimes their misuse, often entails great labor and hardship for them.

Islam's directives in this respect are very specific, as the few Ahadith we will cite show: "The Prophet once passed by a camel whose belly clave to its back. 'Fear God,' said he, 'in these dumb animals, and ride when they are fit to be ridden, and let them go free when it is meet they should rest.'"[11]

The following Hadith lays down the principle that animals should be used only for the purpose for which they are meant and only for the necessities of life: "Abu Huraira reports that the prophet said: 'Do not use the backs of your beasts as pulpits, for God has made them subject to you in order that they may bring you to a town you could not otherwise reach without fatigue of body.'" [12]

Daily prayer is one of the five pillars of the Islamic faith. The following Hadith shows that even this very important obligation used to be deferred by the Prophet and his companions in favor of the comfort of animals: "Anas says: 'When we stopped at a halt, we did not say our prayers until we had unburdened the camels.'" [13]

5. Experiments on Animals

During the pre-Islamic period, certain pagan superstitions and polytheistic practices involving acts of cruelty to animals used to be in vogue in Arabia. All such practices were condemned and stopped by Islam. The following few verses of the Quran and a few Ahadith deal with this theme:

> It was not Allah Who instituted [the heretical
>   practices such as] a
> slit-ear she-camel,
> Or a she-camel let loose for free pasture
> Or camels let loose.

> (ch. 5 v. 106.)

This verse was cited in condemnation of the pagan superstition that the she-camels, ewes, and nanny goats who had brought forth five young ones, the last of which was a male, should have their ears slit. In the next verse, such practices were declared as Satanic aids in sharp words:

> Allah cursed him [Satan], but he [Satan] said:
> "I will get hold of some of your men,
> And I will lead them [human beings] astray
> And I will excite in them vain desires;

And I will incite them to cut off the ears of cattle;
And most certainly I will bid them to alter the Nature
Created by Allah."

(ch. 4 vv. 118, 119.)

When the Prophet came to Medina, after his flight from Mecca in 622 C.E., the people there used to cut off camels' humps and the fat tails of sheep. The Prophet ordered this odious practice stopped and declared: "Whatever is cut off an animal, while it is alive, is carrion and must not be eaten."[14] These verses refer to cutting living animals for food or as an offering to idols or gods. But the Islamic prohibition against cutting live animals, especially when pain results, can be extended to vivisection in science. However, vivisection should not be confused with the dissection of a living animal, amputation of parts of its body, and other surgical operations that become imperative as medical treatment, even if they disfigure the animal. We are able to support this interpretation of Islamic teaching by referring to a number of representative traditions of the Prophet Muhammad. In them we find expressed the principle that any interference with the body of an animal that causes pain or disfigurement is contrary to Islamic precepts.

Jabir reported the Prophet as saying, when an ass which had been branded on its face passed him by; "God curse the one who branded it."

Jabir told that God's Messenger forbade striking the face and branding on the face [of animals].[15]

The Prophet forbade setting animals against one another.[16]

Abi Huraira narrates that the Holy Prophet said: "Do not store milk in [the dug or udders of] animals."[17] (Storing milk in the dug of animals was perhaps done to beguile a prospective buyer.)

One might also appeal to Islamic law to oppose using animals in military research in general and in the so-called wound labs in particular. The following Hadith would seem to support this position: "Abus Abbas reported the Prophet as saying:/ 'Do not set up any living creature as a target.'" [18] Though Islamic thought, as interpreted here, prohibits any and all painful or disfiguring use of animals in science, it does not prohibit all animal use in science. If anesthetic is used and the body of the animal is not disfigured, the scientist's use of the animal cannot be faulted on these grounds. However, to kill animals to satisfy the human thirst for inessentials—cosmetics or yet another "new" household cleaner or brake fluid, for example—is a contradiction in terms within the Islamic tradition. Think of the millions of animals killed in the name of commercial gain in order to supply a complacent public with trinkets and products they do not need. And why? Because we are too lazy or too self-indulgent to find substitutes. Or to do without. It will take more than religious, moral, or ethical sermons to quell the avidity and greed of some multinational corporations and their willing customers.

Some research on animals may still be justified, given the traditions of Islam. Basic and applied research in the biological and social sciences, for example, is allowed if laboratory animals are not caused pain or disfigured and if human beings or other animals benefit as a result of the research.

The basic and most important point to understand about using animals in science is that the same moral, ethical, and legal codes should apply to the treatment of animals as are applied to humans. According to Islam, all life is sacrosanct and has the right of protection and preservation. The Prophet Muhammad laid so much emphasis on this point that he declared: "There is no man who kills [even] a sparrow or anything beyond that, without its deserving it, but God will ask him about it." (Narrated by Ibni 'Umar-Ahmad, Nasai and Darimi.) [19]

Like all other laws of Islam, the Islamic laws on the treatment of animals have been left open to exceptions and are based on the criterion that "Actions shall be judged according to intention." [20] Any kind of medical treatment of animals or experiments on them become ethical and legal or unethical and illegal according to the intention of the people who perform them. If the life of an animal can be saved only by the amputation of a part of its body, it will be a meritorious act in the eyes of God to do so. Any code of law, including religious law, which is so rigid as not to leave any scope for exceptional circumstances, results in suffering and breeds hypocrisy.

According to all the religions of the world, all life, including animal life, is a trust from God. That is why, in the case of human life, suicide is considered the ultimate sin. Animals, however, do not possess the freedom of choice to willfully terminate their own lives. They have to go on living their natural lives. When a human being subjects an animal to unnecessary pain and suffering and thus cuts short its natural life, he actually commits a suicidal act on behalf of that animal, and a spiritual part of his own life dies with the animal.

Most of our problems and arguments about the use of animals in science as well as about their general treatment would be far easier to solve if only we could acknowledge the realism of nature and learn to treat all life on earth homogeneously, without prejudice and double standards.

Consider, for example, a high security prison where thieves, murderers, rapists, and other such criminals are imprisoned and compare it with a so-called research laboratory where innocent and helpless animals are cooped up in cages. By what stretch of imagination can we justify the difference in the living standards of these two places? What moral or ethical justification is there for the difference in their treatment? In the case of human prisoners you are not allowed even to prick a pin in their flesh, while the animal captives are allowed to be lacerated and hacked by surgical instruments in the name of science and research, most of which is for commercial purposes.

These and many other such disparities are being allowed by the so-called humane societies only because of the double standards of our moral, ethical, and religious values. The real and ideal approach to this problem would involve setting forth for ourselves the criterion that any kind of medical or scientific research that is unlawful to perform on humans is unlawful to perform on animals.

Conclusion

After all is said and done, one wonders why, in our so-called civilized society today, man's cruelty to animals is on the increase. Why is it that human attitudes toward animals are hard to change? The organized religious institutions could have played an important role in educating the people. Almost 90 percent of the world's population owes allegiance to one of the major religions. Each of these religions has the benefit of platforms whereupon captive audiences could be influenced and educated. But one never hears from their pulpits any sermons preaching the word of God about animals. The dictum "Love thy neighbor" embraces all neighbors, including animals. Perhaps the clerics of our religions are too busy preparing their respective laities for the life hereafter to spare any thought for the "poor dumb beasts."

Most of the sermons from our religious pulpits are admonitions against sin. If someone were inclined to choose a subject pertaining to animal welfare, there is enough material in every scripture to choose from. For example, there are two sayings of Prophet Muhammad that would make very appropriate themes for such sermons. In the following Hadith, the Prophet placed the unauthorized killing of animals as second on the list of the seven deadly sins: "Avoid ye the seven deadly things; Polytheism; the killing of breathing beings which God has forbidden except by right." [21]

In the following Hadith it has been placed as third in the list of four sins: "The grievous things are: Polytheism; disobedience to parents; the killing of breathing beings; . . ." [22]

One of the reasons why most of our religious, social, and cultural education in this respect is wasted when the effort to educate is made is that it is aimed at adults, whose character has already become unyielding and unresponsive to new attitudes and values. If only we could start education on animal welfare at a tender and more responsive age, perhaps the results could be better. An international movement of children such as "Friends of Animals," more or less along the lines of the Boy Scouts and Girl Guides, deserves serious consideration.

To end this paper, there could not be a better conclusion than the following aphoristic Hadith of the Holy Prophet Muhammad:

"Whoever is kind to the creatures of God, is kind to himself." [23]

Comments

(i)   A.C. = *Anno Christum*, i.e., the Christian era or year. Muslims prefer not to use A.D., which means *Anno Domini*, or "the year of our Lord." Muslims believe in Jesus Christ as a messenger of God and not as the son of God or as the Lord.

(ii)   A.H. = *Anno Hijrae*, i.e., the year of migration (622 A.C.), when the Holy Prophet Muhammad[S] had to flee from Mecca to Medina. This date has been established as the first year of the Islamic era.

(iii) (S) = It is considered highly meritorious and obligatory for a Muslim to pronounce a reverential *Salam* whenever the name of the Messenger of God is uttered or written. S stands for "peace be upon him."

(iv)   Muslim means one who submits to God. Believers in Islam prefer to be called Muslims and not Muhammadans or by any other name or spellings.

(v)   Many of the quotations cited within this chapter are incomplete, since the originals are too long to fully reproduce.

(vi)   In the Quranic references, the first number stands for chapter and the second for verse. In some English translations the verse numbers may be different. In this article the numbers quoted are from the translation by A. Yusuf Ali, (Lahore, Pakistan, Sh. Muhammad Ashraf, 1938). In case the reader's edition gives a different number, please look for the verse one or two verses above or below.

(vii) In the Hadith references, the name of the book is given.

(viii) The Quranic references are given in the text following the quotations. All other references and notes are in the following list.

Notes

1. Bukhari and Muslim.

2. *Maxims of Ali*, translated by A. Halal from the famous book *Nahj-ul-Balagha*, Elmi (Lahore, Pakistan, Sh. Muhammad Ashraf, 1963), p. 436. Hereafter referred to as *Maxims*. The Imam, Hazrat Ali bin Abi Talib, was the son-in-law of the Holy Prophet Muhammad[S] and the fourth successor (*caliph*) (644–656 A.C.—22–34 A.H.).

3. *Maxims*, p. 203.

4. *Maxims*, p. 381.

5. For further study of this theme, the following verses of the Quran are recommended: 7:73; 16:5–8 and 66; 25:48–50; 26:155, 156; 31:10; 32:27; 35:28; 40:79, 80; 42:29; 45:3, 4; 55:10; 79:27–33; 81:1–18; and 88:17.

6. Muslim. Alfred Guillaume, *The Traditions of Islam* (Beirut, Lebanon, Khayats Oriental Reprinters, 1966), p. 106. Hereafter referred to as Guillaume, *Traditions*.

7. Narrated by Shaddad bin Aus. Muslim, vol. 2, ch. 11, section on "Slaying," 10:739, verse 151. Also "Mishkat al-Masabih," p. 872. English translation by James Robson, in four volumes (Lahore, Pakistan, Sh. Muhammad Ashraf, 1963). Hereafter referred to as Robson.

8. I have been informed that the Government of Saudi Arabia has recently made some arrangements to freeze the meat of the sacrificed animals during the festival of Hajj in order to distribute it among the poor. Unfortunately, I have not been able to get detailed and authentic information of this development.

9. *Maxims*, p. 436.

10. Sayyid Abu a'la Maududi, *Towards Understanding Islam*, English translation by Dr. Khurshid Ahmad (a Muslim of renown in Western literary and religious circles), (Lahore, Pakistan, Islamic Publications Ltd., 1967), pp. 174–176.

11. Narrated by Abu Huraira. Guillaume, *Traditions*, pp. 106, 107.

12. Guillaume, *Traditions*, pp. 106, 107.

13. Guillaume, *Traditions*, pp. 106, 107.

14. Narrated by Abu Waqid al-Laithi. Tirmidhi and Abu Dawud. Robson, p. 874.

15. Muslim, vol. 1, ch. 3, section 9:265 on "Duty Towards Animals." Also Yusuf al-Kardawi, *The Lawful and Unlawful in Islam* (in Arabic), (Cairo, Mektebe Vahba, 1977), p. 293 and Robson, p. 872.

16. Narrated by Ibn Abbas. Tirmidhi and Abu Dawud. Also Robson, p. 876.

17. Bukhari and Muslim. Also Muhammad Manzur Ilahi, *Holy Traditions*, vol. 1 (Lahore, Pakistan, Ripon Printing Press, 1932), p. 149.

18. Narrated by Abu Abbas. Muslim. Also Robson, p. 872.

19. Narrated by Ibni 'Umar. Musnad of Ahmad. Also narrated by 'Abdallah bin 'Amar bin al-'As, Robson, p. 874.

20. The Arabic version: *"Al-'Amālo bil-niyyah."*

21. Narrated by Abu Huraira. Bukhari and Muslim.

22. Narrated by Abdallah bin 'Amru. Bukhari and Muslim.

23. Muhammad Amin, *Wisdom of Prophet Muhammad* (Lahore, Pakistan, Sh. Muhammad Ashraf, 1965), p. 200.

7 Hindu Perspectives on the Use of Animals in Science

Basant K. Lal

Questions about our use of animals in science are of comparatively recent origin. Therefore we will be disappointed if we expect to find definitive and pointed answers in Hinduism. It could not even have occurred to the Hindu seers when they were trying to formulate the Hindu doctrines that such questions would ever demand their attention. Therefore, the Hindu perspective on the use of animals in science must be extrapolated from the general tenor of Hindu thought. This paper intends to fulfill that task, and it proceeds under the conviction that it is possible to do so authentically. For the Hindu code offers a general perspective toward animals, enjoining us to develop a distinctively religious attitude toward them. It is on the basis of an analysis of this attitude, I hope to show, that the Hindu perspective on the use of animals in science can be determined.

There is, however, an important limitation under which the present deliberation must proceed. Hinduism is a very old religion, with a history extending for thousands of years. In the course of its evolutionary growth, a distinction has developed between what may be called doctrinal Hinduism and popular Hinduism. Doctrinal Hinduism, interpreted strictly, continues to be rigidly faithful to its venerated traditions and consequently maintains inflexible articles of faith. Popular Hinduism, on the other hand, has changed with the demands of changing times, and as such, at least in its practical outlook and conduct, is more liberal and less rigid. There are, then, two different perspectives on the use of animals in science that need to be worked out—the doctrinal and the popular perspectives. And, as we shall see below, even the doctrinal viewpoint may have to be further divided into the transcendental and the empirical.

1. The Hindu Attitude Toward Animals and *Mokṣa*

If we are to understand the Hindu attitude toward animals, one basic fact must be kept in mind: The Hindu recommendation to cultivate a particular kind of attitude toward animals is based *not* on considerations about the *animal* as such but on considerations about how the development of this attitude is a part of the purificatory steps that bring men to the path of *mokṣa* (salvation). The primary religious goal of the Hindu is *mokṣa*, and the fulfillment of every religious prescription, if it is valid, must aid in the realization of that goal. Consequently, in Hindu tradition such recommendations have only a this-wordly value and not an ultimate or transcendental value. They are like rungs on a ladder: each has value only in the sense that, by mounting them, the climber goes higher.

When, therefore, the Hindu talks of the sacrifice of animals or of cultivating an attitude of sacredness toward the cow, he believes that these steps will help him in disciplining himself. Even the talk of *ahiṃsā* (nonviolence) refers merely to a kind of virtue that must be cultivated if one is to be a sincere seeker of salvation. To embody these attitudes, however, is but one stage—a stage that is ultimately to be superceded as one ascends the ladder of self-purification and self-development. The importance of this point cannot be overemphasized. There are references to animal sacrifice in the Hindu ritual, but there are also recommendations to cultivate positive attitudes toward domestic animals. From the ultimate or transcendental point of view, however, neither the sacrifice nor the attitude has any value or disvalue in itself: From that point of view, like the rungs of a ladder, neither has any intrinsic significance.

2. Five Areas of Hindu Thought

The general Hindu attitude toward animals can be determined on the basis of an exploration of five areas of Hindu thought. These areas are not mutually exclusive, and none concerns animals to the exclusion of all else. However, each one addresses some of the ways leading to salvation and in the process, each is suggestive of ideas which, considered collectively, coalesce in the Hindu attitude toward animals. Let us try to summarize them briefly.

(i) The most obvious point we must consider is the Vedic reference to *animal sacrifice*. It is a fact that the Vedas place great emphasis on sacrificial ritual, and at times they recommend the sacrifice of animals such as goats, oxen, and horses. Indeed, even to this day animal sacrifice has not disappeared from Hindu practice. But—and this is the most interesting point about the Hindu sacrificial ritual—the sacrifice of an animal is *not really the killing of an animal*. The ritual does not proceed with the understanding or intention that an *animal* is going to be killed. The animal to be sacrificed is not considered an animal; it is, instead, a *symbol*, a symbol of those powers for which the sacrificial ritual stands. Even a casual look at the sacrificial rituals will establish this.

What is important for sacrificial ritual is not the object to be offered in sacrifice but following the elaborate rites and scrupulously observing the traditional rules.[1] The offerings can be *soma*, *ghee* (melted butters), *grain*, *animals*, or *even humans*. There are very elaborate rites regarding the choice of the place for sacrifice, such as preparation of the altar, chanting of the hymns, raising the fire, and so on. The most minor departure from the strict regulation of the ritual vitiates the sacrifice. That is why these rituals gave rise to rich and varied mythologies. The rituals were understood not only to affect the cosmos but also to cause the emergence of new gods. There are passages in the Vedas and other scriptures that suggest that the universe itself originated by sacrificing a cosmic animal (a horse or cow) or a cosmic *purusa* (man). In *Satpath Brāhmana*,[2] the sun, the sky, the wind, the dawn, the earth, and so forth are all said to come out of the sacrificial horse. Moreover, *animal sacrifice* is not a necessary feature of every sacrifice. In fact sacrifices are offered daily and also on special occasions; animal sacrifice is generally absent from the daily sacrificial ritual.

The logic behind this seems plain. The sacrificial rituals are believed to serve special purposes. As the importance of these purposes increases, the nature of the offerings also tends to assume greater importance. That is why on rare occasions, for specific purposes, even a human being is sacrificed. The entire ritual, therefore, proceeds under the conviction that it is not a "deliberate killing" because, unlike ordinary killing, here there is no motive or intention to *kill*. Whatever we are to make of these teachings, it should at least be clear that animal sacrifice, as sanctioned in Hinduism, does not justify killing or torturing animals outside a special ritualistic context.

(ii) The Hindu attitude toward animals can be further understood by appreciating its attitude toward pets. Hindu families commonly keep birds and other animals as pets. That may be a legacy of the primitive life, but what is significant is that Hindus generally treat these pets as members of their families, that it is considered a pious and religious duty to tend and feed these animals. In certain cases the observance of daily *dharmas* includes this activity, and the householder is asked to begin his own routine only after feeding these pets. It is difficult to find doctrinal justification for this kind of attitude toward pet animals, but it is noteworthy that it is expressed in the myths regarding gods and goddesses, in which almost every deity is said to have a symbolic pet bird or animal as company or even as conveyance. We are not in error if we regard these myths as showing that the Hindu naturally has a loving attitude toward some animals.

(iii) This general attitude of caring is dramatically heightened in the case of the cow. It is difficult to determine precisely when the cow came to be regarded as a specially sacred animal. But it is a fact that veneration of the cow is a very widespread and ancient feature of Hindu religious life. In fact, even in the *Atharva Veda*[3] there is a hymn that suggests that it is the cow that has been transformed in the visible universe and that both gods and mortals depend for life and being on the cow. In popular Hinduism the cow is regarded as the most sacred of all animals, and cow dung is considered so pure that it is used not only as fuel and disinfectant but also to wash floors, walls, and even places of worship. A man on his deathbed is supposed to have a smooth passage to the next form of existence if he holds the tail of a cow and makes a gift of it to the deserving Brahman. The killing of a cow is considered a sin,[4] and the sentiment attached to this is so strong that at times it leads to communal riots. Even now, in certain parts of India, one day is reserved for worshipping cows as deities. At times the sacredness of the cow passes over to the ox and the bull. This special feature of Hindu belief and practice clearly shows that the attitude of the Hindus toward animals can be one of extreme affinity rather than selfish hostility.

(iv) Hinduism, generally speaking, has come to accept the great merit of recognizing our affinity with nature and animals. It is interesting to note that the truths of Hinduism were apprehended, grasped, and formulated by seers who were invariably forest dwellers. The central truth of Hinduism is that emancipation lies in the realization of the ultimate truth of *unity*. Such a realization requires an extension of consciousness, which cannot take place if nature and other creatures are regarded as alien. What is recommended is *a life in nature*, lived with other creatures. That is why even great epics and other literary writings of the creative periods of the history of Hinduism are replete with descriptions of life in nature, usually in the forests. Hinduism thus enjoins us to experience our affinity with all aspects of existence. As we achieve this state of awareness, we cannot in any way be hostile or even indifferent to animals, since they are a very prominent part of nature, with which the knowledgeable seek to be united.

(v) There is still another feature of Hindu thought that has a direct bearing on the problem at hand. This is the emphasis on *ahiṃsā*, which has been present in almost every phase of the development of Hinduism. It is said that in Hinduism the emphasis on nonviolence is not as great as it is in Jainism and Buddhism. Scholars speculate and suggest that the later Hindu emphasis on nonviolence is a direct result of the influence of Jainism and Buddhism. It is true that nonviolence is not central to the teachings of the Vedas. It is also true that in other writings—even in the *Gita*—killing (even war) is justified under certain conditions. But there is an opposite side of the picture. If we survey the Hindu literature, we find that *ahiṃsā* has occupied a prominent place in most sacred writings. Even in the Vedas, *ahiṃsā*, in the sense of positive love, finds a mention. In the Upanishads there are various explicit references to the nonkilling of animals. The *Cāndogya Upanishad*[5] forbids killing animals except for the purposes of sacrifice. *Ahiṃsā* and *satya* are often referred to as cardinal virtues. Moreover, both in *Mahābhārata* and in *Dharmaśāstras*, *ahiṃsā* is one of the *yama*. The *purānas* at times speak of tortures that one would have to face in the future if one killed an animal in one's lifetime. Thus it appears that Hinduism exalts *ahiṃsā* as a virtue but permits "killing" in certain very special circumstances. The logic behind this apparently paradoxical attitude is very simple. *Ahiṃsā* has to be practiced not because there is a definite *dharma* toward other creatures but because it is a way to develop self-restraint and thus self-development. Every practice ultimately aims at salvation, and it is this aim that makes an act sacred. That is why even animal sacrifice sometimes is recommended. *Ahiṃsā* is both nonkilling and positive love. It is recommended because such an attitude is necessary for the progress of the soul. In certain cases where *him sā* (violence) is recommended, it, too, is recommended because it outweighs the spiritual effects that would otherwise result.

With the preceding as prologue, we are now in a position to make certain generalizations. First, Hindu doctrines recommend an attitude of affinity with and compassion for animals—this despite the fact, to be explained below, that they teach that animal life has a status inferior to that of human life. Second, this attitude of affinity is rooted not in considerations about the animal as such but in considerations about man's own salvation. As a third and final reminder, we can also assert that the ritual of animal sacrifice cannot be used as a plea or justification for harming animals outside recognizable religious rituals.

3. Duties Regarding Animals vs. Duties to Animals

From what has been said above, we can perhaps anticipate the importance, for Hindu thought, of the distinction between *duties regarding animals* and *duties to animals*. As we shall see, the Hindu accepts the former and rejects the latter. We need not enter fully into the intricacies of this distinction; commonsense illustrations will serve our purposes.

When we say that a mother has *duties to* her newly born child, we imply that the child has a right to receive certain things (for example, food and attention) from the mother. The mother's duties and the child's rights are opposite sides of the same coin. In contrast, when we speak of our having *duties regarding* certain things (for example, *duties regarding* the preservation of works of art), we do not imply that these things themselves have rights or that these duties are owed directly to them. Our duties regarding the preservation of works of art, for example, are duties we have, not to these works themselves, but to future generations of human beings; we owe it to our descendants to preserve for them what is best in our art and culture.

Hinduism in all its forms teaches that we have no duties to animals and thus implicitly denies that they have any rights. We have only duties regarding animals, given the Hindu perspective, which means that these duties are owed to someone other than the animals themselves. Who is this? The Hindu answer is that it is the agent himself. When, for example, we are enjoined to practice *ahiṃsā* toward animals, the basis of this prescription is the role the development of this attitude plays in the individual's search for salvation. Those animals who are the recipients of our positive expression of *ahiṃsā* are undeniably the better for it, but their benefits are not the basis of our duties. The basis is the necessity of developing this attitude in the course of man's religious quest for salvation.

At this point someone may object that Hindu teachings concerning reincarnation imply that we have duties to and not merely duties regarding animals. It is true, as is well known, that the Hindu mythology sometimes portrays rebirth in the form of animals, which does suggest that just as the mother has duties to the child and the child rights in relation to the mother, we have duties to animals and they have rights in relation to us. But Hindu mythology, it seems, avoids this implication. It is believed that human life is a privilege because it is intrinsically superior to other forms of life, including animal life. Thus, if a soul migrates to an animal form from a human life, it moves from a superior to an inferior form of life, and it does so because of its misdeeds while in the human form. Animal ensoulment, the fruits of bad *karma*, thus is spiritually regressive. This inferior life cannot demand duty from us. Our duties regarding animals are based on the demands of our spiritual quest in the human form, and this is true even if a dog or a cat, say, are the material homes of unfulfilled, reincarnated souls.

4. Three Uses of Animals

One preliminary point must be made before we can explore the Hindu positions on the use of animals in science. A distinction must be made between three kinds of uses. Let us call them the *medical use*, the *exploratory use*, and the *cosmetic use*. The medical use includes surgery and the various kinds of research (on cancer, birth defects, and the like) associated with the medical research establishment. The aims of these endeavors are to make society happier, healthier, and disease-free. The exploratory use refers to using animals in such fields as biology and physiology, where research is conducted with the aim of acquiring greater knowledge of the structure and function of the biological and physiological systems. These are called exploratory because their basic concern is acquisition of information and knowledge. The cosmetic use includes the use of animals in the manufacture and testing of articles of use, fashion, and luxury.

Our problem comes down to this: What has Hinduism to say about these three kinds of uses of animals in science? Though the ancient sacred works of Hinduism do not address the questions explicitly, we have been able to discern the general outlines of their teaching regarding our proper relationship to animals, and on this basis we can attempt to say how Hinduism will view these different uses of animals. These answers, however, must be worked out at two levels—the doctrinal and the popular. And even at the doctrinal level, as will be explained more fully below, a division will have to be drawn between the transcendental and the practical views. At the transcendental level the demands of Hindu doctrine are very strict, but at the practical level the doctrinal demands relax somewhat, giving some consideration to the demands of everyday life.

Doctrinal Hinduism

Doctrinal Hinduism, very strictly speaking, *does not permit any of the three uses of animals in science.* The reason is simple. All considerations concerning these uses of animals in science are rooted in man's condition of bondage—that is, our attachment to the material world—and therefore are sources of distraction from man's primary concern: the transcendence of this world. Our primary concern is *mokṣa* (salvation), and everything that stands in the way of its attainment is distracting at best and illusory at worst. Doctrinal Hinduism, interpreted strictly, teaches that the permanent solution of problems such as disease, death, and suffering lies in rising above these occurrences and in bringing about a basic attitudinal change toward them. The worldly solutions of the problems of disease and suffering (drugs, surgery, and the like) are not final solutions, according to the strict Hindu, because they do not aim at transcending this world and its suffering. To seek better medical cures and treatments so that human life will be "better" is itself symptomatic of a failure to understand what human life is. Doctrinal Hinduism, strictly interpreted, teaches that the attainment of final bliss and peace is possible if and only if one transcends *all* worldly considerations.

But that is the *pārmārthika drsti* (the transcendental point of view). The practical point of view of Hinduism, associated with a less strict interpretation of doctrine, recommends a self-controlled, virtuous, and happy life for the individual. Therefore, viewed from this side of the Hindu doctrine, the problem would receive a somewhat different solution. Viewed thus, the Hindu doctrine *does* permit medical uses of animals in science. But this sanction is not unconditional. The restraint and virtue Hinduism recommends limit the use of animals in the name of human happiness. *Medical uses are permitted if and only if* (1) *the benefits humans receive far outweigh the pain animals endure, and* (2) *the use of animals is necessary* (that is, the benefits are not otherwise obtainable).

Here an objection can be anticipated. Why should such experiments be done on animals and not on humans themselves, especially since human experiments would probably give more accurate information? This question seems particularly acute for Hinduism. One of the most well-known Hindu doctrines, propounded in the *Gītā*, is the injunction to perform good acts without any attachment to their fruits. To experiment on human beings for humanitarian reasons, especially if one were to volunteer oneself, would seem to be quite consistent with the dictates of the doctrine of nonattachment. Why, then, should the experiments be performed on animals rather than on people?

Hinduism's answer here is reminiscent of the answer

given to another difficult question in our earlier discussion of reincarnation. Our life, it is believed, is a privilege because it is superior to the lives of animals and plants. Life, in order to sustain itself, has to feed on life itself. But if a still higher religious life is to be led, this tendency to feed on life must be kept in check, and to the minimum, and then only the lowest forms of life may be killed. That is how the Hindu argues in favor of vegetarianism, even though eating vegetables and fruits also takes life away. In the same way it can be argued that if very beneficial results for humans can be achieved by performing experiments on lower forms of life (animals), then there is no reason to perform the same experiments on higher life forms. It is true that in this sense Hinduism is open to the charge of speciesism, but then it would not consider it a charge and would give its approval to medical uses of animals, provided, of course, the previously mentioned conditions are fully satisfied.

Even in its milder form, however, doctrinal Hinduism will not approve of the other two uses of animals in science. It will not approve exploratory uses because the knowledge gained would not appear to the Hindu to be significant or valuable. Hindu doctrines approve of only that kind of knowledge that has spiritual significance. Research in the exploratory realms is not of any use in man's spiritual quest, and, indeed, is a hindrance to this quest because it signifies attachment to the physical world. Moreover, in the case of exploratory uses, there is no direct balance of human good over the physical suffering of the animals. Likewise, doctrinal Hinduism, even in its more relaxed interpretation, positively opposes experiments on animals for cosmetic use. Because these uses are clearly rooted in physical vanity, they are a further weighty obstacle to the spiritual quest.

Popular Hinduism

Popular Hinduism, however, responds differently to the questions before us, since it has softened with the practical demands of the time and to a notable extent has relaxed

the rigors of the doctrinal demands. One special feature of
Hinduism is that it has always tried to assimilate the good fea-
tures of other teachings, including those of other religions.
Popular Hinduism assumed its present shape as a result of this
process of assimilation, and some of its current teachings are
traceable to influential exponents of a reformed Hinduism, active during the last two centuries. Many of the religious practices of the past have either disappeared or have changed in
accordance with the demands of the time. *Satī* (burning of the
widow on the funeral pyre of her husband) has become a thing
of the past. Widow marriages and intercaste marriages are
being accepted. Provision has been made for divorce. Un-
touchability has been abolished. Foreign travel is no longer ta-
boo. Moderation in the forms of worship and fasting have
been introduced. In the course of this process of change and
reform, popular Hinduism has developed two prominent tendencies. First, it is now commonly asserted that spirituality
does not consist of or require divorcing oneself from the concerns of this world. It is said that the reality of this world must
be accepted and faced, and that religious pursuits must give
due regard to this-worldly and not just other-worldly demands. That is why some advocates of popular Hinduism believe that the religious way of life and the demands of science
can be reconciled. Second, some of the most influential representatives of popular Hinduism offer a new interpretation of
mokṣa. The individual's goal remains the same: personal salvation. But the achievement of this goal, it is claimed, is not possible on an individual basis. *Nobody is really saved unless the
whole race is saved.* That is why thinkers such as Sri Auro-
bindo speak of a *divine life* and why Radhakrishnan writes of
sarvamukti (redemption of all) as the ultimate goal of the religious life. It is in this way that these thinkers attempt to meet
the charge of unbridled individualism that is often brought
against Hinduism.

The differences we find in the general teachings of doctrinal and popular Hinduism are bound to make a difference in
how each will answer some of the questions before us. Both,

however, are in agreement concerning the medical use of animals, popular Hinduism supporting it because it will sanction the sacrifice of a lesser for a much greater good. Moreover, this view increasingly recognizes that *this* world must be made a better, happier, healthier place in which to live if the goal of redemption of all is to be achieved. Our individual spiritual pursuit cannot take place in a vacuum. The religious *ideal* remains human salvation, but the *concern* of religion is man, living and suffering in this world. For we cannot make our spiritual pilgrimage unless we are first fit in mind and body.

In the case of the exploratory use of animals in science, popular Hinduism's attitude is less clear because there appears to be no way to assess, in general, whether or not the knowledge gained outweighs the suffering of the animals used in its pursuit. We do know that popular Hinduism will not give its approval merely on the grounds of the researcher's theoretical inquisitiveness; theoretical curiosity does not necessarily outweigh moral considerations. Perhaps, then, a case-by-case approach, in which each research proposal is evaluated in terms of the likelihood of the relevance of its findings to important human interests, is the best approach to the exploratory use most in keeping with the discernible tendencies of popular Hinduism.

Whatever uncertainties we may have concerning the exploratory use of animals pale in comparison with the crystalline clarity of popular Hinduism's beliefs about their use for cosmetic purposes. This use must be categorically condemned because the human interest it serves (our vanity), far from being vital or important, is in fact ignominious. Popular Hinduism cannot approve of the death and suffering of animals so that we may adorn ourselves with objects of luxury and fashion. Despite the many differences noted among the varieties of Hinduism current in the world today, therefore, all of them, popular Hinduism included, condemn the cosmetic use of animals as essentially and ineradicably irreligious and immoral. One must assume that all the world's religions and their members at least can agree on that.

Notes

1. *The Hymns of the Rig Veda*, translated by Ralph Griffith and others (Benares, Lazarus & Co., 1896), especially VI–23.6.7.

2. Satpath Brāhman in *The Sacred Book of the East*, translated by Maurice Bloomfield (Oxford, Clarendon Press, 1879–90), vol. XLIII, X–6.4.1. Hereafter referred to as *The Sacred Book of the East*.

3. Atharva Veda, in *The Sacred Book of the East*, vol. XLII, The Hymns of the Atharva Veda, X–10.

4. Manmathnath Datta (ed.), *The Dharmaśāstras* (in 6 volumes), (New Delhi, Cosmo, 1978), especially Yajnavalkya Samhitā in vol. 1, 264.

5. See S. Radhakrishnan (ed.), *The Principal Upaniṣads* (New York, Harper & Bros., 1953); also, R. E. Hume (ed.), *The Thirteen Principal Upaniṣads* (Oxford, Oxford University Press, 1934).

8 Noninjury to Animals: Jaina and Buddhist Perspectives

Christopher Chapple

The view of animals held by those in the Indian milieu differs radically from that held by those living in the European-Western technological matrix. Similar views are found in Hinduism, Jainism, and Buddhism, influencing Asian attitudes and offering a unique perspective on the role of animals in the drama of human life. In the material that follows, I will discuss the treatment of animals in two traditions: Jainism, which has remained confined primarily to the Indian subcontinent for reasons we will see below, and Buddhism, which spread from India to Central Asia, China, Japan, Korea, and Southeast Asia.

In approaching the religious traditions of Asia, two key interrelated concepts contribute to an understanding of the animal domain. The first, noninjury to living beings, is more of a practice than a concept, and is the first precept in virtually all Indian traditions. The second is more theoretical: the notion of repeated, cyclical embodiment, best described by the Sanskrit word *saṃsāra*, which means "passing through a succession of states." Various schools have offered different interpretations of both of these; we will concentrate here on communicating an understanding of the concepts of noninjury and rebirth strictly as they apply to animals in the Jaina and Buddhist traditions. At the close of the discussion, we will explore how these religious traditions might respond to the modern dilemma of utilizing animals in scientific research.

1. Jainism

Jainism is one of the most ancient indigenous traditions of India. The name Jainism is derived from the term *jina*, which means conqueror or victor; hence, the Jainas are followers of the path established by the Jinas, those who have conquered the suffering (*duḥkha*) inherent in attachment. The most recent Jina, Vardhamāna Mahāvīra, lived from 599 B.C. to 527 B.C. His immediate predecessor, Pārśvanatha, has been dated at 850 B.C. Twenty-two other Jinas (also known as *Tīrtaṅkaras*) are said to have preceded Mahāvīra and Pārśvanatha, but no historical evidence exists to prove or disprove their existence.

At the heart of Jainism is the doctrine that all being (*sat*) is divided into nonliving (*ajīva*) and living (*jīva*) forms. The former includes what we might consider principles: motion, rest, space, matter, and time. The latter, the living forms, includes almost everything regarded as animate or inanimate by non-Jainas, from a rock and a drop of water up to men and women. Each life form, including mountains, lakes, and trees, is said to have consciousness (*caitanya*), bliss (*sukha*), and energy (*vīrya*). Living beings are classified in a hierarchical fashion according to the number of senses they possess. Earth, water, fire, air, and vegetables, the simplest forms of life, are said to possess only the sense of touch. Worms have both touch and taste. Bugs, lice, and ants have touch, taste, and smell; moths, bees, and flies add the sense of seeing. Snakes are said to have all the senses, including hearing, while beasts, birds, fish, and humans are said to have six senses: seeing, hearing, tasting, smelling, touching, and thinking.[1] Hence, the human order is, technically speaking, equivalent to that of fish and animals.[2]

A *jīva*'s status in this hierarchy is not fixed but is in a constant state of flux, indicated by the Sanskrit term *saṃsāra*. The universe is filled with living beings that have no beginning but that, because of unquenched desires, continually take on new embodiments. These embodiments or states of being fall into four categories (*gati*): gods, humans, hell beings, and animals and plants. The last of these—animals and plants—is divided into three parts, the lowest form of life being the *nigoda*, which "are so undifferentiated that they lack even individual bodies; large clusters of them are born together as colonies which die a fraction of a second later."[3] They are said to reside in flesh, among other places. Above these are the earth bodies, the water bodies, the fire bodies, and the air bodies. The third and highest division of this plant and animal group includes plants and the various beasts mentioned in the preceding paragraph.

The most important state to achieve is that of the human being, as it is the only state in which the living being (*jīva*) can be freed from the bondage of action (*karma*). For the Jainas, *karma* is a physical entity, a viscous mass that adheres to the *jīva* and causes attachment and suffering. The average person is filled with *karma*, which obstructs one's true nature of infinite knowledge, bliss, and energy. The influx (*saṃvara*) of new *karma* must cease if a person is to achieve the pinnacle of all life, the state of liberation (*mukta*), wherein there is no more attachment to passion and impurity.

Noninjury to Living Beings

In order to overcome the negative influence of *karma*, Jainas take on a series of vows, the practice of which aids in the purging (*nirjarā*) of the residue accumulated during repeated deleterious activity. The first and foremost of these is the vow of noninjury (*ahiṃsā*). The word *ahiṃsā* comes from the Sanskrit root *hiṃs*, a desiderative form of the verb *han*, to kill or injure or strike. Prefixed with the privative "a," it is best translated as "absence of the desire to kill or harm."[4] This is the prime practice in Jainism for overcoming past actions, and all dimensions of the religion and the philosophy, including logic, reflect a concern for *ahiṃsā*. Acts of violence are to be avoided because they will result in injury to oneself at some future time, even perhaps in another embodiment. The *Ācārāṅga Sūtra* states the need for *ahiṃsā*, as follows:

Injurious activities inspired by self-interest lead to evil and darkness. This is what is called bondage, delusion, death, and hell. To do harm to others is to do harm to oneself. "Thou art he whom thou intendest to kill! Thou art he whom thou intendest to tyrannize over!" We corrupt ourselves as soon as we intend to corrupt others. We kill ourselves as soon as we intend to kill others.[5]

In order to uphold the vow of *ahiṃsā*, two paths of practice were developed: one for the Jaina monks, who adhered to greater vows (*mahāvrata*), and another for the Jaina lay community, who followed a less rigorous discipline (*anuvrata*). Four types of violence were acknowledged: intentional, nonintentional, related to profession, and self-defense. The monks lived according to rules that avoided all types of violence; lay persons, as we will see, were allowed to take life in some instances. All Jainas are strict vegetarians, living solely on one-sensed beings (vegetables) and milk products. Alcohol, honey, and certain kinds of figs are also prohibited, because they are said to harbor many forms of life, especially *nigoda*.

Ahiṃsā is said to be practiced in five ways: restraint of mind, control of tongue, carefulness on roads, removing beings from the road, and eating in daylight (to avoid ingesting bugs).[6] In order to observe these forms of *ahiṃsā*, several rules are required, including care in movement, speech, eating, placing and removing, and evacuation. An additional rule suggests that one limit the area of one's activities, thus renouncing potential harm one may cause in far-off places.[7] This last rule contributed to the regional nature of Jainism: monks face strong prohibitions against travel. These concerns have led the Jaina community to pursue limited means of livelihood: government and farming are acceptable but not desirable occupations; writing, arts, and crafts are encouraged; and commerce is the most desirable, as long as trade is not conducted in tools of violence such as weapons.[8] For the most advanced monks, the disciplines become increasingly rigorous. In addition to limited food intake, restraint from sexual desire, and the renunciation of all possessions (in the case of the Digambara sect, any form of clothing is renounced), no digging, bathing, lighting or extinguishing of fires, or fanning is allowed in order to protect earth, water, fire, and air bodies, respectively.[9]

As evidenced by these prohibitions, the world view of the Jainas present an unparalleled concern for life. "All beings are fond of life; they like pleasure and hate pain, shun destruction and like to live, they long to live. To all, life is dear."[10] With this basic orientation, the Jaina community exerted a great deal of influence on Indian society as a whole, though it has consistently remained a tiny minority.[11] They have protested vigorously against the Hindu practice of animal sacrifice. One text declares: "Those terrible ones who kill animals under the guise of making an offering to the gods, or the guise of sacrifice, are bereft of compassion and go to a bad fate."[12] Largely as a result of their efforts, vegetarianism is practiced in all parts of India, and animal sacrifice is now illegal in most states. The Jaina monk Hīravijaya-Sūri persuaded the Muslim emperor Akbar (1556–1605) "to prohibit the killing of animals on certain days."[13] Akbar eventually renounced hunting and very nearly became a vegetarian.

These prohibitions are primarily statements about what *not* to do and convey little of the immense affection the Jainas hold for animals. We have mentioned that the tradition attributes a thinking faculty (*manas*) to animals; this special ability has spawned the proliferation of numerous stories in which animals make reasoned choices, particularly in regard to nonviolent behavior, which subsequently advances them from animal to human status. One such story was recently told to me by Professor Padmanabh Jaini:

> Long ago, there was a large forest fire, and all the animals of the forest fled and gathered around a lake, including a herd of elephants, deer, rabbits, squirrels, etc. For hours the animals crowded together in their small refuge, cowering from the fire. The leader of the ele-

phant herd got an itch, and raised his leg to scratch himself. A tiny rabbit quickly occupied the space vacated by
the elephant's foot. The elephant, out of an overwhelming desire not to hurt the rabbit, stood on three legs for
more than three days until the fire had died down and
the rabbit scampered off. By then, his leg was numb and
he toppled over. Still retaining a pure mind and heart,
the elephant died. As a reward for his compassion he
overcame the need for embodiment as an animal and was
born as a prince by the name of Megha and eventually
became a disciple of Mahāvīra, taking the vows of monk-
hood in hopes of transcending all forms of existence.

This fanciful story is noteworthy for its confidence in animal
abilities, illustrating the Jaina emphasis on the link between
the human and animal orders.

2. Buddhism

Buddhism, like Jainism, originated in India as a religious movement easily distinguishable from Hinduism in its
nonallegiance to Vedic texts and its disdain for animal sacrifice.
Unlike Jainism, however, Buddhism spread far from its native
India, reaching virtually all parts of Asia. Its founder, the Buddha, lived from 563 to 483 B.C. and is said by some to have
been a contemporary of Mahāvīra, the founder of Jainism.
References to animals abound in the teachings of both the
Buddha and the later Buddhists. In this discussion we will examine some passages from phases of Buddhist history and then
see how the traditional Buddhist views might contribute to
the modern issue of animal rights.

Like Jainism, Buddhism does not allow for a creator god;
the cycle of life has been present from beginningless time. It
differs from Jainism, however, in that it does not posit an abid-
ing life force (*jīva*) but asserts that all phenomena are without
lasting self-nature. The pinnacle of human achievement is *nir-*

vāna, the transcendence of passions, often referred to as a realization of emptiness (*śūnyatā*) that releases one from all attachment. This is the state of Buddhahood and, depending
upon the school, is said to be accessible to any and all beings
who undergo the rigors of meditation.

Rebirth

Although Buddhism does not posit a permanent, fixed
self-nature, it does advance a doctrine of *karma* as the process
causing the continuation of *saṃsāra*. *Saṃsāra*, also referred to
as the wheel of existence, is divided into six domains, into
which anyone may be born, depending upon his or her past
actions: animals, hungry ghosts, hell beings, demons, humans, and gods. The world of animals is one of the three lesser
destinies (*gati*), along with the hell beings and hungry ghosts.
According to the *Jewel Ornament of Liberation*, a medieval Tibetan text, animals continually suffer the misery of "servitude,
slaughter, and devouring each other."[14] Birth as an animal is
said to be punishment for evil deeds. Quoting the *Ratnāvalī*,
Sgam-po-pa states that

> as a rule, through cupidity one becomes a spirit (hungry
> ghost); through malevolence one is born in hell; through
> deludedness one becomes an animal. . . . By constantly
> committing evil deeds we are reborn in hell, by doing
> many we become spirits and when we do only a few we
> are reborn as an animal.[15]

Graphic stories have been told to communicate the need to act
properly to avoid birth as an animal. In the *Avādana Śataka*, a
group of lazy and indolent students is said to have been reborn
as parrots and swans "as a punishment for their indifference to
duty."[16] Another student who failed to keep a fast is said to
have been reborn as a snake.[17] Animal existence is not regarded as a desirable state by the Buddhists, but this observation, rather than denigrating animals, sees animalhood as a
possible alternative to human existence.

Respect for Animals

Animals are also presented in a very positive manner in Buddhist literature. For instance, in the *Jātakamālā*, didactic tales told by the Buddha drawn from his past lives, he portrays himself as a rabbit, a swan, a fish, a quail, an ape, a woodpecker, an elephant, and a deer. Animals are said to have contributed to his desire for *nirvāṇa*; seeing animals and humans suffer caused Buddha to seek enlightenment. In one such story, the future Buddha nurses back to health a goose that had been shot by his cousin Devadatta. In another anecdote, he feels compassion when he sees a tired farmer ploughing the earth, a bird eating a worm dredged up by the plough, the welts inflicted on the back of the ox by the farmer, and the weariness of both the gaunt farmer and the overworked ox. The sufferings of both beast and man helped initiate his quest for total awakening.

In some instances in Buddhist literature, animals are portrayed as sacrificing their lives for the sake of human beings. In other cases, humans are seen as giving up their own flesh and sometimes their very lives so that animals may survive. The *Avadāna-kalpalatā* tells of an elephant who throws himself off a rock in the desert to rescue starving travelers. A lion and an elephant rescue some men from a dragon, sacrificing their lives in the process.[18] In the *Śaśa Jātaka*, a rabbit offers his body to a Brahman for food, jumping into a fire piled up by the rabbit himself. The Brahman was in fact the god Indra in disguise, who then placed the figure of the rabbit in the moon.[19] But these stories are only half the picture. Several parables and birth stories tell of humans sacrificing their flesh so that animals may keep living. In the *Jātaka Mālā*, the *Suvarṇaprabhāṣa*, and the *Avadāna-kalpalatā*, a story is told in which a Buddhist throws himself before a hungry tigress so that she may feed her cubs.[20] The 16th minor precept in the *Fan-wang-ching* (*Brahmajāla Sūtra*), a text popular in China, graphically states that "One should be willing to forsake one's entire body, one's flesh, hands and feet as an offering to starv-

ing tigers, wolves, lions, and hungry ghosts."²¹ Although this
example is undoubtedly overstated, the message is clear that
animals are to be treated with great respect.

The treatment of animals is included in the first Buddhist
precept—not to harm or injure living things (*prāṇātipātād
viratiḥ*). In some instances, the qualifier "needlessly" is added
to this precept. The *Daśabhūmika Sūtra* states that a Buddhist "must not hate any being and cannot kill a living creature
even in thought."²² Kṣemendra writes, "I cannot endure the
pain even of an ant."²³ In the *Bodhisattva-bhūmi* discussion of
giving (*dāna*), the first of the six perfections (*pāramitā*), the
Buddhist is not allowed to give anything that "may be used to
inflict injury on other living beings," nor is he allowed to give
"poisons, weapons, intoxicating liquors, and nets for the cap-
ture of animals." He should not bestow upon others a piece of
land on which the animals may be hunted or killed."²⁴ In the
Mahāvagga, the ᴾuddha proclaims: "A *bhikkhu* [monk] who
has received ordination ought not intentionally to destroy the
life of any living being down to a worm or an ant."²⁵ This concern for animal and plant welfare shaped monastic life. In the
early days of the Buddhist community, the monks traveled
during all three seasons, winter, summer, and the rainy season. The public, however, protested that "they crush the
green herbs, they hurt vegetable life, they destroy the life of
many small living beings," particularly when traveling during
the rainy season.²⁶ Subsequently, the Buddha required that
all monks enter retreats and stop wandering during the
monsoons.

One *Jātaka* tale is particularly instructive in regard to the
importance of noninjury to life:

> Once upon a time, a goat was led to a temple and was
> about to be sacrificed by the presiding Brahman. Sud-
> denly, the goat let out a laugh and then uttered a moan-
> ing cry. The Brahman, startled by this odd behavior,
> asked the goat what was happening. The goat responded
> as follows: "Sir, I have just remembered the history of

what has led up to this event. The reason I have laughed
is that I realized this is the last of 500 births I have suffered as a goat; in my next life I will return again as a
human. The reason I have cried is out of compassion for
you. You see, 500 births ago I was a Brahman, leading a
goat to the sacrifice. After killing the goat, I was condemned to 500 births as a goat. If you kill me, you will
suffer the same fate." The Brahman, visibly shaken, immediately freed the goat, who trotted away. A few min-
utes later, lightning struck the goat and he was free to
again become human. The Brahman likewise was spared,
due to the goat's compassionate intervention.[27]

This story includes multiple facets of Buddhist teachings,
including *karma*, rebirth, noninjury, and compassion. Its
graphic indictment of animal sacrifice, a topic to be discussed in more detail later, holds particular importance for
this volume.

Animal Protection

The concern for animal welfare was not confined to the
Buddhist monastic community. Aśoka, one of the best-known
Indian emperors (*ca.* 274–232 B.C.), converted to Buddhism
and established several laws that required kind treatment to
animals. These included restricting meat consumption, cur-
tailing of hunting, and establishing hospitals and roadside wa-
tering stations for animals. Excerpts from Aśoka's inscriptions
are as follows, translated from rocks and pillars still standing
throughout India:

Formerly, in the kitchen of the Beloved of the gods,
King Priyadarśin (Emperor Aśoka), many hundred thousands of animals were killed everyday for the sake of
curry. But now when this Dharma-rescript is written,
only three animals are being killed (everyday) for the
sake of curry (*viz.*) two peacocks (and) one deer (and) the
deer again, not always. Even these three animals shall
not be killed in the future.[28]

Everywhere in the dominion of the Beloved of the gods, King Priyadarśin (Emperor Aśoka), and likewise among (his) Borderers, such as the Colas, the Pāṇḍyas, Satiyaputra, Keralaputra, up to Tāmraparṇī, the Yona king of Antiyaka, and also those kings who are the neighbours of that Antiyaka—everywhere (provision) has been made by the Beloved of the gods, King Priyadarśin, (for) two (kinds of) medical treatment (*viz.*) medical treatment for men and medical treatment for animals.

And wherever there are no (medicinal) herbs that are suitable for men and suitable for animals, everywhere (such) have been caused to be brought and caused to be planted.

And wherever there are no (medicinal) roots and fruits, everywhere (such) have been caused to be brought and caused to be planted.

And on the road, wells have been caused to be dug and trees have been caused to be planted, for the use of animals and men.[29]

On bipeds and quadrupeds, on birds and aquatic animals, various benefits have been conferred by me, (even) as far as the grant of life.[30]

The Beloved of the gods, King Priyadarśin (Emperor Aśoka), spoke thus:

(When I am) crowned twenty-six years, these various (animals) are declared by me inviolable, *viz.* —

Parrots, mainas, the *aruṇa*, ruddy geese, wild ducks, the *nandīmukha*, the *gelāṭa*, bats, the *ambā-kapīlikā*, small tortoises, boneless fish, the *vedaveyaka*, the *Gaṅgā-pupuṭaka*, the *sankuja* fish, large tortoises and porcupines, squirrels, young deer, bulls, the *oka-piṇḍa*, wild asses, white pigeons, village pigeons, (and) all quadrupeds which are neither useful nor edible.

Those she-goats, ewes and sows (which) are either with young or are giving milk (to their young), are inviolable, and (so) also (are) those (of their) young ones which are less than six months old.

Cocks are not to be caponised.

Husks containing living beings (*i.e.*, insects) are not to be burnt.

Forests are not to be burnt, either uselessly or for killing animals.

One animal is not to be fed with another animal.

On the three *çāturmāsīs*, on (these) three days during the Tiṣyā full moon, (*viz.*)—the fourteenth, the fifteenth, (and) the first (tithi)—and invariably on every fast-day, fish are inviolable and are not to be sold.

On these very same days, those other classes of animals (that live) in elephant-parks (and) in fishermen's settlements, are also not to be slain.

On the eighth (tithi) of every (lunar) fortnight, on the fourteenth, on the fifteenth, on *Tiṣyā*, on *Punarvasu*, on the three *cāturmāsīs*, (and) on auspicious days, bulls are not to be castrated, (and) he-goats, rams, boars, and other animals that are usually castrated are not to be castrated.

On Tiṣyām in Punarvasu, on the *cāturmāsīs*, (and) during the fortnight of (every) *cāturmāsī*, the branding of horses and bullocks is not to be done.[31]

Though in many ways only a partial assertion of animal rights, these inscriptions nonetheless reveal a highly unusual compassion on the part of a temporal ruler toward his subjects, both human and natural.

This policy of animal protection spread with Buddhism to China and Japan, where it periodically gained favor as a means of earning merit. The twentieth precept of the *Fan-wang-ching* (*Brahmajāla Sūtra*) declares:

If one is a son of Buddha, one must, with a merciful heart, intentionally practice the work of liberating living beings. All men are our fathers, all women are our mothers. All our existences have taken birth from them. Therefore all the living beings of the six *gati* are our parents, and if we kill them, we kill our parents and also our former bodies; for all earth and water are our former bodies, and all fire and wind are our original substance.

> Therefore you must always practice liberation of living
> beings (*hōjō*) (since to produce and receive life is the
> eternal law) and cause others to do so; and if one sees a
> worldly person kill animals, he must by proper means
> save and protect them and free them from their misery
> and danger.[32]

The influence of this and other texts such as the *Suvar-naprabhāṣa Sūtra* caused Chinese and Japanese leaders to declare the institution of *hōjō-e* or "meetings for liberating living beings." In the sixth century, the monk Chi-i reportedly convinced more than 1,000 fishermen to give up their work. He also purchased 300 miles of land as a protected area where animals could be released. In 759 A.D. the Chinese Emperor Suh-tsung established 81 ponds where fish could be released; this was followed by similar actions on the part of Emperor Chen-Tsung (1017 A.D.). In Japan, Emperor Temmu Tennō restricted the use of certain hunting devices and the eating of cow, horse, dog, and monkey meat in 675 A.D., and he ordered that various provinces "let loose living things" the following year. In 741 the Emperor Shōmu Tenno ordered prohibitions against hunting and fishing on the fast days of the month. His daughter, the Empress Kōken, issued several similar decrees.[33] The release of living beings continues to be practiced in the East Asian world, primarily as a ceremonial event,[34] and has even been practiced in North America.[35]

Although vegetarianism was not a strict requirement for all Buddhist monastic communities, some sects particularly emphasize the importance of not eating meat. The *Lan kāvatāra Sūtra*, one of the early texts of the Mahāyāna school (and especially linked to Zen Buddhism), makes an eloquent appeal for vegetarianism and respect for animals in its eighth chapter.[36] Grounded in the theory of *karma*, the small excerpt below expresses the sentiment that prompted a concern for nonviolence in diet:

> In the long course of *saṃsāra*, there is not one among
> living beings with form who has not been mother, father,
> brother, sister, son, or daughter, or some other relative.

> Being connected with the process of taking birth, one is
> kin to all wild and domestic animals, birds, and beings
> born from the womb.[37]

The viewpoint that all life is interrelated was used to promote
the abstention from meat, and within a Buddhist context
serves as a basis for protesting all maltreatment of animals.

Classical Buddhist literature consistently places a high
value on the importance of animal life, from the words of the
Buddha, to references made in the canonical texts on monastic
discipline, to the later Mahāyāna Sūtras. In the present era,
Buddhists still have the same concerns regarding the sanctity
of all life. The 14th Dalai Lama, exiled leader of the Tibetan
people and an important contemporary world religious figure,
has summarized the Buddhist attitude toward life in the following passage, taken from a book published in 1980:

> In our approach to life, be it pragmatic or other-
> wise, a basic fact that confronts us squarely and un-
> mistakably is the desire for peace, security and hap-
> piness. Different forms of life at different levels of
> existence make up the teeming denizens of this earth of
> ours. And, no matter whether they belong to the higher
> groups such as human beings or to the lower groups
> such as animals, all beings primarily seek peace, com-
> fort, and security. Life is as dear to a mute creature as it
> is to a man. Even the lowliest insect strives for protec-
> tion against dangers that threaten its life. Just as each
> one of us wants happiness and fears pain, just as each
> one of us wants to live and not to die, so do all other
> creatures.[38]

3. Use of Animals in Scientific Research

We have considered the Jaina and Buddhist attitudes
toward animals from a variety of textual sources. From the evidence surveyed, noninjury to animals clearly holds a prominent place in both traditions. However, scientific research
using animals—the focus of the present volume—did not

take place when these texts were written, and no clear statement that could be applied to this problem can be found. One related issue that can be cited is that of animal sacrifice, performed by the Hindus and strongly condemned by both Buddhists and Jainas. The early Hindu community performed intricate rituals that culminated in the sacrifice of live animals. One such ritual, the horse sacrifice (*aśvamedha*), entailed releasing a horse for one year, following it as it wandered throughout India, and then killing and dismembering it. This ritual eventually became internalized and the process was visualized but not enacted.[39] For years, Buddhists and Jainas labored against all animal sacrifice, using the argument that such activities violated the first and most important ethical principle: nonviolence. They were successful in many respects. Within many later Hindu texts, nonviolence is accorded the same respect it is given in Jainism.[40] However, goat sacrifices continue to be practiced in Nepal though the Jainas have successfully lobbied for the ban of this practice in most states of India.[41]

How might the classical Jaina and Buddhist positions contribute to the current debate over the use and abuse of animals for scientific research? First, these traditions both view animals as sentient beings. Animals are said to have feelings and emotions and to be able to improve themselves, at least in some of the various parables that were cited. This is not necessarily a naive anthropomorphism but rather indicates a deeply rooted cultural perspective. In seeing animals as kin, that is, in accepting the theory of repeated birth as increasingly or decreasingly sophisticated animals, depending upon one's deeds, the entire kingdom, humans included, becomes an extended family. For the Jainas, even rocks and streams are within the same continuum. By contrast, the one-life orientation of the prophetic religious traditions regards animals in an entirely different light and has allowed for their sacrifice in the laboratory environment. For a Jaina or a Buddhist, this would be unthinkable. To kill is a great infraction against the religious precepts and certainly would result in future suffering.

The theory of *karma* as presented above is interpreted as

a linear process; acts are committed by and accrue to one, individual life. "If I do this good act now, I will earn merit which will be rewarded in the future" would be one expression of this reading, as would "the reason I am so unfortunate now is because of evil acts I committed in the past." This mechanistic view unfortunately does not directly relate the effects of human action to society, though threats of karmic punishment are used to advocate socially acceptable behavior. A modern reading of *karma*, which would dispose of the need for belief in reincarnation and hence be more accessible to the superstition-wary Westerner, would be to view it as horizontal instead of sequential. An action does not necessarily remain confined to one life, but its influence spreads out to the lives of others. If one acts violently and is imprisoned as a result, an entire family is affected. Similarly, actions by scientists affect society at large. This interpretation does not seek to dismiss the personal responsibility one carries but emphasizes the social dimensions of action. The rise of science gave birth to medicines and luxuries that have greatly eased human misery. But these same advances now plague the world with nuclear weaponry and chemical warfare, increased rates of cancer and heart disease, and tragedies such as thalidomide and Agent Orange. It might be said that the violence that was required for the development of these various substances is now being experienced indirectly as the widespread effects of the technological age are being felt.

Despite the abnegation of animal sacrifice by the Buddhists and the Jainas, both traditions affirm the nobleness of animals and humans who have given their lives to others, as seen in the story of the elephant who spared the rabbit and the story of the rabbit who jumped into the fire to feed a traveler. These fantastic tales are myths designed to encourage humans to improve their own behavior. It might be construed that these anecdotes could legitimize the loss of animal life for the sake of science. But in each of the stories, the animals were not coerced into their acts of compassion but surrendered their lives out of their own will and desire. In the modern context, it is highly doubtful that any animal would march into a corporate research laboratory or volunteer to overdose on drugs or be injected with carcinogens.

It might be argued that medicines are needed to protect the human order, that we are waging a war against disease and need to enlist the aid of animals in this just war. The Jainas, as we have seen, do in fact include within their system a provision for committing violence out of self-defense. An elder monk would not place himself or herself in a situation that would require such an activity, but lay persons continually encounter a need for violence, however subtle, in order to survive. Would the threat of disease such as a plague that would undoubtedly kill thousands of people but can only be counteracted by medicines tested on animals be an acceptable justification for restricted violence in "self-defense?" The response within the context of Jaina logic is not simple. The Jaina would not deny the validity of the argument for using animals in such research. According to their philosophies of *anekāntavāda* (literally, "not only one solution") and *naya* (partial expression of truth), there is never one valid perspective in a given situation: all truths are partial truths. The Jaina philosophy of nonabsolutism, an outgrowth of the *ahiṃsā* doctrine, would not allow a Jaina to hold an opinionated or rigid attitude about this or any other situation. Hence, a Jaina would probably not deny that the scientist who conducts such experiments has a legitimate viewpoint within the scientific milieu. However, the Jaina precepts would prohibit a Jaina from accepting the utility of killing animals for himself or herself. Because of the doctrines of *karma* and *ahiṃsā*, the Jaina would refuse to be directly involved. However, he or she may follow the example of earlier Jainas and attempt to make the other side see the validity of the Jaina perspective and perhaps, at minimum, declare days of abstinence of destruction, as was achieved through Jaina influence at Akbar's court.

From a Buddhist perspective, the endeavors of experimental science might be regarded as useful in a limited way, being primarily concerned with manipulations on the level of *saṃsāra*. From the ultimate point of view, which is the prime concern of the Buddhist, such work would not ultimately prove worthwhile. Neither scientists nor disease victims nor animals have independent self-natures. All are composed of parts and are subject to decay and dissolution. All three need to be helped, not merely to live longer or to live a more comfortable life but also to see their nonsubstantiality, their impermanence. For the Buddhist, avoidance of death, the *telos* of the scientific realm, would not be the highest value. Rather, the quality of death is most important, and this can only be determined by one's understanding of life. This is not to say that Buddhism looks forward to death; the earlier passages affirm the sanctity of life. We saw that Aśoka instituted the planting of medicinal herbs for both animals and humans. Medical and surgical cures are mentioned in the early Buddhist canon, and later Buddhism includes healing deities (Bhaiṣajya-rāja and Baiṣajya-samudgata) who assist in curative processes.[42] But when death becomes imminent it must be accepted, and the Buddhist must attempt to die freely, without attachment or fear.[43]

Putting these philosophical considerations aside, our problem remains: How might the Buddhist religion approach the modern practice of killing animals in research laboratories, given the long history of Buddhist kindness to all living things? Before passing judgment on any issue, Buddhism requires that three factors be taken into consideration: the intention of the act, the means used to execute it, and its consequences. This formula has been illustrated with a story told by the Buddha in which a ship with 500 people on board is threatened by an evil man who has the ability to kill all 500. The captain must decide whether to act against this man or not and, after having considered the intention and consequences of performing an act of violence, he kills the evil man, thus saving everyone else on board.[44] Could similar considerations be used by a contemporary Buddhist to agree to or support the killing of animals in research laboratories? Three factors would have to be considered: intention, means, and consequences. The first category eliminates the bulk of possible circumstances: destruction of animals for instruction in high school biology classes would be deemed unnecessary, as would research conducted by cosmetic companies aimed at enhancing human vanity. Only in an extreme case would the intention be deemed acceptable, such as the testing of a vaccine desperately needed to stave off an epidemic. Then the means would have to be considered. Can the pain be minimized? Are the animals well treated? Finally the consequences have to be considered. Will lives in fact be saved? Will other reactions occur, such as genetic damage or increased risk of cancer on the part of the humans who use the product? Will the test merely lead to the proliferation of more tests and endanger more lives, both animal and human?

The responses of modern Buddhist leaders and organizations in North America are quite clear in their position regarding animal welfare. Roshi Philip Kapleau, Director of The Zen Center in Rochester, New York, has written several articles and the book *To Cherish All Life* in defense of animals. In California, students of the Tassajara Zen Monastery have founded the organization Buddhists Concerned for Animals, which lobbies for animal rights in farming, scientific experimentation, war research, and trapping. These movements, though operating on a small scale through limited publications, have the potential to influence a larger population. As the BCA newsletter points out, "As Buddhist monks and lay people, we are finding ourselves able to reach people who may otherwise not be involved in the effort to liberate animals from suffering. We aim to point out the relationship of the current Animal Rights Movement to the traditional Buddhist path, and to a sometimes overlooked but present aspect in other religions." Such efforts may appear insignificant but must not be dismissed. The gentle persuasion of the Jainas, which has endured for centuries, has convinced major segments of the Indian population that the protection of living beings is both meritorious and desirable; similar efforts in the modern world might prove equally effective.

Notes

1. Section 43, *Puruṣārtha-siddhyupāya* of Amritchandra, translated by Ajit Prasada (Lucknow, Abhinadan, 1933). Hereafter referred to as *Puruṣārtha*.

2. The Jaina system attributes a thinking faculty to animals, in contrast to the Cartesian model current being questioned by Donald Griffin, Tom Regan, and others.

3. *Gommaṭasāra-Jīvakāṇḍa*, pp. 191–193, as quoted in Padmanabh S. Jaini, *The Jaina Path of Purification* (Berkeley, University of California Press, 1979), p. 109. Hereafter referred to as Jaini, *The Jaina Path*.

4. Madeleine Biardeau, as quoted in Louis Dumont, *Homo Hierarchicus: The Caste System and Its Implications* (Chicago, The University of Chicago Press, 1970), p. 148.

5. *Ācārāṅga Sūtra* I.1.2, I.5.5, as excerpted and translated by Nathmal Tatia, *Studies in Jaina Philosophy* (Banaras, Jain Cultural Research Society, 1951), p. 18.

6. As given in Koshelya Wadia, *The Conception of Ahiṃsā in Indian Thought According to Sanskrit Sources* (Varanasi, Bharata Manisha, 1974).

7. "The pure minded, who thus confines the extent of his activities, practices absolute *ahiṃsā* for that time by renouncing all *himṣā* possible in the vast space which has been given up." *Puruṣārtha*, p. 140.

8. Jaini, *The Jaina Path*, p. 171.

9. *Ācārāṅga Sūtra* I.1, in *Jaina Sūtras*, translated from *Prākrit* by Hermann Jacobi (Delhi, Motilal Banarsidass, 1973; first published by Oxford University Press, 1884). Hereafter referred to as *Jaina Sūtras*.

10. *Jaina Sūtras*, I.2.3.

11. The current Jaina population in India is estimated at four million, less than one percent of the total.

12. *devopahāravyājena yajñavyājena ye 'thavā*
    ghanti jantūn gataghṛṇā ghorāṃ te yanti durgatim
    Yogaśāstra of Hemacandra, II.39.

13. Vincent A. Smith, "The Jain Teachers of Akbar," in *Essays Presented to Sir R. G. Bhandarkar* (Poona, 1917), as quoted in Jaini, *The Jaina Path*, p. 284.

14. Sgam-po-pa, *The Jewel Ornament of Liberation*, translated by Herbert Guenther (Berkeley, Shambala Publications, 1971), p. 63. Hereafter referred to as Sgam-po-pa, *Liberation*.

15. Sgam-po-pa, *Liberation*, p. 79.

16. As cited in Har Dayal, *The Bodhisattva Doctrine in Buddhist Sanskrit Literature* (London, Kegan Paul, Trench, Trubner, and Co., 1931), p. 221. Hereafter referred to as Dayal, *Boahisattva Doctrine*.

17. Dayal, *Bodhisattva Doctrine*, p. 221.

18. Dayal, *Bodhisattva Doctrine*, p. 187.

19. "Animals," in *Encyclopaedia of Buddhism*, edited by G. P. Malalasekara (Government Press, Ceylon, 1965), Fascicle 4, pp. 667–672.

20. Dayal, *Bodhisattva Doctrine*, p. 182.

21. *The Buddha Speaks the Brahma Net Sūtra*, translated into English by Dharma Realm Buddhist University (Talmage, California, Buddhist Text Translation Society, 1981), p. 150.

22. Dayal, *Bodhisattva Doctrine*, p. 199.

23. Dayal, *Bodhisattva Doctrine*, p. 199.

24. Dayal, *Bodhisattva Doctrine*, p. 175.

25. *Mahāvagga* I.78.4, in *Vinaya Texts*, translated from Pāli by T. W. Rhys-Davids and Hermann Oldenberg (Delhi, Motilal Banarsidass, 1974; first published at Oxford University Press, 1882). Hereafter referred to as *Mahavāgga* in *Vinaya Texts*.

26. *Mahāvagga* in *Vinaya Texts*, III.1.1.

27. Jātaka Tale 18, retold from *Jataka Tales*, Selected and Edited with Introduction and Notes by H. T. Francis and E. J. Thomas (Cambridge University Press, 1916), pp. 20–22.

28. Rock Edict I, as translated in *Asoka's Edicts* by Amulyaçhandra Sen (Calcutta, The Institute of Indology, 1956), p. 64. Hereafter referred to as *Asoka's Edicts*.

29. Rock Edict II, *Asoka's Edicts*, p. 66.

30. Pillar Edict II, *Asoka's Edicts*, p. 146.

31. Pillar Edict V, *Asoka's Edicts*, pp. 154–156.

32. M. W. deVisser, *Ancient Buddhism in Japan: Sūtras and Ceremonies in Use in the Seventh and Eighth Centuries A.D. and Their History in Later Times* (Leiden, E. J. Brill, 1935), p. 198. Hereafter cited as deVisser, *Ancient Buddhism.*

33. deVisser, *Ancient Buddhism*, pp. 198–212.

34. Holmes Welch, *The Practice of Chinese Buddhism, 1900–1950* (Cambridge, Mass., Harvard University Press, 1967), pp. 378–382.

35. Philip Kapleau, "Animals and Buddhism." *Zen Bow Newsletter: A Publication of the Zen Center* (vol. V, no. 2, Spring, 1983), pp. 1–9. This and other writings by Roshi Kapleau were very helpful in the preparation of this paper.

36. According to D. T. Suzuki, this chapter is probably a later accretion to the text.

37. . . . *anena dhīrgenādhvanā saṃsaratām prāṇinām nāstyasau kaścitsattvaḥ sulabharūpo yo na mātābhūtpītā vā bhrātā vā bhaginī vā putro vā duhitā vānytarānyataro vā svajanabandhabandhūbhūto vā tasyānyajanmaparivṛttāśrayasya mṛgapaśupakṣiyonyantarbhūtasya bandhorbandūbhutasya . . .*

38. Tenzin Gyatso, the 14th Dalai Lama, *Universal Responsibility and the Good Heart* (Dharmasala, India, Library of Tibetan Works and Archives, 1980), p. 78.

39. See *Bṛhadāraṇyaka Upaniṣad* I.1–2.

40. For instance, the *Sāṃkhya Kārikā* of Īśvarakṛṣṇa dismisses Vedic sacrifices as ineffective means to alleviate suffering because of the destruction they entail. The description of *ahiṃsā* in Patañjali's *Yoga Sūtra*, similar to that in Jaina texts, condemns violence whether done, caused, or approved, and claims that the Great Vow (*mahāvrata*) is not limited by time, place, or circumstance.

41. Jaini, *The Jaina Path*, p. 285n.

42. For a discussion of Buddhist medical practices, see Raoul Birnbaum, *The Healing Buddha* (Boulder, Colorado, Shambhala, 1979).

43. See *The Tibetan Book of the Dead*, translated by W. Y. Evans-Wentz (London, Oxford University Press, 1927) and *The Wheel of Death* by Philip Kapleau (New York, Harper & Row, 1971).

44. This story is recounted in the *Ārya-Sarvabuddha-mahārahasyopāyakauśalyajñānottarabodhisattvaparipṛcchāparivarta*, Sūtra 38 in the *Mahāratnakūta* collection. It is translated in Garma C. C. Chang (general ed.), *A Treasury of Mahāyāna Sūtras: Selections from the Mahāratnakūta Sūtra* (University Park, Pa., Pennsylvania State University Press, 1983), pp. 456–458.

9 Of Animals and Man: The Confucian Perspective

Rodney L. Taylor

1. Classical Confucianism: Heaven, Man, and Moral Virtue

The Classical Confucian tradition is distinctive in part because it emphasizes a specific set of moral relations within which the involved individuals are enjoined to develop appropriate moral virtues. This set of relations is usually described as the five human relationships: king-subject, father-son, husband-wife, elder brother–younger brother, and friend-friend.[1]

Conspicuous for their absence from this list are animals and other living things, a fact that goes some way toward explaining the prevailing tendency to classify the Confucian ethic as just another species of humanism. In its religious teachings, however, Confucianism does not restrict the realm of value or the scope of moral relations only to human beings. *T'ien* (Heaven) is the source of ultimate religious authority, and *T'ien-li* (the Principle of Heaven) permeates all living things, animals as well as humans, plants as well as animals. The natural order, the Confucian *Tao*, is a moral order. Though not identical, macrocosm and microcosm are similar because each is permeated by the principle of Heaven. Viewed in terms of the religious teachings of Confucianism, then, the religious agent (one who is guided by religious teachings) is simultaneously and inescapably a moral agent. Since the religious teachings of Confucianism involve ethical precepts, and since, as just noted, these teachings affirm the fundamental similarity of all living things, it is a mistake to assume that classical Confucianism is "just another form of humanism." How far this is from the truth will be clearer once we have examined representative passages from *Lun Yü* (the Analects of Confucius), *Meng Tzu* (the works of Mencius), and *Hsün Tzu* (the works of Hsün Tzu).

Lun Yü, *Confucian Analects*

The *Analects* are regarded as the primary source of the teachings of Confucius (551–479 B.C.). There are, of course, other writings that purport to represent Confucius, but for a variety of historical-critical reasons the *Analects* are considered our most historically authentic record. The work itself consists primarily of recorded conversations between Confucius and his disciples, but some passages deal mainly with the acts and character of Confucius. This is true of the first passage that concerns us, one of a small number that deal with human-animal relationships.

"The Master fished with a line but not with a net; when fowling he did not aim at a roosting bird."[2] Passages of this kind became for the later Confucian tradition descriptions of the wisdom of Confucius, and they instruct via example; since this is something that Confucius himself considered important, it is something we ought to take seriously and emulate. Personality characteristics of this kind were also considered to be part of the make-up of the general image of the sage (*sheng*) or, the phrase Confucius himself uses most frequently, of *chün-tzu* (the noble or moral man).

The point of this particular passage is not that Confucius refrains from taking life—such an attitude is not a major part of the early tradition—but rather that he does not take "unfair advantage" of the fish and the birds. There is, then, no judgment that catching fish and birds is morally culpable; culpabil-

ity is restricted to the *methods* used to catch them. To take
unfair advantage reflects poorly on the character of the agent;
indeed, to do so, Confucius implies, would be to violate his
own moral nature, particularly that aspect of the moral nature
identified as *i* (righteousness). Righteousness for Confucius is
part of human nature, its function being to determine our
moral relationships. Here he is suggesting that righteousness
also includes proper relations with fish and birds.

At a deeper level the authority of this moral system is
T'ien (Heaven). Within the framework of their religious ethic,
Confucians will argue that man's moral nature is itself a reflection of *T'ien*. The *chün-tzu* reflects the religious authority of
T'ien in his way of life, and humaneness (*jen*) is action taken in
conscious understanding of the relation of man to Heaven.
Acting reasonably and sensitively toward other forms of life,
such as Confucius does in the passage just quoted, is expres-
sive of the relation between the moral nature of humans and
that of Heaven. Thus sensitivity to animals is not only ethi-
cally suitable but also carries religious authority. However,
though sensitivity to other forms of life is suitable, it is not un-
qualified. As other passages in the *Analects* show, such sensitivity to other forms of life does not override the special
moral relations that obtain between human beings.

The clearest passage on this point is one that depicts the
character of Confucius. "When the stables were burnt down,
on returning from Court, he said, Was anyone hurt? He did
not ask about the horses."[3] The passage shows Confucius' obvious concern with the potential loss of human life. As the disciple who recorded this incident appears to point out, Confucius could have asked about the horses but did not. Thus we
may infer that he believed in the priority of human life.

This interpretation is consistent with the dominant tenor
of Confucius' teachings. The traditional set of special moral relations focuses on the moral responsibilities human beings
have to other human beings. However, we have also seen that
moral relations to living things other than humans are not excluded; human life and relations are simply more important.

Another issue we must address, made more difficult than those considered up to now because it involves religious sources of authority, is that of animal sacrifice. "Tzu-kung wanted to do away with the presentation of a sacrificial sheep at the Announcement of each New Moon. The Master said, Ssu! You grudge sheep, but I grudge ritual."[4]

The issue addressed in this passage is the maintenance of traditional sacrificial codes of state religion. In this particular ritual an announcement is made to the ancestors at the start of each new month, accompanied by a sacrifice that includes a sheep. Tzu-kung, one of Confucius' disciples, felt that the sacrifice of the sheep was an unnecessary part of the ceremony. Unfortunately we are not told why, although the tradition has tended to interpret Tzu-kung's comments as suggesting his feeling for the life of the sheep. Confucius' response to Tzu-kung emphasizes his view that it is far more important that the ritual (*li*) be maintained than that the sheep be spared. The explanation of Confucius' attitude is one that bears on his attitude toward the traditional state religion of China and the institutions of the ancient period. For Confucius, the primary task was to restore the moral order that prevailed in China during the reigns of the founding fathers of the Chou dynasty (1122–256 B.C.). Confucius taught that the institutions, thought, and practices preserved in the Chinese Classics (*ching*) represented these early times. The term "state religion" applied to the religious practices associated with the maintenance of the authority of the ruler, a ruler who was seen as ruling by the authority of *T'ien-ming* (the Mandate of Heaven) and who was viewed as an intermediary between man and Heaven, an *axis mundi*, as suggested by his title, *T'ien-tzu* (Son of Heaven). At the center of this state religion was a strict ritual code, *li*, which, particularly to the Confucians, guaranteed the religious significance of ritual, its propriety for the individual and society, and its relation to Heaven itself. Confucius did not attempt to change this traditional religious point of view. Just the reverse. He says of himself in an often-quoted phrase: "I am a transmitter and not a creator. I believe

in and have a passion for the ancients."[5] Of course we know
him to be a creator as well, but the passage is consistent with
the importance he attached to the restoration of the ways of
the ancients, including their elaborate ritual and ceremonial
codes—even when, as ritual frequently required, a sacrifice of
cooked meat (sheep, oxen, and pig) was made.[6]

In the passage quoted concerning the use of the sheep
in sacrifice, the only significant question for Confucius is
whether its use is required for the particular sacrifice. Feelings for the sheep are totally secondary and, indeed, quite irrelevant if ritual demands that a sheep be used. While in many
contexts the *chün-tzu* will show sensitivity to the feelings of
other living things as part of the application of the general virtue of humaneness (*jen*), this sensitivity is not to exceed its
proper place. When, as in this case, sensitivity toward animals
conflicts with ritual, the maintenance of ritual prevails. Since
the basis of ritual is to be found in the practices of the sages of
antiquity, and since these sages represent the ultimate paradigm of moral reflection and activity, the details of ritual en-
capsulate their informed moral guidance and *must* be viewed
as authoritive.[7]

Another passage from the *Analects* that bears on the classical Confucian's beliefs about man and animals concerns those
humans who withdraw from the world:

> Under Heaven there is none that is not swept along by
> the same flood. Such is the world and who can change
> it? As for you, instead of following one who flees from
> this man and that, you would do better to follow one
> who shuns the whole generation of men. And with that
> he went on covering seed. Tzu-lu went and told his mas-
> ter, who said ruefully, "One cannot herd with the birds
> and beasts. If I am not to be a man among other men,
> then what am I to be? If the Way prevailed under
> Heaven, I should not be trying to alter things."[8]

This passage is one of a series in which either Confucius or his
disciples encounter individuals who have essentially given up

on any reform efforts in the world. For them there is nothing that can be done other than to find some out-of-the-way place, settle down, and try to live out their years in a peaceful manner. To such individuals Confucius appeared as someone who was trying to do the impossible; his efforts were simply worthless. Confucius' attitude toward such individuals is obvious from the passage. They are condemned for fleeing their moral responsibilities of serving and, when necessary, of reforming the world. Such individuals receive the wrath of Confucius, and he says of them that they differ little from the birds and the beasts.

Why are these individuals compared to the birds and the beasts? A person who withdraws from the human community thereby fails to act as a reasonable moral agent. The moral nature of such a person remains unfulfilled. As such he is not truly a moral agent and, by extension, given the degree to which our moral nature is itself definitive of human nature, such a person might very well be said to be something *less* than human. What does that make him like? The answer is clear: he has become as the birds and beasts.

We must, however, be certain not to be misled by this answer. The rustics who are the subject of this passage have *chosen* to ignore moral responsibilities that by nature they possess. Thus at one level they may be said to be little different from birds and beasts. By not employing their moral natures they function at the same level as those who, owing to their natural endowment, have only a rudimentary capacity to act morally. On the other hand, and this is where the analogy of birds and beasts can mislead, the rustics *do wrong* by choosing to ignore their moral responsibilities. Their conscious decision to ignore this responsibility is obviously *different in kind* from having only rudimentary capacities for reflection and action to begin with.

How then can we describe Confucius' position with regard to animals? At the heart of his teaching is the moral development of both the individual and society; responsibility for performing individual acts is determined by reference to these ends. At the level of individual moral development, Confucius teaches sensitivity to the life of animals. Such sensitivity may even be said to be characteristic of the *chün-tzu* as a reflection of moral responsibility. It remains true, however, that the primary measure of those moral virtues we are to develop is tied largely to those special moral relations that bind members of the human species together—whether they are king-subject, father-son, elder brother-young brother, husband-wife, or friend-friend. If these relations are fulfilled, *then* feelings can be extended outward to all people and, eventually, to all living things. But we are not to attempt to do the latter before we have successfully completed the former.

Meng Tzu, *Mencius*

Usually considered the second major Confucian thinker, Mencius (372–289 B.C.) is now regarded as the primary interpreter of Confucius, a position he came to occupy as part of the Neo-Confucian movement beginning in the 13th century. It was at this point that his work was canonized as part of the collection of basic Confucian scripture. By developing and expanding upon basic themes represented only in the briefest of terms in the *Analects*, Mencius admirably clarifies the teaching of Confucius. His most basic teachings concern human nature. Confucius suggested, but never stated, that man's nature was morally good. Mencius is explicit in making this idea basic to Confucian teaching. Mencius says of human nature, *hsing*: it has the beginnings of moral goodness. He is specific about the nature of the beginnings, stating that it possesses the *ssu-tuan* or Four Beginnings—*jen* (humanity), *i* (righteousness), *li* (propriety), and *chih* (wisdom).[9] According to Mencius, these constitutive parts of human nature are endowed in us by heaven at our birth. But they are merely beginnings, they are not yet fully developed. Such development is necessary before human beings can act morally to the fullest extent.

Mencius illustrates the universal nature of our natural goodness by referring to a child about to fall into a well.[10] To Mencius it is a plain matter of fact that humans possess moral goodness because any person who sees the peril of the child will spontaneously act to save him.

One's ability to develop one's moral nature will ultimately depend upon the use of the mind (*hsin*). The learning and self-cultivation necessary to perfect the moral nature, Mencius seems to believe, will eventually yield a level of moral awareness that is all-encompassing. It is a state hinted at in Mencius' comment that all things are complete within him.[11] What are the moral implications of this kind of vision, especially as they relate to our relations with other living things?

Let me begin to answer this question by considering one of the classic discussions of animals in all of Confucian literature. The passage opens in the following way. While sitting in his hall, a king sees a man leading an ox. The king asks the man where he is taking the animal, and the man responds that he is on his way to consecrate a new bell with the blood of the ox. The king asks the man to let the ox go. The man in turn responds by asking the king whether the consecration of the bell is thereby to be omitted. The king responds that it was not his purpose to omit the consecration; rather, he ordered the release of the ox because "I cannot bear its frightened appearance, as if it were an innocent person going to the place of death."[12] In the place of the ox, the king orders that a sheep be used to consecrate the bell.

As he discusses the issue with Mencius, the king acknowledges the apparent arbitrariness of his choice. Was the sacrifice of a lesser order and therefore a smaller animal could be used? Was the sheep to suffer less than the ox? Was it less worthy of being reprieved from suffering than the ox? Was the king less culpable because he allowed the sacrifice of a sheep instead of an ox? Mencius gives the following response:

> Your conduct was an artifice of benevolence. You
> saw the ox, and had not seen the sheep. So is the supe-

rior man affected towards animals, that, having seen them alive, he cannot bear to see them die; having heard their dying cries, he cannot bear to eat their flesh. Therefore he keeps away from his cookroom.[13]

Mencius' response suggests that the king is a man of moral virtue and sensitivity and his behavior is an example of *jen*, here translated as benevolence. For the king acted in behalf of the ox, having seen its fright; the sheep, having had no direct contact with the king, remained an abstraction.

The discussion returns to the king's inability to bear the frightened appearance of the ox. The similarity between the king's reaction and the case of the child about to fall into the well is clear. In both cases it is said that by nature humans are unable to see others suffer, or, as it is stated at a later point in the text, "All men have a mind which cannot bear to see the sufferings of others."[14] This is the basic, quintessential ethical claim that is made about human nature. The goodness of human nature described technically in terms of the four beginnings of goodness must ultimately stand or fall on this claim. And in a formulation that parallels Bentham's plea for recognizing the suffering of others,[15] we have as basic a statement of Confucian ethics as will be found. The *chün-tzu* cannot bear to see the suffering of others; moreover, the scope of this moral perception encompasses not only fellow humans but also the lives of other sentient creatures.

True to the classical Confucian tradition, however, the special moral relations between humans have priority over the sensitivity to the suffering of animals and others. In particular, Mencius states that such feelings will be misplaced if they are not accompanied by a proper understanding of moral relations. For the king, for example, the most important moral relations are his obligations as ruler to his people. If these are overlooked, then the moral responsibility of the ruler is skewed. As Mencius says, "Now here is kindness sufficient to reach to animals, and no benefits are extended from it to the people—How is this?"[16] For Confucianism the first and foremost measure of the cultivation of the moral nature is the perfection of the classical set of special moral relations. If, as the philosopher Mo Tzu (470–391 B.C.) taught, one should practice universal love, *chien-ai*, then according to the Confucians there would be no love. And there would be no love because it would have no beginning, no first special moral relation from which to develop. It would remain only an abstraction, nothing more. If, however, special moral relations are developed, then man's natural goodness will develop. And with the development of this goodness, the sphere of moral reflection and action will increase, including, for the *chün-tzu*, all living things.

A later passage in Mencius' writings speaks directly to this point: "In regard to inferior creatures, the superior man is kind to them, but not loving. In regard to people generally, he is loving to them but not affectionate. He is affectionate to his parents, and lovingly disposed to people generally. He is lovingly disposed to people generally and kind to creatures." [17] The differences in this passage in terms of feelings toward animals, people in general, and people in special moral relations are expressed as the differences between *ai* (kindness), *jen* (humaneness or loving), and *chin* (affection). The *chün-tzu's* moral nature has the capacity to act in all these ways. But there is a natural order to moral development, and natural feelings are associated with the different compartments of the moral life.

Mencius adds much to the discussion of Confucian ethics and the specific relationships of humans and animals. He defends the appropriateness of feelings of kindness toward animals in far more detail than Confucius and with a more clearly formulated basis. Ultimately he uses the same helping principle for animals as used for assisting human strangers—the inability to bear the suffering of others. But while it is appropriate to show kindness to animals, it is most inappropriate if in the process one fails to fulfill his special responsibilities to human beings, and, in particular, those in a special relationship.

Hsün Tzu

In many ways Hsün Tzu (*fl.* 298–238 B.C.) is the most systematic of the early Confucian thinkers. His text is a model of the early method of argumentation. He is also more concerned than Mencius with the need for strict and unwavering attention to the process of learning. For Hsün Tzu as well man *can* perfect himself, he *can* become a sage, but a life-long commitment to learning is essential. As such, Hsün Tzu makes a greater effort to distinguish man from other forms of life. The distinction is drawn in terms of the uniquely human capacity to learn, with the implication that the goal of sagehood is obtainable only if one devotes one's life to learning.

Having drawn a sharp line between the realms of humans and animals, Hsün Tzu nevertheless also displays an extraordinary sensitivity to animal behavior and urges that humans emulate it. He writes:

> All living creatures between heaven and earth which have blood and breath must possess consciousness, and nothing that possesses consciousness fails to love its own kind. If any of the animals or great birds happens to become separated from the herd or flocks, though a month or a season may pass, it will invariably return to its old haunts, and when it passes its former home, it will look about and cry, hesitate and drag its feet before it can bear to pass on. Even among tiny creatures the swallows and sparrows will cry with sorrow for a little while before they fly on. Among creatures of blood and breath, none has greater understanding than man; therefore man ought to love his parents until the day he dies.[18]

We still find the statement that man is the highest form of life, but the statement is qualified by pointing to the basic moral responses shared by animals. Though technically they would not be of the same order as human moral responses, they are nevertheless a *kind* of moral response. This reaffirms the Confucian teaching that humans and animals differ in degree, not in kind. Even animals have a rudimentary moral sense. This is an interesting perspective—all the more because it comes from the sternest of Confucian philosophers and portends something of the direction in which Confucian tradition moves in the hands of the Neo-Confucians. For though the Neo-Confucians still insist upon the superiority of humans in the scheme of things, they also insist, as we shall see shortly, on the unity of all living things.

2. The Neo-Confucian Ethical Vision

Neo-Confucianism refers to the form of Confucianism that arose during the Sung dynasty (960–1269) and has continued until recent times. While there is much here that simply echoes the basic teachings of Confucianism, there is also a new-found interest in philosophical issues, in particular a metaphysical tendency that has as its goal the grounding of the Confucian moral virtues in a developed metaphysical system. There is also a new emphasis on the individual's religious quest for *sheng* (sagehood). These points will be explained as we proceed.

Neo-Confucianism functions in both the public and the private sector. In the former it is state orthodoxy, a role it plays in China, Korea, and Japan. In the latter, the instruction it gives to the individual is at the very center of the cultures of these countries. In its role as state orthodoxy it holds a prominent position as ideological authority, while its instructional role provides a profound religious and ethical orientation for the individual. It is hard to overestimate the importance of Neo-Confucianism in East Asia, where it continues to play a major role in sustaining the value systems of both individuals and groups.

Mind and Nature: Metaphysical Models for Moral Action

Within Neo-Confucianism there are two major schools of thought: the School of Principle (*li-hsüeh*), or the Ch'eng-

Chu School, named after its two major thinkers, Ch'eng I (1033–1107) and Chu Hsi (1130–1200), and the School of Mind (*hsin-hsüeh*), or the Lu-Wang School, named after Lu Hsiang-shan (1139–1192) and Wang Yang-ming (1472–1529). The School of Principle believes that principle (*li*), or the Principle of Heaven (*T'ien-li*), is to be found in all things, including human nature. Its thinkers follow a scheme of learning exemplified by the *Ta Hsüeh* (Great Learning) that instructs the learner·to investigate the principle in things (*ko-wu*). As this process of investigation is extended to a wider and wider circle of things and activities (*chih-chih*), the person who understands principle will develop his nature (*hsing*) to the point of sagehood (*sheng*). The focus of much of this effort for the School of Principle is upon the meaning of *ko-wu*, the investigation of things, and how one discovers principle inherent in them.

Moral development also requires investigating "things" (*ko-wu*). But in addition it demands that the individual sincerely intend to internalize the principle as it exists in the particular case—for example, in *his* relation to *his* parents. Through this process the basic moral virtues, the Four Beginnings of Mencius, traditionally considered to be constitutive of human nature, are tied to a deeper metaphysic.

The School of Mind, on the other hand, finds principle to be inherent in the mind (*hsin*), not just in nature (*hsing*), and as a result *the act of thinking* itself is a proper object of study of principle. The pedagogical schema changes dramatically as a result. Emphasis is placed not on the first two steps of the *Ta Hsüeh* (*ko-wu*, the investigation of things, and *chih-chih*, the extension of knowledge) but on the third step, *ch'eng-i* (sincerity of intention). The search for principle becomes thoroughly internalized.

The relevance of these differing models to the relationship of humans and animals can be overestimated; there *is* a difference in emphasis, but little difference in the nature of how we should act. Like the Classical Confucians before them, Neo-Confucianists continue to teach the superiority of humans over animals. Chou Tun-i (1017–1073), for example, says that it is man who receives material force (*ch'i*) in its highest form.[19] And Shao Yung (1011–1077) states that "man occupies the most honored position in the schema of things because he combines in him the principle of all species."[20] Though accounts of man's superiority differ, it is clear that it has a metaphysical basis.

It is Chu Hsi, however, who puts the argument in its tightest form, and it is his teachings that may be viewed as the orthodox Neo-Confucian interpretation of the relation of man to animals. The argument is developed within the framework of a comparison of the nature of humans and the nature of animals. "The nature of man and the nature of things," it begins, "in some respects are the same and in other respects different."[21] First, as regards the creation of things, there is a similar aspect and a different aspect. In the basic Neo-Confucian cosmogony things are created from a beginning (or first) point, called the Great Ultimate (*T'ai-chi*). The actual creation of things comes about through the intermingling of the two modes of material force (*ch'i*), the forces of *yin* and *yang*. Man and animals may be said to be similar, for they are both products of the intermingling of *yin* and *yang*. On the other hand, the intermingling of *yin*, *yang*, and the five elements (*wu-hsing*), another structure of metaphysical influences, produces inequalities in separate things. On the basis of the inequalities produced, humans and animals may be said to be unequal.

In this respect the issue of equality and inequality may be interpreted in terms of the distinction between the material force (*ch'i*) and the principle (*li*) of things: animals and humans are similar as regards their principle but different in terms of material force. This point is made in the following passage:

> From the point of view of principle, all things have one source, and therefore man and things cannot be distinguished as higher and lower creatures. From the point of view of material force, man receives it in its perfection and unimpeded while things receive it partially and obstructed. Because of this they are unequal, man being higher and things lower.[22]

There is, however, a qualification to be noted. As the argument continues, we find that man is said to differ from animals even in terms of the principle that "constitute(s) (his) nature."[23] In man's case principle confers the capacity for moral reflection: "Thus consciousness and movement proceed from material force while humanity, righteousness, decorum, and wisdom proceed from principle. Both man and things are capable of consciousness and movement, but though things possess humanity, righteousness, decorum, and wisdom, they cannot have them completely."[24] In this part of the argument we find the suggestion that animals do not differ from humans in material force, at least in terms of consciousness and movement, while they do differ in principle, humans possessing the capacity for moral reflection that animals lack.

If this line of reasoning has been followed, then it will appear that Chu Hsi has contradicted himself. Initially he argues that humans and animals are similar with regard to principle but differ in material force. In the end he argues that they are similar with regard to material force but differ in terms of principle. But there is no real contradiction. Chu Hsi is writing from two different perspectives. On the one hand, to say that animals and humans are similar in principle but differ in material force is to stress the Neo-Confucian cosmology that places the Great Ultimate as the source of creation of all things. On the other hand, to say that animals and humans are similar in terms of material force but differ in terms of principle is to speak from the axiological perspective.

When one assesses the argument that is put forth by Chu Hsi, an argument expressed in the categories of Neo-Confucian metaphysics, the conclusion reminds one of something that Mencius said, though in far simpler terms. "That whereby man differs from the lower animals is but small," he writes. "The mass of people cast it away, while superior men preserve it."[25] Is there a clear-cut distinction between man and animal according to Chu Hsi? There seems to be little that one could point to that would justify saying that man possesses this but animals do not. As regards material force, for example, there is no categorical difference between humans and animals. The

closest the argument comes to making a hard distinction is
when it is said that man receives material force in a clear form,
while animals receive it in a turbid form. That, however, is not
a distinction that is terribly meaningful, nor is it one that Neo-
Confucians emphasized.

As far as principle is concerned, because both animals
and humans share in it, they are similar. However, we are also
told that principle is constitutive of human nature to a degree
different from that of animals; man has a full capacity for moral
virtue as part of his nature. Does this mean that animals do
not? Surprisingly, it does not mean this. Man is said to have a
fuller moral nature, but animals possess moral virtue too,
even though it is not in a "complete" form. Man is capable of
thorough-going moral reflection, while animals are only capable of a rudimentary kind of moral reflection. The difference
between humans and animals, again, is not a difference in
kind, as we have seen in the earlier tradition as well, but, as
always, a difference in degree. Thus we find Chu Hsi writing:

> Heaven and earth reach all things with this mind. When
> man receives it, it becomes the human mind. When
> things receive it, it becomes the mind of things (in gen-
> eral). And when grass, trees, birds, or animals receive it,
> it becomes the mind of grass, trees, birds and animals
> (in particular). All of these are simply the one mind of
> Heaven and earth.[26]

A Vision of Unity

The fact that there is no difference in kind between humans and animals allows Neo-Confucianism to teach the unity
of all forms of things. Ch'eng Hao (1032–1085) states that "the
humane man forms one body with all things comprehensively.
. . . All operations of the universe are our operations."[27]
Ch'eng I said, "The humane man regards Heaven and earth
and all things as one body. There is nothing which is not part
of his self. Knowing that, where is the limit (of his humanity)?"[28] Lu Hsiang-shan said, "The universe never separates it-

self from man; man separates himself from the universe."[29] And the *Chin-ssu lu* directs one to enlarge the mind in order to be able to enter into all things in the world: "Combine the internal and the external into one and regard things and self as equal. This is the way to see the fundamental point of the Way."[30]

Probably more than any other work, however, Chang Tsai's (1021–1077) *Hsi ming* (Western Inscription) has captured the imagination of Neo-Confucian ethical thought. The first few lines read:

> Heaven is my father and earth is my mother, and even such a small creature as I finds an intimate place in their midst. Therefore that which extends throughout the universe I regard as my body and that which directs the universe I consider as my nature. All people are my brothers and sisters, and all things are my companions.[31]

The vision is clear: animals and humans share in the same material force and the same principle. Men embody these in their highest or fullest form, but this only makes greater demands upon our ethical reflections and action. All living things, not just human beings, stand in *moral* relation to man, and man in turn fulfills his own moral nature by standing in moral relation to all living things.

The degree to which this was taken literally as a directive to moral action can be seen in several poignant examples. In a short biographical note about Chou Tun-i (1017–1073), the *Chin-ssu lu* states that he "did not cut the grass growing outside his window. When asked about it, he said, '[The feeling of the grass] and mine are the same.'"[32] In the commentary to this passage a question is raised about the meaning of the statement that the feeling of the grass and Chou Tun-i's feeling are the same. The first response simply states, "You can realize the matter yourself. You must see wherein one's feelings and that of the grass are the same."[33] A second response is recorded and gives more explanation.

"If we say that one's feelings and that of the grass are the same, shall we say that one's feeling and those of trees and

leaves are not the same? And if we say that one's feeling toward
the donkey's cry and one's own call are the same, shall we say
that a horse's cry and one's own call are not the same?"[34] Once
we recognize that we share the same material force and the
same principle with all that lives so that we form one body together, we will grasp the moral need to see and listen for
others in distress. Thus we return to the essential Confucian
moral vision: The man of moral insight cannot bear to see the
suffering of others, and it is this inability to bear the suffering
of others that culminates in moral action.

The great Neo-Confucian of the School of Mind, Wang
Yang-ming, specifically ties this sense of moral responsibility
to the basic ethical teaching of Mencius: the inability to bear
the suffering of others. In his "Inquiry on the Great Learning," Wang Yang-ming makes the following statement:

> Therefore when he sees a child about to fall into a
> well, he cannot help a feeling of alarm and commisera-
> tion. This shows that his humanity forms one body with
> the child. It may be objected that the child belongs to
> the same species. Again, when he observes the pitiful
> cries and frightened appearance of birds and animals
> about to be slaughtered, he cannot help feeling an "in-
> ability to bear" their suffering. This shows that his hu-
> manity forms one body with birds and animals. It may
> be objected that birds and animals are sentient beings as
> he is. But when he sees plants broken and destroyed, he
> cannot help a feeling of pity. This shows that his human-
> ity forms one body with plants.[35]

If this moral nature can be developed, then man will have
formed a true sense of "one body" with all things.

> Everything from ruler, minister, husband, wife, and
> friends to mountains, rivers, spiritual beings, birds, ani-
> mals, and plants should be truly loved in order to realize
> my humanity that forms one body with them, and then
> my clear character will be completely manifested, and I

will form one body with Heaven, Earth, and the myriad things.[36]

In Wang Yang-ming's view, these statements are of particular significance for specific moral action and culminate in one of the basic principles of his thought, the unity of knowledge and action—*chih-hsing ho-i*. The two, knowledge and action, form a unity because each is ultimately dependent upon the other. To speak of knowledge without action is empty talk, according to Wang Yang-ming, while to speak of action not motivated by knowledge is to speak of action of no consequence. Moral knowledge, the inherent or innate knowledge of the good (*liang-chih*), is inseparable from moral action. To know the good, as Socrates had taught, *is* to do it. Moral knowledge is not "abstract knowledge."

For the Neo-Confucian ethics is a way of thinking that leads to a way of living, though Wang Yang-ming would suggest that the thought and the action are even more closely tied together. To stop with only the thought is to engage in empty and useless talk.

I would like to end this section with a quote from Kaibara Ekken (1630–1714), a Japanese Neo-Confucian of the Chu Hsi school, *Shushi-gaku*. Kaibara Ekken, perhaps more than any other figure, brought Confucian ethics to the forefront of discussion in the school and the home alike. The passage I want to quote is from his *Shogaku-kun* (Precepts for Children) and stresses the ethics that flow naturally from the philosophical and religious position of the unity of all things.

No living creatures such as birds, beasts, insects, and fish should be killed wantonly. Not even grass and trees should be cut down out of season. All of these are objects of nature's love, having been brought forth by her and nurtured by her. To cherish them and keep them is therefore the way to serve nature in accordance with the great heart of nature. Among human obligations there is first the duty to love our relatives, then to show sympathy for all other human beings, and then not

to mistreat birds and beasts or any other living thing.
That is the proper order for the practice of benevolence
in accordance with the great heart of nature. Loving
other people to the neglect of parents, or loving birds
and beasts to the neglect of human beings, is not
benevolence. [37]

Here, in a statement that builds upon the monism of *ch'i*
(*ki* in Japanese), Kaibara Ekken identifies specific forms of
ethical action. Nature itself is said to manifest loving kindness
(*jen, jin* in Japanese), and we are to see that we are a part of
the basic ethical goodness of nature. Thus our own actions
must bear the quality of loving kindness. The loving kindness
of nature is not a misplaced anthropomorphism but a manifestation of the moral nature shared by all. We in turn must
recognize the moral obligations of being human, obligations
that engage us in the lives of those closest to us in the most
profound way but ultimately involve us in the lives of all living
things. From the common perception of shared life comes the
perception of shared moral feeling and the injunction not to
cause suffering to others.

Such is the development of the Neo-Confucian tradition,
its moral injunctions perpetuating the basic Classical Confucian stance that humans possess a mind that is incapable of
bearing the suffering of others. I want now to bring the tradition into a contemporary context and inquire into its implications for the issues around which this collection of essays has
been organized—the use of animals in science.

3. A Neo-Confucian in Modern Japan

Virtually nothing has been written about the relation of
Confucianism to the moral problems created by contemporary
technological societies. Recognizing the large historical role
the Confucian tradition has played in the creation of East
Asian cultures and yet knowing, too, how little its teachings
are articulated in the affairs of contemporary Asia, it struck me

that it would be appropriate to discuss its applications to these affairs with one of the last major Confucian thinkers in Japan. This I did during the summer of 1983, spending five weeks with Okada Takehiko in Fukuoka, Japan. Part of our conversation touched on the relation between humans and animals and, in particular, the use of animals in science. What follows is a record of our conversation on this topic.

Taylor: I want to turn now to the discussion of respect for life and the relation of respect for life to the development of science.

Okada: Since science has developed, it has reached a position where it has come to threaten the very existence of life itself. Nevertheless, we can't stop the continued development of science because it appears necessary as the basis for the continued development of the human community. Science needs to be made aware of the degree to which it has to develop for the benefit of the human community. To make science develop in this way, both scientists and nonscientists have to come to understand the importance of the human community and human life itself. I think that Confucianism is the most suitable of teachings for this purpose because it emphasizes as a central idea the forming of one body with all things. One can live only by living with others. Confucian ethics are fundamental in this respect—one must consider the other person's heart. If we extend the concept, then we must consider nature itself as well, that is, all living things.

Taylor: You have talked about the extraordinary importance of respect for human life and the degree to which science, and for that matter humanity, if they are to survive, must reach toward the emergence of respect for human life. Therefore you have essentially said that science must be grounded in ethics if it is to be ultimately useful. I wonder to what degree you as a Confucian can speculate upon the importance of not just human life, but all life. Do we have ethical responsibilities to all forms of life, not just human life?

Okada: Yes I think we do, and such an idea should be extended to all forms of life, animal life and plant life. The Confucian idea of forming one body with all things could be interpreted to mean one with animals and plants. . . . All mankind has a mind that cannot bear to see the suffering of others and this is something that should be applied to all life.

Taylor: One of the issues that has become increasingly important in Western culture is what is called cruelty to animals. It refers primarily to the mistreatment of animals, and a large part of the question revolves around the issue of the use of animals in scientific research. I wonder the degree to which this mind that cannot bear to see the suffering of others, in being extended to all forms of life, does in fact provide a foundation for non-cruelty and at least for not overusing animals in scientific research?

Okada: Of course, according to the idea of the mind that cannot bear to see the suffering of others, we should not mistreat animals. As regards the overuse of animals in science, this is a very difficult problem. On the one hand, science seems to need such experiments in order to advance. In addition, at times benefits are brought to the animals as well, for example, new medicines or something of this kind. On the other hand, because animals are required, animals suffer. If, however, we truly have a mind that cannot bear to see the suffering of others, then perhaps the problem will be solved. Here in Japan we eat large quantities of fish from the rivers as well as the sea. At times we hold a memorial service in honor of the fish. Thus even when one kills animals or fish, there can still be a mind that cannot bear to see the suffering of others.

Taylor: In terms of these questions in America, and especially in Europe, where they are discussed at great length, there tend to be two extreme positions and, of course many shadings between, on the issue of the ethics of animal use. On the one hand are those who say that there should be no use of animals at all. On the other hand are those who feel that the use of animals is thoroughly justified and ought not to involve any ethical questions. It seems to me that what you are suggesting is a deep feeling of compassion through the mind that cannot bear to see the suffering of others, recognizing that for the advancement of humanity and the advancement of science animals must be used but that they must be used with care for their suffering, in as limited ways as possible, and always with respect.

Okada: The idea of unlimited use of animals as well as the position that no animals may be used, both of these are extreme ideas. With the mind that cannot bear to see the suffering of others the problem will resolve itself. In some cases we need to differentiate man and animals, in other cases it is important to see man and animals as the same. Thus the cases themselves change and we need to be able to respond to such circumstances based upon the mind that cannot bear to see the suffering of others.

The theme of this anthology is the use of animals in science. Thus it would be helpful to be able to distinguish different types of uses and their appropriateness or inappropriateness according to the religious ethics of Confucianism. The discussion with Okada is, however, as close as one can get to this at present. In East Asia issues of animal rights simply have not arisen to the degree that one finds in the West. Thus while it is possible that Confucianism can still be described as the primary mode of ethical thinking in much of East Asia, little can be seen in terms of concrete action directed toward animals. Much of the reason for this is simply that the questions themselves have not been posed. Okada himself was very surprised by my questions concerning animals, and he said repeatedly that these are not questions that are asked in

Japan. Thus the kind of detailed study of uses of animals such as Ryder's *Victims of Science*[38] or Singer's more general statement in *Animal Liberation*[39] carries the issue much further than the present state of Confucian thinking. In many ways Confucianism has been in eclipse as a dominant voice in East Asia in recent times. There are signs, however, that this is changing, and with such change I would anticipate a greater correlation with the level of discussion of ethical responsibilities to animals in the West.

It is important to remember that the Confucian tradition remains committed to certain special moral relationships, relations that place the priority strongly with humans and only after with animals. The descriptions of sensitivity to animals have been reflective of one who has perfected his moral nature. Such people are able to extend their sensitivities to all life *after* they have perfected special moral relations. This bears upon the actual historical reality of treatment of animals in China, Korea, and Japan. Were animals treated with due respect for the mind that cannot bear to see the suffering of others? The answer is that for some it was an important consideration, while for others it was not. In this respect it is similar to the Confucian claim that anyone would rescue a child about to fall into a well. Certainly for some this was an informing ethical statement, but for others it would need to be adjudicated with the practice of infanticide.

Okada's position is representative of a contemporary Confucian response. It is extremely sensitive to the ramifications of the Confucian tradition for contemporary issues, even if it lacks the specific and detailed categorization of the problem as found in the West. Okada interprets the issue of the use of animals in science in terms of the very ideas that have been most basic to the development of Confucian and Neo-Confucian ethics. From Mencius he adopts the idea of the mind that cannot bear to see the suffering of others, and from the Neo-Confucians he adopts the idea of forming one body with all things. Combined, they form the foundation for arguing that sensitivity to all life is appropriate and, in fact, morally demanded. But like Confucians before him, he also suggests that the relation between humans and animals is a complex one. In his comments he suggests that there are times when humans and animals are to be viewed as the same and other times when they are to be viewed as different. The criterion for such differentiations is the mind of compassion itself. *Man* is morally bound to the plight of animals, and he is morally bound to the suffering and plight of his fellow humans. There are times when these two obligations will come into conflict with each other. When they do, it is the mind that cannot bear to see the suffering of others that must adjudicate the proper moral course of action. The priority remains with the special moral relationships, but for the Confucian the mind of compassion feels all suffering and every loss of life as its own moral responsibility. As Okada himself said to me, there is so much suffering in this world that the man who cannot bear to see the suffering of others must bear it and try to reform human and animal alike.

Notes

1. While Confucius referred to several of the relationships (see, for example, *Lun-yü*, 12:11), it was Mencius who first referred to the basic set of relationships (*Meng-tzu*, 3A:4).

2. *Lun-yü*, 7:26, quoted in Arthur Waley, *The Analects of Confucius* (New York, Vintage, 1938), p. 128. Hereafter cited as *Lun-yü*, Waley.

3. *Lun-yü*, 10:12, Waley, p. 150.

4. *Lun-yü*, 3:17, Waley, p. 98.

5. *Lun-yü*, 7:1, quoted in W. T. deBary, *Sources of Chinese Tradition* (New York, Columbia University Press, 1960), p. 25. Hereafter referred to as deBary, *Sources*.

6. The great sacrifice, *t'ai-lao*, was considered central to the maintenance of the state religion. It consisted in part of a cooked meat offering of all three animals, sheep, oxen, and pig. For a fuller description of the sacrifice and a discussion of its incorporation into Confucian practice, see R. L. Taylor, *The Way of Heaven: An Introduction to the Confucian Religious Life* (Leiden, E. J. Brill, 1985).

7. The nature of religious authority of the sages is closely related to the development of the idea of scripture and scriptural authority. For a discussion of Confucian scripture, see R. L. Taylor, "Scripture and the Sage: The Holy Book in Confucianism," in F. M. Denny and R. L. Taylor (eds.), *The Holy Book in Comparative Perspective* (Columbia, University of South Carolina Press, 1984).

8. *Lun-yü*, 18:6, Waley, p. 220.

9. *Meng-tzu*, 2A:6.

10. *Meng-tzu*, 2A:6.

11. *Meng-tzu*, 7A:4.

12. *Meng-tzu*, 1A:7, quoted in James Legge, *The Four Books* (Shanghai, Chinese Book Company, 1930), p. 450. Hereafter referred to as *Meng-tzu*, Legge.

13. *Meng-tzu*, 1A:7, Legge, p. 453.

14. *Meng-tzu*, 2A:6, Legge, p. 548.

15. See Tom Regan and Peter Singer (eds.), *Animal Rights and Human Obligations* (New York, Prentice Hall, 1976), p. 130.

16. *Meng-tzu*, 1A:7, Legge, p. 454.

17. *Meng-tzu*, 7A:45, Legge, p. 974.

18. Hsün-tzu 19:18, quoted in Burton Watson, *Hsün-tzu: Basic Writings* (New York, Columbia University Press, 1963), p. 106.

19. Chou Tun-i, "T'ai-chi-t'u shuo," *Chou Lien-ch'i chi*, 1: 2a–b, quoted in deBary, *Sources*, p. 513.

20. Shao Yung, *Huang-chi ching-shih shu*, 8B:16a–17b, quoted in deBary, *Sources*, p. 518.

21. *Chu Tzu ch'üan-shu*, 42:27b–30a, quoted in deBary, *Sources*, pp. 548–549.

22. *Chu Tzu ch'üan-shu*, 42:27b–30a, quoted in deBary, *Sources*, pp. 548–549.

23. *Chu Tzu ch'üan-shu*, 42:27b–30a, quoted in deBary, *Sources*, pp. 548–549.

24. *Chu Tzu ch'üan-shu*, 42:27b–30a, quoted in deBary, *Sources*, pp. 548–549.

25. *Meng-tzu*, 4B:19, quoted in Legge, p. 744.

26. *Chu Tzu ch'üan-shu*, 49:23b–24a, quoted in deBary, *Sources*, p. 542.

27. *Erh Ch'eng i-shu*, 2A:3a–b, quoted in deBary, *Sources*, pp. 559–560.

28. *Erh ch'eng ts'ui-yen*, 1:7b, quoted in deBary, *Sources*, p. 530.

29. *Hsiang-shan ch'üan-chi*, 34:5b, quoted in deBary, *Sources*, p. 567.

30. *Chin-ssu lu* 2:83, 105, quoted in W. T. Chan (tr.), *Reflections on Things at Hand* (New York, Columbia University Press, 1967), pp. 74–75, 85. Hereafter referred to as *Chin-ssu lu*, Chan, *Reflections*.

31. Chang Tsai, "Hsi Ming," *Chang Heng-ch'ü chi*, 1:1a–5b, quoted in deBary, *Sources*, p. 525.

32. *Chin-ssu lu*, 14:18, quoted in Chan, *Reflections*, p. 302.

33. *Chin-ssu lu*, 14:18, quoted in Chan, *Reflections*, p. 302.

34. *Chin-ssu lu*, 14:18, quoted in Chan, *Reflections*, p. 302.

35. *Wang Wen-ch'eng Kung ch'üan-shu*, 26:1b–5a, quoted in W. T. Chan (tr.), *Instructions for Practical Living and Other Neo-Confucian Writings by Wang Yang-ming* (New York, Columbia University Press, 1963), p. 272. Hereafter referred to as *Wang Wen-ch'eng Kung ch'üan-shu*, Chan, *Instructions*.

36. *Wang Wen-ch'eng Kung ch'üan-shu*, 26:1b–5a, Chan, *Instructions*, p. 273.

37. Kaibara Ekken, "Shogaku-kun," *Ekken zenshu* 3:2–3, quoted in R. Tsunoda and W. T. deBary, *Sources of Japanese Tradition* (New York, Columbia University Press, 1958), p. 377.

38. Richard Ryder, *Victims of Science* (London, Davis-Poynter, 1975).

39. Peter Singer, *Animal Liberation: A New Ethic for Our Treatment of Animals* (New York, Avon, 1975).

About the Authors

J. DAVID BLEICH, PH.D. is *Rosh Yeshivah* (Professor of Talmud), Rabbi Isaac Elchanan Theological Seminary, Yeshiva University; Tenzer Professor of Jewish Law and Ethics, Benjamin N. Cardozo School of Law; Rabbi, The Yorkville Synagogue, New York City; has taught at Hunter College, Rutgers University, and Bar Ilan University; ordained, Mesivta Torah Vodaath; graduated in talmudic studies from Beth Medrash Elyon, Monsey, New York, and Kollel Kodshim of Yeshiva Chofetz Chaim of Radun; *Yadin Yadin* ordination; is a Woodrow Wilson Fellow; a post-doctoral fellow, Hastings Institute for Ethics, Society and the Life Sciences; a visiting scholar, Oxford Center for Post-Graduate Hebrew Studies; an editor in the Halakhah Department, *Tradition*; a contributing editor to *Sh'ma*; past chairman of the Committee on Medical Ethics, Federation of Jewish Philanthropies; a contributor to the Encyclopedia of Bioethics; a fellow, Academy of Jewish Philosophy; past chairman of the Committee on Law, Rabbinical Alliance of America; a member, Executive Board of COLPA (National Jewish Commission on Law and Public Affairs); a member, Board of Directors of Union of Orthodox Jewish Congregations of America; a member, National Academic Advisory Council of the Academy for Jewish Studies Without Walls; a member of Committee on Ethics, Hospital for Joint Diseases and Medical Center; a member of Bioethics Committee, Metropolitan Hospital; author of *Contemporary Halakhic Problems* (2 vols.), *Providence in the Philosophy of Gersonides, Judaism and Healing,* and *Bircas Ha-Chammah*; editor of *With Perfect Faith: Readings in the Foundations of Jewish*

Belief; editor (with Fred Rosner) of *Jewish Bioethics*; and has
written extensively on topics of Jewish law and ethics in publications such as *Ha-Ma'ayan, Ha-Ne'eman, Or Ha-Mizrah,
Ha-Pardes, Moriah, Shanah ba-Shanah, Jewish Observer,
Tradition, Sh'ma, Jewish Life, Judaism, Jewish Quarterly Review, Hastings Center Report,* and *Hospital Physician.*

JOHN BOWKER is a graduate of Oxford University.
After a period as a lecturer at Cambridge University, he became Professor of Religious Studies at Lancaster University. A
frequent visitor to the United States, he has been Vice Presi-
dent of the Institute on Religion in an Age of Science and is
Honorary President of Stauros and Adjunct Professor of Reli-
gion at North Carolina State University. He is now Dean of
Chapel at Trinity College, Cambridge, England. Among his
books are *Problems of Suffering in Religions of the World, The
Sense of God, The Religious Imagination and the Sense of
God,* and *Worlds of Faith: Religious Belief and Practice in
Britain Today.*

CHRISTOPHER CHAPPLE grew up in Lyndonville
and Avon, New York. He graduated from the State University
of New York at Stony Brook in 1976 and received a Ph.D. in
the history of religions from Fordham University in 1980. He
served for five years as Assistant Director of Institute Services
at the Institute for Advanced Studies of World Religions, during which time he also taught Sanskrit and religions of India at
the State University of New York at Stony Brook. At present he
is Assistant Professor of Theology at Loyola Marymount University in Los Angeles. He is the author of *Karma and Creativity* and of several articles exploring the implications that
Indian philosophy holds for the modern world.

JAMES GAFFNEY was born in New York City in 1931.
He graduated from Spring Hill College and received an M.A.

from Fordham University and an S.T.D. from the Gregorian University in Rome. He has taught at Gonzaga University in Florence, Illinois Benedictine College, the University of Liberia, the University of Notre Dame, and Loyola University in New Orleans, where he is currently Professor of Ethics. He is the editor of *Essays in Morality and Ethics* and the author of *Moral Questions, Focus on Doctrine, Biblical Notes on the Lectionary, Newness of Life, Sin Reconsidered,* and numerous articles.

SIDNEY GENDIN is Professor of Philosophy at Eastern Michigan University. His Ph.D. is from New York University (1965). He taught at the State University of New York at Stony Brook for five years before coming to Eastern Michigan in 1970. He is co-editor of *Philosophy: A Contemporary Perspective* and has published dozens of articles and book reviews in leading philosophical journals such as *The American Philosophical Quarterly, The Journal of Philosophy, Australasian Journal of Philosophy,* and *Philosophia.* He has just completed a book-length study of the Arrow General Impossibility Theorem. He has been cited several times by his university for teaching and research awards.

BASANT K. LAL is Professor and Chairman of the Department of Philosophy, Magadh University, Bodhgaya, India. He was born in Ranchi, India, in 1928. He graduated from Patna College and received his M.A. and Ph.D. degrees from Patna University. He has been in the teaching profession for the last 35 years and has written extensively on the philosophy of religion, metaphysics, and epistemology. He has had over 120 articles and papers published in anthologies and journals all over the world. Among his books are *Contemporary Indian Philosophy, Man, A Study in Indian Thought from an Existentialist Standpoint, Impact of Science and Technology on Values, A Short History of the Indian Philosophical Congress,* and a few books in Hindi. He was the editor of the Indian

Philosophical Congress for several years and has edited a number of publications, including *Proceedings I.P.C. 1967, Proceedings I.P.C. 1968, Ethics, Religion and Subjectivity,* and *Philosophy and the Social Sciences.* He has lectured and participated in conferences at different universities throughout the world and has organized various international and All India seminars, conferences, and teacher-orientation courses. Along with others, he has just completed the work of editing two encyclopedias being prepared by the Ministry of Education and Social Welfare, Government of India, one relating to world religions and the other to the philosophers of the world.

ANDREW LINZEY was born in Oxford, England, in 1952 and educated at King's College, London, and University College, Cardiff. He trained for the ministry at St. Augustine's College, Canterbury, and was ordained an Anglican priest in 1975. He has taught religious studies at the North East Surrey College of Technology and for the Open University and is currently chaplain to the University of Essex. His doctoral research is on "The Doctrine of the Non-human Creation in the Thought of Karl Barth." He is the author of *Animal Rights: A Christian Assessment of Man's Treatment of Animals* (1976) and has since written extensively on Christian theology and the human use of animals.

AL-HAFIZ B. A. MASRI was born in India in 1914 and was educated at the University of Punjab. (*Hafiz* means one who has memorized the whole of the Quran.) He received his B.A. degree (Honors in Arabic) from the Government College, Lahore, in 1938. From 1941 to 1961 he lived in British East Africa, where he became actively involved in animal welfare work, holding very responsible positions in the international organizations of animal welfare. In 1964 he was appointed as the first Sunni Imam of the Shah Jehan Mosque in Woking, Surrey, England. For three years (1968–71), accompanied by his wife, he toured the various Islamic countries by car. As a journalist, he keeps himself busy in his retirement by writing about animal welfare from the Islamic point of view.

TOM REGAN, a native of Pittsburgh, Pennsylvania, received his undergraduate education at Thiel College and was awarded the M.A. and Ph.D. degrees from the University of Virginia. Since 1967 he has taught philosophy at North Carolina State University, where he has twice been elected Outstanding Teacher and, in 1977, was named Alumni Distinguished Professor. He has lectured extensively on moral issues and has served as Distinguished Visiting Scholar, University of Calgary, and Distinguished Visiting Professor of Philosophy, Brooklyn College. He is co-editor, with Peter Singer, of *Animal Rights and Human Obligations* and, with Donald Van-DeVeer, of *And Justice for All: New Introductory Essays in Ethics and Public Policy*, and sole editor of *Matters of Life and Death: New Introductory Essays in Moral Philosophy, Earthbound: New Introductory Essays in Environmental Ethics*, and *Just Business: New Introductory Essays in Business Ethics*. His other books include *Understanding Philosophy, All That Dwell Therein: Essays on Animal Rights and Environmental Ethics, The Case for Animal Rights*, and *Bloomsbury's Prophet: The Moral Philosophy of G. E. Moore* (in press).

RODNEY L. TAYLOR was born in Hollywood, California, in 1944. He received his B.A. degree from the University of Southern California, his M.A. from the University of Washington, and his Ph.D. from Columbia University. He has taught at the University of Virginia and, since 1978, at the University of Colorado at Boulder, where he is Chairman of the Department of Religious Studies. He is author of *The Cultivation of Sagehood As a Religious Goal in Neo-Confucianism* (1978), *The Way of Heaven: An Introduction to the Confucian Religious Life* (1985), *The Holy Book in Comparative Perspec-*

tive (with F. M. Denny, 1985), and at present he is finishing a volume, *The Confucian Way of Contemplation.* He is also the author of numerous scholarly articles and the editor of the *Journal of Chinese Religions.*